Behold the Lamb!

E.J. Dold

First published under the title We Would See Jesus in 2018
Second edition, Behold the Lamb, 2023

info@gatesofpearl.com.au

Cover image by artist Phil McKay.
www.philmckay.com

John 1:29

The next day John seeth Jesus coming unto him, and saith, Behold the Lamb of God, which taketh away the sin of the world.

Preface

This book is the result of my personal struggle to understand what it means to be saved. What is God's part? What is mine? As a young college student I remember listening to a preacher talk about justification and sanctification, and using terms such as 'forensic', 'intrinsic', 'imparted', and 'imputed' when referring to the salvation process. What did all this mean? I felt like jumping up on my seat and crying out, 'Just tell me what all this means to you personally. How are you experiencing the salvation process? How does this impact your practical everyday living? What difference has it made to your life?' But of course, I was too shy for that, and so, without answers, I eventually wandered away from God.

Years later, I decided to read the Bible through from cover to cover. The stories in Genesis and the early part of Exodus were interesting. I enjoyed reading them, but when I got to the description of the Old Testament sanctuary with all its minute detail, I was tempted to skip it altogether.

However, I had made a resolution and was determined to persevere. As I read, I became more and more interested and began making notes and drawing diagrams and flow charts in the margins of my Bible. My interest led me to explore other books on the subject. For the next 12 months the Mosaic sanctuary totally absorbed me until at last God's wonderful plan to save humanity gradually unfolded. This book is my journey of discovery as I attempted to answer for myself the age-old question, 'What must I do to be saved?'

God providentially gave me 12 months in which I was relatively free to explore the subject of redemption. I made extensive notes and filed them according to topic. All this note taking gradually morphed into a book, which at first was written so that I could record all the information I had gathered in an organised way. From here, the realisation came that this material was not meant for me alone, so began the journey into book publishing.

The first edition of this book was called "We Would See Jesus" in which I included nearly all the information I had gathered. This second edition is a slimmed down, reformatted, more focused, warmer, and more attractive edition. I pray that the reader will be as blessed in reading it as I was in writing it.

Contents

Behold the Lamb!

It is a balmy spring afternoon in the year AD 31. Trees blossom with the promise of a rich harvest, and the hillsides are carpeted with a profusion of delicately tinted flowers. The westward sinking sun bathes the countryside in its gentle radiance. Winter's grip has been broken, and all nature rejoices as life returns to the Palestinian hills and valleys. However, peace and tranquility are only an illusion, for dark clouds of grief, disappointment, and fear hang over the small nation.

It was the time of the annual Passover festival. A time for rejoicing and fellowship as all Israel gathered to remember its miraculous deliverance from Egyptian bondage and its birth as a nation. This festival also reminded them of a still greater deliverance – that promised by the coming of the long-awaited Messiah. The Messiah! How the heart of every true Israelite throbbed with longing. But year after year slipped by and the Messiah had not come. Gradually the ceremonies pointing to the coming Deliverer deteriorated imperceptibly into predictable and meaningless rituals.

But hope still flickered in the hearts of many. Did not the prophet Daniel point to this very hour as the time when the Messiah would come? But where was He? Could Daniel have been mistaken? Rumours regarding a miracle-working teacher from Nazareth had engulfed the small nation. Could He be the one? With hopeful hearts thousands of pilgrims from around the world poured into Jerusalem.

As they entered the gates of the Holy City more rumours greeted them. The teacher from Nazareth they are told, the one they hoped would be Israel's Messiah, had been arrested during the night and condemned to death. He was to die that very day! As the news spread, jostling, curious crowds spilled into the narrow streets and alleyways of Old Jerusalem. They wanted to see this teacher, this 'would-be' Messiah, as he passed on his way to the place of execution.

*   *   *   *

Here he comes - Israel's king! A sudden hush descends upon the excited people. Is this the man everyone is talking about? Is this man indeed Israel's Messiah - this man who comes staggering along the rough, uneven pavement, carrying a heavy cross like a common criminal? He is stripped to the waist, and his back is lacerated by the cruel whip. Blood pools in the dust with each painful step. As the people gaze in astonishment, the man suddenly staggers and falls under the weight of the cross, and the crowd once again finds its voice. Some cry out in sympathy; others jeer and mock. This is NOT the king they want. He deserves to die for deceiving the people. They spit upon him as he passes.

The careless multitude, having passed its hasty and superficial judgment, now falls in behind the sufferer as he wends his painful way through the gates of the city to a nearby hill called Golgotha. Here the most degraded and hardened of criminals are hung upon Roman crosses to die the long agonising death of crucifixion. Here the crowd of curious spectators now gaze in silence as unfeeling soldiers pound nails through the quivering outstretched hands of the world's Redeemer. Momentarily they draw breath as the cross, bearing its precious burden, is roughly raised by strong Roman arms and allowed to fall heavily into place.

With the cross now in position and secured, the guards take their stations and wait. The crowd starts to drift away, but some, not yet tired of the sport, stay to mock. Others watch and wait silently - their hearts breaking in anguish. Six long, agonising hours later it is all over.

The Passover ceremonies continue throughout the day and into the Sabbath hours, but they are not the same. Strange and fearful forebodings fill the hearts of the people. What was the meaning of the violent earthquake that shook the city as the Man died? What about the strange darkness which engulfed the cross at midday? And the thick temple curtain! Why did it suddenly rip from top to bottom as if torn by an unseen hand? Could this Man have been the Messiah after all?

It is now Sunday afternoon. People from the surrounding countries have long since departed, but the city remains tense and troubled. With heavy hearts Cleopas and his companion turn their steps towards home in nearby Emmaus. Their hopes are shattered. Their beloved Teacher is now dead. He could not have been the Messiah. Overcome with grief, they murmur softly together regarding the strange events of the past few days as they trudge unseeingly toward Emmaus.

Suddenly a stranger appears and falls instep beside them. Absorbed in their misery they are hardly aware of his presence until he speaks. Tactfully he breaks in on their conversation and questions them as to the reason for their great sadness. Cleopas is amazed to find someone who does not seem to be aware of recent events in Jerusalem, so he quickly relates the story of Jesus of Nazareth. He tells the stranger about their shattered hopes and breaking hearts.

The stranger listens politely. Then with words of gentle authority he says, *"O foolish ones, and slow of heart to*

believe in all that the prophets have spoken! Ought not Christ to have suffered these things, and to enter into His glory?" The attention of Cleopas is now fully aroused. Who is this man? What does he mean? Surely they have understood and believed the prophets. Respectfully he waits for the stranger to continue. The sun is now sinking below the horizon in a blaze of glory, but Cleopas and his companion hardly notice. The real sun, the Son of Righteousness, Jesus Christ Himself, has their full attention. The greatest of all Teachers now begins to take them on a walk through the Scriptures, on a journey they will never forget. Beginning with the books of Moses, He explains to them all things written there concerning Himself - **the Lamb of God**. As Cleopas and his friend listen, their hearts burn within them and faith revives.

Intent on what the Stranger is saying, they are surprised when He suddenly stops. Looking up they see that they are standing at the door of their humble cottage. With true Eastern hospitality they entreat the Stranger to stay and eat with them. He graciously consents, and when asked to bless the food He takes the bread, and lifting His eyes to heaven, thanks God for His wonderful provisions. The way He does this is strangely familiar. Memory revives. Suddenly the eyes of these disciples of Christ are opened, and they behold at last their risen Lord! Overcome with joy and amazement they fall down to worship Him - but He is gone! Leaving the meal untouched, they grab their coats and run back toward Jerusalem, stumbling and falling in the semi-darkness. They have a story to tell and cannot contain it. Jesus of Nazareth has risen from the dead! He is indeed the Messiah! Everyone must hear the wonderful news.

*   *   *   *

The plan of redemption, with Jesus as its central figure, was the story Christ told that evening. It is the story of the *"the Lamb of God which taketh away the sin of the world."* As we begin to comprehend something of our Saviour's incomprehensible love for humanity, and of His marvellous plan to rescue us from Satan's grasp, our hearts also will *'burn.'* We too will have a story to tell.

The Greek believers who came seeking Jesus during the Passover celebrations had but one request. *"We would see Jesus"* was their cry. This cry of the human heart has been echoed by every sincere seeker for truth ever since. But how do we see Jesus? Where do we begin? Jesus tells us about Himself in the Word of God, the Holy Bible. From beginning to end it contains His story. *''And beginning at Moses and the prophets, He expounded unto them in all the Scriptures the things concerning Himself"* Luke 24:27.

This book is an attempt to tell the story of Jesus from the beginning of the sin problem until that great and glorious day when sin and pain will be forever eradicated from the universe. By the time you reach the end of the book the big 'picture' will have taken shape, and you will be astonished and humbled by the profound, yet simple plan God has devised or saving the human family.

Of course there are far greater depths to the plan of redemption than have been presented here. It will be a subject of study throughout the endless ages of eternity. As we take this journey together, may our response be, as was that of Cleopas, *"Did not our hearts burn within us, while He talked with us by the way, and while He opened to us the Scriptures?"*

Acknowledgments

I wish to acknowledge the following authors, whose writings on the plan of redemption have been a great inspiration to me, and whose thoughts I have often borrowed in the preparation of this book. These authors are as follows:

M. L. Andreasen
W. D. Frazee
E C. Gilbert
Clifford Goldstein
Leslie B. Hardinge
Stephen N. Haskell
Sarah Peck
John L. Shuler
Julius G. White
E. G. White
The inspired authors of the Holy Bible.

Especially am I indebted to Sarah Peck for her magnificent book on the subject, *"The Path to the Throne of God."* Her insights throw a flood of light upon the plan of salvation, and open the mind to a greater understanding and appreciation of Jesus' love for humanity.

I wish to also acknowledge with love and gratitude, the encouragement and technical support given by my husband Terry and my son Robert. I thank also my nephew Joel Ridgeway of Revealer Media (*revealermedia.com*), for re-formatting this 2nd edition and presenting it in a 'reader friendly' and attractive format.

My heartfelt gratitude also goes to Pr Priebe of Dennis Priebe Ministries, USA, who took time from his busy schedule to review this book and to offer some excellent advice for its improvement.

To Pr Mike Brownhill of QLD, Australia, editor extraordinaire! Thank you! Nothing seems to escape your eagle eyes. And thank you so very much for reviewing the material and taking time to write a recommendation.

To Ray and Marie Richter, thank you so very much for helping to make the publication of this second edition possible. To write a book is lonely work, but it takes a team to bring it to fruition.

May God bless you all!

How to Study the Bible

There is only one way to study the Bible, and that is to follow the example of the Bereans who were *"more noble than those in Thessalonica in that they received the Word with all readiness of mind, and searched the Scriptures daily, whether these things were so"* (Acts 17:11). We must take no man's word regarding the Scriptures, but study these things for ourselves.

We must dig deep into the Word of God searching for its truths as for buried treasure, but never without first asking the Holy Spirit to guide us in our search. Spiritual things are spiritually discerned, and without the Holy Spirit's guidance we are in danger of misinterpreting them to suit ourselves (1Corinthians 2:14).

 The Bible tells us how to study - *"precept upon precept, line upon line, here a little, there a little"* (Isaiah 28:10, 13). If you do this, you will find the pieces of the puzzle will come together in perfect harmony. We are not to base a whole doctrine upon one text, or part of a text. Read each text in its setting and lay aside preconceived ideas and opinions. Do not try to prove your point from the Bible. Let the Bible reveal its own truth. Pray, humbly pray, for light and guidance to seek and know only the truth.

-E.J.D.

*　　*　　*　　*

Chapter 1

"In The Beginning God..."

Who is God? How can we begin to understand Him? To begin our search for God, let us go outdoors one clear and cloudless night and spend a quiet, thoughtful hour, gazing up into the heavens. Here we will see law and order displayed in the movement of the planets, stars, and galaxies. Our solar system, with its planets orbiting around our sun, and its moons orbiting around the planets, is but a small glimpse of the whole.

Let our imaginations now grasp countless billions of galaxies all moving in perfect order around the throne of God who *"upholds all things by the word of His power"* Hebrews 1:3. The things we know about the universe tell us that we live in a little corner of a huge well-regulated kingdom. As Job said many years ago, *"Indeed, these are the mere edges of His ways, and how small a whisper do we hear of Him!"* (Job 26:14, NKJV).

> *"The heavens declare the glory of God, and the firmament shows His handiwork"* (Psalm 19:1).

> *"Lift up your eyes on high, and behold who has created these things? . . . Have you not known? Have you not heard, that the everlasting God, the Lord, the Creator of the ends of the earth . . . there is no*

searching of His understanding" (Isaiah 40:26, 28).

Yes, who has created all these things? Looking into God's limitless universe, we are bewildered and overwhelmed by what we see. Astronomers tell us that if we look at the sky through a hole the size of a 10-cent piece, there are approximately 1,500 galaxies composed of billions upon billions of stars in that one area alone. The vastness, the clock-like precision, the balance and harmony of space defy the imagination.

The constellation Orion is considered by many astronomers to be the most majestic of them all. The appearance of the Orion nebulae is described as that of *"light shining and glowing behind Herculean walls of ivory or pearl."* Its walls are *"studded with millions of diamond points"* each one a shining star. And each one of these stars is a giant blazing sun! Many of them dwarf our own in size and brilliance. Betelgeuse, the second brightest star in Orion, is *"classified as a red supergiant of spectral type M1-2, the star is one of the largest and most luminous stars visible to the naked eye. If Betelgeuse were at the centre of the Solar System, its surface would extend past the asteroid belt, wholly engulfing the orbits of Mercury, Venus, Earth, Mars, and possibly Jupiter"*[1]. The diameter of our sun is only 1,384,036 km by comparison. Here is a star so large that if it were as close to us as our sun, it would completely fill our horizon, making it impossible to see beyond its circumference. Yet Betelgeuse is only one of the millions of stars shining down on us from Orion.

Did all these wonders happen just by mere chance? Does design, organisation, and plan come out of chaos? Edwin Conklin, a scientist from Princeton University, does not think so. He is on record as saying that *"the probability of life originating from an accident is comparable to the probability of an unabridged dictionary resulting from an explosion in a printing factory."* Or as Edward Hoyle wrote in *Nature*, November 12, 1981, *"The chance that higher*

---

1   https://en.wikipedia.org/wiki/Betelgeuse

forms of life arose by evolutionary processes is comparable with the chance that a tornado sweeping through a junk yard might assemble a Boeing 747 from the materials therein." [2]

In 1996 Michael Behe, a biochemistry professor at Lehigh University, Bethlehem, Pennsylvania, published a book in which he admitted, *"In the face of the enormous complexity that modem biochemistry has uncovered in the cell, the scientific community is paralysed. No one at Harvard University, no one at the National Institutes of Health, no member of the National Academy of Sciences, no Nobel prize winner - no one at all can give a detailed account of how the cilium, or vision, or blood clotting, or any complex biochemical process might have developed in a Darwinian fashion. But we are here. Plants and animals are here. The complex systems are here. All these things got here somehow: if not in a Darwinian fashion, then how?"* [3]

"All that exists upon this earth and in the heavens testifies to one unshakable fact - intelligent design . . . The natural world has a precision, an intricacy, a remarkable infiniteness that defies ultimate understanding. For numerous decades the great minds of the world, expending billions upon billions of dollars, utilising the most sophisticated scientific tools ever known, have explored the mysteries of nature. Annually new secrets of nature are discovered in an ever expanding plethora of scientific discoveries. The end of scientific discovery is not in sight. We believe it never will be, for God is infinite in wisdom. Each new discovery provides further evidence of His wisdom and creatorship . . . All testify to the fact that God created the heavens and the earth." [4]

As Sir Isaac Newton, the father of modern science once observed, *"The most beautiful system of the sun, planets,*

---

2   Vandeman, G., Planet in Rebellion, p. 18

3   Behe, M., Darwin s Black Box: The Biochemical Challenge
         to Evolution, p. 187

4   Standish, R & C., The Big Bang Exploded , p. 6

and comets, could only proceed from the counsel and dominion of an intelligent and powerful Being" [5]

Let our minds now journey back through past ages to a time before our planet came into existence. Try to imagine the Sovereign of the universe sitting upon His glorious throne, the centre of His government, and surveying His vast, endless kingdom. He is laying plans to expand and enrich it. He desires to make it even more glorious - a place of exceeding beauty, a place to be enjoyed not only by God Himself, but by beings created in His image. Such things cannot be explained by science. What science can explain the mystery of life?

In the creation of this world, God was not dependent upon pre-existing matter.

> *"By the word of the Lord were the heavens made; and all the hosts of them by the breath of His mouth . . . For He spoke, and it was done. He commanded, and it stood fast"* (Psalm 33:6, 9).

> *"By faith we understand that the worlds were framed by the word of God, so that things which are seen were not made of things which do appear"* (Hebrews 11:3).

> *"I form the light, and create darkness . . .*
> *I the Lord do all these things . . .*
> *I have made the earth,*
> *And created man upon it:*
> *I, even My hands have stretched out the heavens,*
> *And all their host have I commanded"*
> (Isaiah 45:7-12).

> *"In the beginning God created the heaven and the earth . . . And God saw everything that He had made and, behold it was very good"* (Genesis 1:1, 31).

---

5   Principia, 1687.

   Image Credit: ESA/Hubble & NASA

Is it possible that life exists on other worlds in this vast, endless universe of ours? Isaiah wrote, *"For thus saith the Lord that created the heavens. God Himself that formed the earth and made it. He has established it. He created it not in vain, He formed it to be inhabited"* (Isaiah 45:18).

If this world in which we live was not created in vain - that is without inhabitants - then it follows that what is true of our world could well be true of other parts of the universe, or as George Vandeman expresses it, "Did God make many houses and put inhabitants in only one? Is this beautiful orderly, intelligent universe a desert of infinite loneliness?" [6]

One of the most interesting statements ever made on the subject is that by Bernard De Fontenelle, *"To think that there may be more worlds than one is neither against reason nor Scripture. If God be glorified by making one world, the more worlds He made the greater must be His glory."* An Astronomer Royal of England is quoted as saying, *"with the universe constructed on so vast a scale, it would seem inherently improbable that our small earth could be the only home of life."* [7]

More recently, evolutionary philosopher and cosmologist, Paul Davies, observed, *"We are led to the startling conclusion that, in an infinite universe subject to the Copernican principle, there must be life elsewhere, in infinite abundance."* [8]

Scientists estimate that there are millions of galaxies each containing billions of planets and stars. If perhaps only one world in each galaxy is inhabited, this means that the number of inhabited worlds could well number in the millions - and of course we have no idea how far our universe extends!

---

6   Vandeman, G., Planet in Rebellion, p. 22

7   Ibid., p. 24

8   Davies P., Are We Alone? p. 21 (Professor of Natural Philosophy; University of Adelaide).

What does the Holy Bible say about the possibility of life on other planets? It tells us that God through Christ, *"made the worlds"* (plural) - (Hebrews 1:1, 2). It further tells us that *"the family in heaven"* and in *"the heaven of heavens with all their <u>hosts</u>"* are preserved by the mighty power of God, and all worship Him (Ephesians 3:14,15; Nehemiah 9:6). The Concise Oxford Dictionary defines 'host' as a *'large number of beings,'* or a *'heavenly army.'*

In the book of Job, God asks the patriarch, *"Where were you when I laid the foundations of the earth? . . . When the morning stars sang together, and all the sons of God shouted for joy"* (Job 38:4, 7). Who were these *'sons of God'* who rejoiced as God laid the foundations of planet earth? Evidently, they were either angels or some other beings created before earth was formed. Adam is called the *"son of God"* (Luke 3:38). Could not similar created beings be called the same? Whatever the answer to these questions may be, we can know for certain that our God is a BIG God!

The Creation of our World.

As the *'sons of God shout for joy,'* and the *'morning stars sing together,'* God speaks our world into existence. Our planet, way out on the edge of the giant Milky Way Galaxy, comes into being by the omnipotent power of our Creator God. It is a wonderland of beauty with everything in it to delight the senses. Its surface is shaped into a variety of land forms - majestic mountains, rolling hills, beautiful valleys, and spreading plains. Scattered throughout are lovely lakes and sparkling rivers. Graceful shrubs and delicate flowers greet the eye at every turn, and the hills are crowned with stately trees. The air is sweet, clean and perfumed with the scent of flowers.

Now God speaks again, and living creatures come into existence. Insects, birds, fish, and animals of all kinds. All are created with the spark of life, all can reproduce themselves, all have built within them laws to govern their being. When God calls to the animals they come running to

Him, eager to hear His voice, to feel the touch of His hand, to shower Him with affection. Bounding with energy and life their antics are a joy to behold - but God is not yet satisfied. The beauty of the natural world is indeed lovely, and the companionship of animals something to be treasured, but God wants more for planet earth. He wants these natural wonders to be enjoyed by beings who can appreciate the things which He has made.

Beings like Himself so that He can communicate with them heart to heart. *"So, God created man in His own image, in the image of God created He him. Male and female created He them"* (Genesis 1:27).

As the parents of mankind came forth from the Creator's hand they were of lofty stature, perfect in form and feature. Their faces glowed with health and happiness. They wore no artificial clothing but were arrayed as were the angels in a covering of light and glory. This was God's crowning act of creation, beings patterned after Himself with minds able to understand Him, to appreciate Him, and to love Him. In the companionship of man God found His greatest joy. *"The Lord takes pleasure in His people"* (Psalm 149:4). God's happiness was, and still is, bound up with the happiness of His created beings.

However, in creating mankind, God took a fearful risk, for to create an intelligent, thinking creature patterned after Himself, He must give him the power of choice. Man must be allowed to govern himself and not be controlled by instinct as were the animals. He must know what God required and be allowed the freedom to obey or not obey. Though a subject of the divine government, he must also be a free moral agent. His obedience must come from a loving heart and must not be the result of force or fear. This is the liberty of which Patrick Henry spoke when he exclaimed, *"Give me liberty or give me death."*

God could have made man without the power to transgress His laws, but this would have reduced him to the level of a robot, programmed to obey. Parents can force their young children to obey but there is no pleasure for them in this. Such children grow up without the ability to think or act for themselves. Without the power of choice there is no development of character. Willing, cheerful obedience which comes from a spirit of love is the only obedience that brings joy to a parent's heart. God is no different. Forced obedience would be abhorrent to Him and unworthy of man as an intelligent being.

God knew full well the risks He took when he made man a free moral agent. There now existed the possibility of rebellion against His government, bringing in its train death and ruin. But God made man upright with noble traits of character, with no bias toward evil. He was given the strongest possible incentives to be true to God and to obey His laws.

The harmony of the whole universe depends upon obedience to law. Natural law governs the movement of the stars and planets, and regulates the life, growth, and reproduction of plants and animals. Only man, of all the inhabitants of this planet, is subject to moral law as well. God's moral law appeals to his reason and is formulated to protect him and to ensure his happiness. The principles of this law are embodied in the Ten Commandments, written by God in stone to underscore the unchanging nature of His requirements. This perfect, unchangeable law comes from a perfect, unchangeable God, who of Himself declares, *"I am the Lord, I change not"* (Malachi 3:6). The principles of the moral law, which forms the foundation of God's universal government, were already in existence when man was created.

To further safeguard man from choosing a wrong course, God placed within him a conscience. This acts like a silent monitor of all his activities. Like traffic lights in the brain, the conscience signals when a wrong act is about to be committed and gives the 'all clear' to acts of obedience.

And to be absolutely fair, God told man what the results of disobedience would be. For a law to be effective it must have a penalty as a law without a penalty is no law at all. And it naturally follows that the penalty must reflect the seriousness of the wrong. The laws of our land follow this principle. If the penalties for traffic offences, theft, or murder were not enforced, we would soon despise the law and the law makers. Anarchy would reign, and our social structure would disintegrate.

And so, with God. If the penalty for breaking His law was of little consequence God's created beings would soon despise His law and God as the creator of the law. They would come to regard sin as a small matter. However, sin, rebellion against God's government, is not a small matter (See 1 John 3:4).

God ensured that mankind had everything he needed. Everything for his happiness and well-being was abundantly provided. There would be no excuse for sin. For man to deliberately choose to break God's law would be an act of rebellion. Rebellion, like a contagious disease, spreads quickly and contaminates all with whom it comes in contact. Consequently, only one possible penalty for sin existed - death, Romans 6:23. The *'sons and daughters of God,'* could obey and live, or disobey and die.

So why didn't God exterminate the first rebel before the whole universe was affected. There are reasons why He did not. We will look at these in the next chapter.

The Chapter in Review

We can summarise the thoughts presented in this chapter by using the following diagram. Each block is dependent upon the block beneath it.

<table>
<tr><td>GOD'S HAPPINESS</td></tr>
<tr><td>MAN'S HAPPINESS</td></tr>
<tr><td>PERSONAL FREEDOM</td></tr>
<tr><td>POWER OF CHOICE</td></tr>
<tr><td>LAW</td></tr>
<tr><td>PENALTY</td></tr>
</table>

"For the wages of sin is death; but the gift of God is eternal life through Jesus Christ our Lord."

Romans 6:23

"And There was War in Heaven..."

"And there was war in heaven. Michael and His angels fought against the dragon; and the dragon fought and his angels, and prevailed not; neither was their place found any more in heaven. And the great dragon was cast out, that old serpent, called the Devil, and Satan, which deceives the whole world. He was cast out into the earth, and his angels were cast out with him" (*Revelation 12:7-9*).

With these few terse words inspiration tells us about a war in heaven, in that pure, utopian environment. Impossible! How could there be war in heaven of all places?

Who is this Satan anyway who was cast out into this world? And why this world, why not some other place?

To find the answers we must again backtrack to a time prior to the creation of this world. It was a time when perfect harmony and peace reigned throughout the universe of God. Love to God was supreme, and love between created beings was trusting and unselfish. There was no note of discord to mar the celestial happiness. But gradually a dark cloud of discontent crept over this euphoric existence. It came imperceptibly at first, but slowly gathered momentum.

There was one who perverted the freedom which God granted His higher order creatures - the freedom to think and choose for oneself. Amongst God's creation was one who was outstanding in perfection and beauty. There was no gift that a loving God did not bestow upon him. He was one of the covering cherubim, first among the angels, next to Christ in authority. The Creator made him very beautiful, as near as possible like Himself. But little by little Lucifer, *"the son of the morning"* (Isaiah 14:12), came to indulge the desire for self-exaltation. Not content with high honours and the devotion of angels, he began to covet the glory which belonged to Christ alone. In the book of Ezekiel, Lucifer is represented under the figure of the Prince of Tyre, flourishing in might and magnificence.

> *"Thus says the Lord God, you seal up the sum, full of wisdom, and perfect in beauty. You have been in Eden, the garden of God. Every precious stone was your covering . . . You were the anointed cherub that covers, and I have set you so. You were upon the holy mountain of God. You have walked up and down in the midst of the stones of fire. You were perfect in your ways from the day that you were created, until iniquity was found in you . . . Your heart was lifted up because of your beauty. You have corrupted your wisdom by reason of your brightness"* (Ezekiel 28:12-17).

Forgetting that he himself was a created being, this prince of angels began to aspire to the power and glory that belonged to Christ alone.

From the little the Bible tell us about this time, we can piece together what might well represent a reasonable picture of events. It probably went some thing like this:

Deliberately ignoring the fact that he himself was a created being, this prince of angels began to aspire to the power and glory that belonged to Christ alone. His jeal-

ousy of Christ led him to dispute the supremacy of the Creator, and to question the very law of God. Laws might be necessary for the inhabitants of the worlds, he reasoned, but angels, being more exalted, did not need such restraints (Hebrews 2:6, 7). They were sufficiently wise to govern themselves.

Working with mysterious secrecy, and concealing his real purpose under a disguise of loyalty to God, he artfully began to insinuate doubts into the minds of the angels under his charge. While secretly fostering discord and rebellion, he, with unsurpassed skill, made it appear that his real purpose was to promote loyalty to God and to preserve the peace of heaven. The spirit of dissatisfaction was now doing its malicious work. Angels, who had previously been in perfect accord with the divine government, became discontented and unhappy because they could not understand all of God's purposes, or be part of His governing councils. The spirit of discontent and resentment had never been known in heaven. It was a new element - strange, mysterious, unaccountable. The perfect harmony of heaven was broken.

We can be sure the Sovereign of the universe warned the angels of Lucifer's bewildering sophistries. We can imagine heavenly councils being called where loyal angels pleaded with Lucifer, and Christ presented before him the greatness, goodness, and justice of God, and the sacred, unchanging nature of His law. No doubt God explained the true position of Christ who shared His throne and authority, and who only could fully enter into His plans and purposes. It was Christ who created all the hosts of heaven, and to Him also belonged the homage and allegiance due to God (Hebrews 1:2-10). After these councils, peace no doubt reigned again in heaven for a while, but within Lucifer's heart a conflict continued to rage. Again, and again he would allow his heart to be filled with pride and with a desire for supremacy. Eventually he reached the point where he aspired to be equal with God Himself.

The time had come for Lucifer to decide. He must either yield obedience to heaven's law and order, or place himself in open rebellion against God. He could not help but see that he was wrong, that he had no reason for complaint. God was just, compassionate, and merciful, but pride prevented Lucifer from retreating from his position. He declared to his sympathisers that they, like he, had gone too far to return. God would not forgive them now. Their only course was to assert their liberty, and gain by force the privileges which had not been willingly granted them. The pleadings of Christ and God were in vain to stay his course. The rebel leader now boldly avowed his contempt for the Creator's law. He denounced the law as a restriction of liberty, and declared it was his purpose to secure the abolition of **all law**. He claimed that he would be like the Most High. He would exalt his throne above the throne of God. This was a declaration of war. In the conflict that followed, Christ, also known as Michael the Archangel, had no choice but to drive the rebels out of heaven. [9]

> *"How are you fallen from heaven, O Lucifer, son of the morning! How are you cut down to the ground . . . For you have said in your heart, I will ascend into heaven. I will exalt my throne above the stars of God. I will sit also upon the mount of the congregation, in the sides of the north* (where God's throne is). *I will ascend above the heights of the clouds. I will be like the most High"* (Isaiah 1 4:12-14).

There was no excuse for Lucifer's rebellion, or for the rebellion of those who sympathised with him and his aims. The knowledge they had of God's character, of His goodness, mercy, and wisdom, made their guilt unpardonable. If they could rebel in the very presence of inexpressible glory, while surrounded by the love, mercy, and goodness of God, there was nothing more that heaven could do for them. Thus Lucifer, the *"son of the morning"* who shared God's glory and attended His throne, became Satan, that old serpent the devil, the enemy of God and those loyal

---

9   Michael means, "Who is like God." See other uses of the name in Daniel 10:13, 21; 12:1; Jude 9; Revelation 12:7.

to Him. He became known as the angel or king of the bottomless pit, '*Abaddon*,' or '*Apollyon*' meaning "*destroyer*" (Revelation 9:11).

Why Didn't God Destroy Satan?

This is a fair question which deserves an answer. After all, was this not God's opportunity to destroy the devil and to rid the universe of the cancer of sin? Was not the sentence of death the penalty for breaking God's law? Why not act quickly to prevent rebellion from spreading? To answer these questions, it must be understood that a serious situation arose when Satan made his charges against God and His law.

God is at a disadvantage in this conflict. He cannot lie or deceive, but Satan can use whatever means his diabolical mind can invent.

"The accusations in reality constituted an impeachment (a charge of misconduct made against someone in public office). Many of the angels - one third, constituting millions of them - believed the charges, and challenged God with their leader. It was no small crisis. It threatened the very existence of God's government. The only way the matter could be satisfactorily settled so that no question would ever rise again as to the fairness and justice of God's government, was for each side to present its evidence, produce its witnesses, and rest its case on the weight of evidence. God is accused and on trial. He has been charged with injustice, with requiring His creatures to do that which they cannot do - keep His law." [10]

God is at a disadvantage in this conflict. He cannot lie or deceive, but Satan can use whatever means his diabolical mind can invent. He makes full use of flattery, deceit, and lies. He falsifies the word of God, and misrepresents His law and government. By subtle arguments he makes mysterious that which is simple, and casts doubts upon the plainest statements of God.

---

10   Andreasen, M. L., The Sanctuary Service, p. 315

At the time of his rebellion, Satan was highly exalted and greatly loved by the heavenly beings. He possessed considerable influence over them and his power to deceive was very great. Everything he did was clothed with a veneer of righteousness so that it was difficult for the angels to fully discern his character and the nature of his work. If God had destroyed him, the inhabitants of heaven and other worlds would not have seen God's justice in this. Some would serve Him out of fear rather than love, and such service is not acceptable to God. The allegiance of His creatures must rest upon faith, trust, and love.

Yes, God could have destroyed Satan at this point, but that would not have destroyed his influence. Before long rebellion would have risen from another source. The deceiver had to be unmasked before the whole universe. His true character and his real motives had to be revealed. Satan's rebellion was to be a lesson to the whole universe for eternity. The terrible results of setting aside divine authority, and the effects of Satan's rule upon men and angels, would provide a perpetual safeguard against future rebellion. The One who sees the end from the beginning could thus confidently declare, *"sin will not rise up the second time"* (Nahum 1:9).

The Example of Absalom

So that we may more fully understand the rebellion of Lucifer, the Bible records the story of Absalom, the son of King David. Like God, David was a good and just ruler. Like Lucifer, Absalom was an outstanding physical specimen. *"In all Israel there was none to be so much praised as Absalom for his beauty. From the sole of his foot even to the crown of his head there was no blemish in him"* (2 Samuel 14:25).

Because of his position as the king's son, and because of his unrivalled beauty, he became very proud. Ambitious, energetic, and unprincipled, he sought to steal the loyalty

Image: www.freebibleimages.org

of the people away from the king. Like Lucifer, he coveted the king's throne. Day by day found him at the gate of Jerusalem where the people met to present their grievances for judgment. He would mingle with the people and sympathise with them, and at the same time foster discontent against the government by his artful insinuations. Having listened to the complaint of a man of Israel, he would reply:

> *"Your matters are good and right; but there is no man appointed of the king to hear you. Oh, that I was made judge in the land, that every man who has any suit or cause might come unto me, and I would do him justice!. . . **So, Absalom stole the hearts of the men of Israel***" (2 Samuel 15:3-6).

Under a cover of secrecy, Absalom continued to foster rebellion against the king. He used every artifice of which he could conceive, even the cloak of religious devotion, to conceal his traitorous designs. Satan found a responsive student in Absalom and implanted in his mind his own methods of deception. In the outcome of Absalom's rebellion, Satan may read his own doom. (Compare 2 Samuel 18:14, 17 and Revelation 20:1-3, 7-10)

The Example of Haman

Haman, prime minister in the kingdom of Persia during the reign of King Ahasuerus, gives us another picture of Satan's aims and ambitions. His story is found in the book of Esther. Haman plotted to exterminate God's people, just as Satan has been trying to do down through the ages.

On one occasion the king asked Haman to tell him what he should do for a certain person whom the king wanted to honour. Haman, full of self-importance and pride, imagined that person could be none other than himself, so he outlined the following program:

Image: www.freebibleimages.org

"Let the royal apparel be brought which the king wears, and the horse that the king rides upon, and the royal crown which is set upon his head. And let this apparel and horse be delivered to the hand of one of the king's most noble princes, that he may array the man whom the king delights to honour. And parade him on horseback through the streets of the city, and proclaim before him, 'Thus shall it be done to the man whom the king delights to honour'" (Esther 6:8, 9).

What does Haman want? The king's robe, the king's horse, the king's crown, the king's authority, and the king's glory. But the king himself is not in the picture. Haman is virtually saying, 'I want to be the king.' This is Satan's agenda. (Read for yourself the whole exciting story in the book of Esther and discover what happens to those who try to destroy God's people. This is another picture of the eventual downfall of Satan.)

The Fall of Man

Barred from causing any more dissatisfaction in heaven, Satan now sought for a new field in which to vent his enmity against God. Looking upon this planet of ours he beheld the peace and happiness of our first parents, and moved by envy, determined to incite them to rebellion.

God warned Adam and Eve of the danger which threatened them. He fully revealed to them the history of Satan's fall and informed them of his plans for their destruction. It was by disobedience that Satan and his angels had fallen, and so the importance of strict obedience to the law of God was urged upon Adam and Eve. We can imagine the loyal angels also warning them to be on their guard. If they steadfastly repelled his first insinuations, they would be secure. While they were obedient to God the devil could not harm them, for every angel in heaven would come to their aid. However, if they yielded to temptation their na-

While Adam and Eve were obedient to God the devil could not harm them, for every angel in heaven would come to their aid.

Image: www.freebibleimages.org

tures would be changed. They would eventually become so morally corrupt that they would possess neither the power or the desire to resist Satan's temptations.

The test of loyalty devised by God for Adam and Eve was a simple one. Like the angels they were placed on probation. Their home in the Garden of Eden could be retained only on condition of obedience to the Creator's law. Everything possible for their happiness and prosperity was theirs. They were given access to the whole Garden of Eden. Only one thing was denied them - fruit from the tree of Knowledge of Good and Evil (Genesis 2:16,17).

Why did God place this tree in the garden? There are four reasons why this tree and the consequent test were essential for humanity:

1. The tree was proof that God had indeed given His creatures the power of choice, despite Satan's accusations to the contrary. God told them not to eat from this tree - they had the choice to obey or not to obey

2. The test gave Adam and Eve the opportunity to develop character by making it necessary for them to choose between right and wrong. It also gave them the opportunity to develop loyalty to God.

3. The tree was a daily reminder of God as Creator and Owner of all things. It was a perpetual reminder that all things belonged to God to do with as He pleased. This was necessary to guard man from making the same mistake as Lucifer, who failed to recognise the distinction between the Creator and the created. He began to imagine that he was equal with God.

4. It provided an arena to which God could restrict Satan, and at the same time allow him access to Adam and Eve if they should choose to disobey God. Satan was not allowed to follow them around with his harassments and temptations. He could have access to them only at the forbidden tree. If they obeyed God and kept away from it, they were safe from his deceptions.

Satan bided his time and waited. He assumed that sooner or later one of them would approach the forbidden tree, and he was ready. He took the form of a serpent, once a most charming winged creature, dazzlingly bright, and enchantingly beautiful. Like a modern-day serpent, he wrapped himself around one of the branches of the tree and waited for his prey. She was not long in coming. Eve had been warned not to separate herself from her husband as together they would be in less danger of falling into temptation. *"Two are better than one . . . for if one falls, the other will lift him up, but woe to him that is alone when he falls. For he has not another to help him"* (Ecclesiastes 4:9,10).

Let our imaginations now picture that fateful day which changed the course of human history. Eve, absorbed in some pleasant task in the garden, unconsciously wanders from Adam's side. On perceiving that she is no longer with him she feels an apprehension of danger, but quickly dismisses her fears. She thinks herself wise enough to discern the temptations of the enemy and to resist him. Here she makes her first mistake. If she had heeded the Lord's warning she would not have proceeded any further. However, she continues her way, and soon finds herself approaching the forbidden tree. Curiosity holds her there one moment too long.

As she gazes upon the beautiful fruit on the tree, she questions in her heart why the Lord has forbidden them to eat from it. Now is the tempter's chance. As if reading her thoughts, he addresses her: *"Has God indeed said, 'You shall not eat of every tree of the garden?"* (Genesis 3:1).

"You will not surely die," was Satan's first lie to the human family, and one which he has repeated ever since.

Surprised and startled, Eve makes her second mistake. Instead of fleeing from this unusual situation, she dares to carry on a conversation, a debate, she has no chance of winning. She responds to the tempter's bait by declaring that God has forbidden them to eat from this tree because if they do so they will die. Satan quickly responds, *"You will not surely die . . . Your eyes will be opened and you will be like God, knowing good and evil"* (Genesis 3:4).

"You will not surely die" was Satan's first lie to the human family, and one which he has repeated ever since. Instead of dying, declared Satan, you will enter into a more exalted state, equal to God Himself. Besides, she could not possibly die, for had she not eaten from the Tree of Life! And was not he himself eating the fruit and still living! She too would gain by breaking God's law. God was keeping this fruit from His creatures, the deceiver alleged, because He did not want them to acquire the powers and wisdom He possessed.

Thus, with the subtlety of the serpent, Satan excited in Eve a spirit of irreverent curiosity, a restless, inquisitive desire to penetrate the secrets of divine wisdom and power. Step by step Eve was led to doubt God's wisdom and love. The serpent had achieved his purpose. All he had to do now was to sit back and await events. Eve was deceived and really believed Satan's lies, but her belief did not save her from the penalty for sin. She disbelieved God, and this is what led to her fall. In the judgment men will not be condemned because they conscientiously believed a lie, but because they refused to believe the truth when it was revealed to them.

Eve, seeing that the serpent did not appear to be suffering any harm, took the fruit he held out and ate. She did not die, but instead imagined herself to be entering a higher state of existence. With a strange, unnatural excitement, she nervously gathered some of the fruit and ran off to share it with her husband. She told him of the new and exhilarating power that was electrifying her whole being.

Eve had been deceived (2 Corinthians 11:3), but Adam was not deceived (1Timothy 2:14). He was alarmed and distressed. He knew that this must be the foe they had been warned about, and that by divine sentence, Eve must die. She had disobeyed the only prohibition God had placed upon them in the garden to test their love and loyalty. What should he do? A terrible struggle took place in his mind. He could not endure the thought of separation from the lovely Eve. All the blessings of God were lost sight of at this moment, even the fact that the Creator could replace Eve. He resolved to share her fate. He would die with her. Seizing the fruit from her outstretched hand he quickly ate it (Genesis 3:6). [11]

At first Adam shared Eve's excitement, but soon the thought of their sin filled them both with terror. The air now seemed strangely chilled, the love and peace which had formerly been theirs had disappeared. Instead they felt a sense of sin, a dread of the future, and a nakedness of soul. Adam now reproached his companion for her folly. She cast blame on the serpent and both ultimately blamed God. Once more, the peace and harmony of paradise was shattered (Genesis 3:12, 13).

God gave Adam and Eve the smallest of tests. If He had given them a very difficult test, many would now excuse their small sins by saying, 'This is a matter so trivial God will not mind.' But in God's dealings with our first parents He has clearly shown that all sin, large or small, is offensive to Him. If God's law is not binding, or if it is impossible for man to obey it as Satan claims, then Adam and Eve should not have been punished.

In God's dealings with our first parents He has clearly shown that all sin, large or small, is offensive to Him.

Meanwhile, back at the tree, Satan exalted in the success of his plan. He now saw himself as the new master of humanity. He had wrested control of the earth from Adam, and now it would be his kingdom. Mankind would be his subjects for *"for by whom a person is overcome, by him also he is brought in bondage"* (2 Peter 2:19). As legal representative head of the human family, Adam's disobedience meant that all his progeny would now inherit his fallen sinful nature.

Thus, Satan became *"the god of this world"* (2 Corinthians 4:4). What he did not know was that God had already formulated a rescue plan for mankind, a plan which God

---

11 White, E. G., Patriarchs and Prophets, p. 55-57

and Christ had devised between them before the creation of beings with freedom of choice. God had foreseen this emergency and had made provision for it. It was time to put the plan into action.

Satan

Who Carries His Business On?

Men don't believe in a devil now,
As their fathers used to do;
They've forced the door of the broadest creed,
To let his majesty through.

There isn't a print of his cloven foot,
Or a fiery dart from his bow,
To be found in the earth or the air today,
For the world has voted so.

They say he doesn't go round about
As a roaring lion now.
But whom shall we hold responsible
For the everlasting row,

To be heard in home and church and state
To the earth's remotest bound,
If the devil, by a unanimous vote,
Is nowhere to be found?

Who mixes the fatal draught
That palsies heart and brain,
And loads the bier of each passing year
With ten hundred thousand slain?

Who blights the bloom of the land today
With the fiery breath of hell?
If the devil isn't, and never was,
Won't somebody rise and tell?

Who dogs the steps of the toiling saint,

And digs the pit for his feet?
Who sows the tares in the fields of time,
Wherever God sows His wheat?

The devil was voted not to be,
And of course the thing is true.
But who is doing the kind of work
The devil used to do?

Won't somebody step to the front forthwith?
And make his bow, and show,
How the frauds and the crimes of a single day spring up?
We want to know.

The devil was fairly voted out,
And of course the devil's gone
But simple people want to know,
Who carries his business on?

- Selected

Chapter 3

The Rescue Plan

It was Satan's hope that Adam and Eve would eat from the Tree of Life so that sin and its terrible consequences would never be eradicated from the universe.

After the fall of Adam and Eve, God commissioned an angel to guard the way to the Tree of Life. Beams of light from the angel appeared like *"a flaming sword which turned every way, to keep the way of the Tree of Life"* (Genesis 3:24). Why was this necessary? For man to live forever he must regularly eat from this tree with its supernatural qualities – something like recharging his eternal life battery. (See Revelation 22:1-2 and Isaiah 66:23). But if deprived of its vitality, he would gradually become weaker and weaker until he died. It was Satan's hope that Adam and Eve would eat from the Tree of Life so that sin and its terrible consequences would never be eradicated from the universe. To prevent this, God quickly dispatched an angel to guard it, and thus ensure that there could never be an immortal sinner (Genesis 3:22-24).

When sin is finally eradicated from the universe, the children of God will once more eat the fruit of the Tree of Life and live forever. *"Blessed are they that do His commandments that they may have right to the Tree of Life, and may enter in through the gates into the city"* (Revelation 22:14). *"To him that overcometh will I give to eat of the Tree of Life, which is in the midst of the paradise of God"* (Revelation 2:7).

Regarding that other tree, the Tree of Knowledge of Good and Evil, God had said, *"In the day that you eat thereof you will surely die"* (Genesis 2:17). On that very day Adam and Eve were separated from the Tree of Life and driven from their Eden home. On that very day they forfeited eternal life, granted on condition of obedience. Their outlook was indeed gloomy and without hope.

Sorrow descended upon heaven and earth. The world was now blighted with the curse of sin, and all its inhabitants were doomed to live a life seperated from God and to die a death from which there was no resurrection. The angels ceased their singing, and mourning filled the courts of heaven.

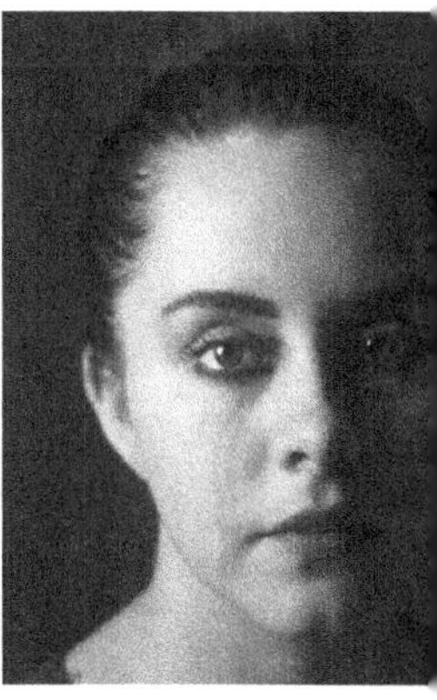

Because of disobedience, the very nature of Adam and Eve was now changed. When created they had no bias toward sin. They had never experienced guilt, they were innocent of all wrong, they were perfect before God. Now their innocence was gone. They experienced guilt, fear, and shame for the first time. Their strength to resist evil was weakened, and they were now unable to maintain their loyalty to God and to keep His law. Their children, instead of being made in the image of God, would now be fashioned in the image of Adam. Like a drug addict who gives birth to a deformed child, all of Adam's children would now be cursed with spiritual birth defects. No wonder the angels wept. What could be done to save mankind? A broken law demanded the life of the sinner. The case for man appeared hopeless. God cannot change His mind or disregard His own rules, for *"His ways are perfect"* (Psalm 18:30).

"God is not a man that He should lie . . . Has He said, and will He not do it? Or has He spoken and will He not make it good?" (Numbers 23:19).

Into this scene of hopeless despair steps Jesus, the Saviour of mankind. Jesus, the Son of God and heaven's glorious Commander, looks with pity upon the fallen race. His heart is touched with compassion. Long before the creation of the world God and His Son had foreseen the fall of man, and in secret counsel had formulated a rescue plan which was then unknown to all created beings. This *"counsel of peace . . . between them both"* (Zechariah 6:13), is described by Paul as *"the mystery which was kept secret since the world began"* (Romans 16:25- 26).

"Sin could not be forced out while His creatures had the power of choice. It could only be loved out."

The plan God and His Son formulated that day offered both **pardon** for sins committed, and **probation** (a second chance for man to prove his loyalty to God). However, God well understood that pardon without punishment would soon undermine the authority and importance of law. If a parent continued to turn a blind eye to the misdemeanours of his child, the time would come when the child would disregard all the rules of the home and treat the parent with contempt. He would go his own wilful way, becoming increasingly bolder in his disregard for all authority. So, how could God pardon the sinner, and at the same time uphold the dignity, authority, and majesty of His law?

It was God's purpose to establish a universal government based on freedom and the power of love, rather than the power of force. Therefore, He proposed to demonstrate His love for His subjects in such a way as to win their hearts forever. *"Sin could not be forced out while His creatures had the power of choice. It could only be **loved** out."* [12]

To impress upon mankind the necessity of obedience to the law of God for his own good, God would not shield him from the natural consequences of sin. If there was no punishment for man to bear, there would be no reminder that sin is wrong. We follow the same policy with law breakers. We do not give such a one a simple reminder by saying, 'That was wrong. Don't do it again', and let him go free of all consequences. That would not be fair. Rather, to impress upon his mind that his behaviour is not acceptable, he is fined, or jailed, and afterwards released on condition that he no longer commit that, or any other crime. He is placed on probation, and by good behaviour

---

12   White, Julius G., The Christians Experience, p. 28

must earn back the respect and trust of society. And so it would be with those who broke God's law. There would be consequences - but there would also be forgiveness, and restoration into the family of God.

§

It was now time to inform the angels of God's plan to rescue the human family.

Amazing Grace - Part I

Deliverance from the PENALTY of Sin

Christ Himself would die as man's substitute, as only the Law Maker could pay the penalty for its transgression. The price paid for man's redemption would cause an infinite amount of suffering to God and to His Son, but there was no other way to maintain the strength of the law and the government of God for all eternity.

The angels could not rejoice as they saw what mankind's redemption would cost their beloved Commander. They listened with grief and amazement to the story of His descent from His position of grandeur as co-Regent of the universe, to the uttermost depths of degradation and cruelty.

> *"Let this mind be in you, which was also in Christ Jesus, who being in the form of God, did not consider it robbery to be equal with God* (counted not being equal with God a thing to be grasped), *but made Himself of no reputation, taking the form of a servant, and was made in the likeness of man. And being found in appearance as a man, He humbled Himself and become obedient unto death, even the death of the cross"* (Philippians 2:5-8).

Christ would Himself become a man so that He would know by personal experience the sorrows and temptations men must endure. And, when His time on earth as man's teacher and example was ended, He would be delivered into the hands of wicked men. These men, under the influence of Satan, would kill Him in a most shameful and cruel way. Before death He would pass long hours of awful agony while the weight of the world's sins pressed upon Him and separated Him from His Father's presence. The angels would not be able to endure the sight. Such are the terrible results of sin, and such is the incomprehensible love of man's Redeemer.

*"He is despised and rejected of men. A Man of sorrows, and acquainted with grief . . . He was wounded for our transgressions, He was bruised for our iniquities: the chastisement of our peace was upon Him; and with His stripes we are healed . . . He was oppressed, and He was afflicted, yet He opened not His mouth. He was brought as **a lamb to the slaughter**, and as a sheep before her shearers is dumb, so He opened not His mouth. He was cut off out of the land of the living; for the transgression of My people was He stricken"* (Isaiah 53:3-11).

"For God so loved the world that He gave His only-begotten Son, that whosoever believeth in Him should not perish, but have everlasting life. For God did not send His Son into the world to condemn the world, but that the world through Him might be saved" (John 3:16,17).

The Author of the law, though innocent of any wrong doing, would be condemned as guilty by that law and punished as a lawbreaker. This would ensure that the authority and importance of the law would not be destroyed by granting pardon to the sinner.

"He shall magnify the law and make it honourable" (Isaiah 42:21).

"Do we then make void the law through faith? God

forbid! Yea, we establish the law" (Romans 3:31).

To pay the penalty for sin the sacrifice must be a perfect one – innocent of all wrongdoing. Imagine a court of law where a convicted murderer has been sentenced to death. Another murderer cannot pay the penalty for his crime because he must die for his own sins, but an innocent man might volunteer to take the sentence on himself. If this is the case, then the man convicted of murder may go free, because the demands of the law, a life for a life, have been met. He goes free, but not to continue in crime. If he does, then he must face the consequences for himself.

And so it would be with Jesus, the innocent would die so that the guilty could have a second chance. Would man appreciate the sacrifice, or would it be in vain?

The astonished angels fall at the feet of the Majesty of heaven and offer to become man's substitute. But only He who has created man has the power to redeem man. However, the angels are assured that they will have a part to play in man's redemption. Jesus would be made *"a little lower than the angels for the suffering of death"* (Hebrews 2:9), and therefore He would need their assistance when He took fallen human nature upon Himself. The angels would minister to Him, strengthen Him, and comfort Him. Likewise, they would minister to God's children (Hebrews 1:14).

Their job would be to guard the future subjects of Christ's kingdom from the power of Satan and his evil angels. They were to protect, strengthen, and comfort them in time of need.

Christ assured the grieving angels that by His death He would not only reconcile man to God but would also recover the kingdom which man had lost by transgression.

Sin and sinners would eventually be blotted out, and never again would the peace and joy of all the universe be disturbed. Now the angels could rejoice. *"Through the celestial courts echoed the first strains of the song which was to ring out above the hills of Bethlehem - 'Glory to God in the highest, and on earth peace, good will toward men (Luke 2:14)."* [13]

Amazing Grace - Part II

Deliverance from the POWER of Sin

In the presence of Adam and Eve God made a strange promise. Addressing Satan, He said, *"I will put enmity between you and the woman, and between your seed and her seed. It will bruise your head, and you will bruise His heel"* (Genesis 3:15). Satan understood from this statement that his work of depraving human nature would be interrupted, and eventually he would be destroyed, but in the process, Christ would also suffer.

The *"woman"* represents God's true church, the *'bride'* of Christ. *"I have likened the daughter of Zion to a comely and delicate woman"* (Jeremiah 6:2). *"I have betrothed you to one Husband, that I may present you as a chaste virgin to Christ"* (2 Corinthians 11:2). The woman's children, or *"seed"* are Christ's true and loyal followers. Satan's *"seed"* are his followers, children of the evil one. The great conflict between Christ and Satan over the loyalty of man and possession of this earth now began in earnest. This was Christ's declaration of war.

There are two parts to God's amazing grace. First, as we have seen, Jesus Christ must come to this earth to die for a broken law as man's substitute. The Sinless One would die for the sins of the guilty. As His death would be sufficient to provide forgiveness for every repenting, believing soul, what more needed to be done for man's redemption? The

---

13   White, E., Patriarchs and Prophets, p. 65

answer lies in the change that occurred in man's nature once he sinned. Before transgression he had no inherited bias toward evil. His nature was holy. He was made in the image of God. Now, as a child of Adam, he was cursed from birth with spiritual deformities. He would find a new law operating in his being which prevented him from giving loyalty and obedience to God even if he wanted to. Satan does not give his subjects the freedom God does. The apostle Paul very aptly describes this conflict in Romans 7:18-24, and 8:7.

"For I know that in me . . . dwells no good thing. For to will is present with me; but how to perform that which is good I find not. For the good that I would, I do not: but the evil which I would not, that I do . . . I find then a law, that, when I would do good, evil is present with me. For I delight in the law of God after the inward man: but I see another law in my members, warring against the law of my mind, and bringing me into captivity to the law of sin which is in my members. O wretched man that I am! Who shall deliver me from the body of this death?"

"The carnal mind is enmity against God. For it is not subject to the law of God, neither indeed can be."

Herein lies a problem for mankind. He is helpless in his fallen condition to find his way back to God. Again, Jesus is the answer to man's dilemma. Not only will He deliver man from the **penalty** of sin, but He will also deliver man from the **power** of sin. He said, *"I will put enmity between you (Satan) and the woman (My* people), *and between your seed and her seed."*

Here Jesus is saying, "I will put hostility toward sin into the hearts of those who want to obey Me. I will change the natural tendencies of their fallen nature so that they will

"Jesus would become the legal representative head of that body of believers He calls His church"

no longer find pleasure in sin. I will give them back their freedom to choose right from wrong which Satan has taken from them. I will break the law of sin and death which now rules in their lives."

In other words, Jesus, our Creator, is promising to re-create us. Just as a skilful surgeon recreates the deformed limbs of a child born physically defective, Jesus, our spiritual surgeon, wants to re-create our hearts, our very natures, because of the damage done by sin. This is the reason why David could pray, *"Create in me a clean heart O God, and renew a right spirit within me"* (Psalm 51:10).

But how could Jesus do this? Adam, as legal representative, and head of the human family had disobeyed God's strict command. He and his descendants had chosen another master, and were now the lawful subjects of Satan because, *"to whom ye yield yourselves servants to obey, his servant ye are"* (Romans 6:16). The prince of darkness is now *"the god of this world."*

"Then the devil, taking Him (Jesus) up on a high mountain, showed Him all the kingdoms of the world in a moment of time. And the devil said unto Him, 'All this authority I will give unto You, and their glory; for this has been delivered to me (by Adam), and I give it to whomever I wish. Therefore, if You worship before me, all will be Yours'" (John 4:5-7 NKJV).

To gain the legal right to break the power of Satan over the human family, Jesus must come to this world as a man born of an earthly mother, experience all of man's temptations and trials, and on man's behalf, break the power of sin by resisting every temptation Satan could throw at Him. In a world of sin and sinners, and possessing man's fallen nature, Jesus would live a perfect, holy life.

It would be a desperate struggle because Satan knew that the outcome of this conflict determined his eternal destiny. If Jesus failed to break the power of sin by His own perfect obedience, this world would be Satan's forever. However, if Jesus succeeded, not only would Satan's power be broken, and his eventual destruction assured, but Jesus would earn the right to take mankind back from Satan's control. He would earn the right to create in every willing and longing heart a new nature - a nature at enmity with Satan and his ways. *"That He might present it to Himself a glorious church, not having spot, or wrinkle, or any such thing, but that it should be holy and without blemish"* (Ephesians 5:27).

The wonderful change made possible in man's nature, is described in the following promises of God:

> *"Come now and let us reason together; saith the Lord. Though your sins be as scarlet, they will be as white as snow. Though they are red like crimson, they will be as wool"* (Isaiah 1:18).

> *"I will put My laws into their mind and write them in their hearts. I will be to them a God, and they shall be to Me a people"* (Hebrews 8:10).

> *"Now Joshua (representing the children of God) was clothed with filthy garments (our sins) and stood before the angel. And He (the Lord), spoke unto those that stood before Him, saying, Take away the filthy garments from him. And unto him (Joshua), He said, Behold, I have caused thine iniquity to pass from thee, and I will clothe thee with change of raiment (the robe of Christ's righteousness)"* (Zechariah 3:3, 4).

> *"I am the Way, the Truth, and the Life. No man cometh unto the Father but by Me"* (John 14:6).

Adam and Eve Leave their Garden Home

It was with unutterable sorrow of heart that Adam and Eve left their Eden home. Here they had communed with angels, and with God Himself, face to face. They had joined angel choirs and united in worship with them on the Sabbath day. Now all had changed. They were outside. No more would they walk with the angels and with God in the same close, familiar way. They were learning the first lesson that sin teaches us. The way of the transgressor is hard! But they went with the promise of redemption ringing in their ears.

What of Jesus Himself? Did He have any feelings at this moment? We are told that He is *"touched with the feelings of our infirmities"* (Hebrews 4:15), so we can be sure that the Creator of the heavens and the earth felt His loss as the two sinners slowly left His presence and the gate shut behind them. No doubt His heart was pained with a sorrow passing the understanding of man. He had created them. He had rejoiced over them with singing. He was already lonely for them. Looking ahead He saw the bloodstained path to Calvary before Him. He saw the rejection and the hatred of those He had come to save. He heard His own piercing cry of despair, *"My God, My God, why hast Thou forsaken Me?"* (Matthew 27:46). But there was no other way, so He did not hesitate.

"Sin had entered - dread sin that would at last nail the Son of God to the cruel tree - and there could be no compromise. The security of the whole universe was at stake. God was already passing through a Gethsemane that would last as long as sin should exist. There must be no hesitancy. God would save man at any cost to Himself." [14]

"It was the marvel of all the universe that Christ should humble Himself to save fallen man. That He who had passed from star to star, from world to world, superintending all, by His providence supplying the needs of every order of being in His vast creation - that He should consent to leave His glory

---

14   Andreasen, M. L., The Sanctuary Service, p. 14

and take upon Himself human nature, was a mystery which the sinless intelligences of other worlds desired to understand. When Christ came to our world in the form of humanity, all were intensely interested in following Him as He traversed, step by step, the bloodstained path from the manger to Calvary.

Heaven marked the insult and mockery that He received, and knew that it was at Satan's instigation . . . They watched the battle between light and darkness as it waxed stronger. And as Christ in His expiring agony upon the cross cried out, "It is finished" (John 19:30), a shout of triumph rang through every world and through heaven itself. The great contest that had been so long in progress in this world was now decided, and Christ was conqueror. His death had answered the question whether the Father and the Son had sufficient love for man to exercise self-denial and a spirit of sacrifice. Satan had revealed his true character as a liar and a murderer. It was seen that the very same spirit with which he had ruled the children of men who were under his power, he would have manifested if permitted to control the intelligences of heaven. With one voice the loyal universe united in extolling the divine administration." [15]

15   White, E. Patriarchs and Prophets, pp 69,70

THE CREATOR-REDEEMER

The Maker of the universe,
As Man, for man was made a curse;
The claims of laws which He had made,
Unto the uttermost He paid.

His holy fingers made the bough,
Where grew the thorns that crowned His brow,
The nails that pierced His hands were mined,
In secret places He designed.

He made the forests whence there sprung,
The tree on which His body hung;
He died upon a cross of wood,
Yet made the hill on which it stood.

The sky which darkened o'er His head,
By Him above the earth was spread;
The sun which hid from Him its face,
By His decree was poised in space.

The spear which spilt His precious blood,
Was tempered in the fires of God;
The grave in which His form was laid,
Was hewed in rocks His hands had made.

The throne on which He now appears,
Was His from everlasting years!
But a new glory crowns His brow,
And every knee to Him shall bow!
- E W. Pitt

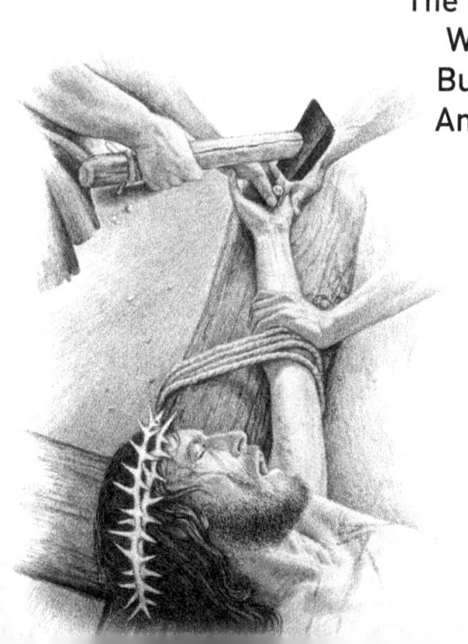

Chapter 4

"Let Them Make Me a Sanctuary..."

Holy angels delight to contemplate the great theme of redemption, but what of man himself? Under the curse of sin, humanity would deteriorate in physical stature, in endurance, and in mental and moral power. Through the indulgence of appetite and passion, he would become incapable of appreciating God's sacrifice. What could be done to keep before him the reality of the gospel? Once again God has the answer.

To provide a lasting reminder of the promised Redeemer, and of the solemn truth that sin causes death, God instituted the sacrificial system. To Adam who had never witnessed death, this was a most painful ceremony. To take a beautiful and spotless lamb and to slay it, *"gave him a deeper and more vivid sense of the greatness of his transgression, which nothing but the death of God's dear Son could expiate. He trembled at the thought that his sin must shed the blood of the spotless Lamb of God."* [16]

Great was his remorse. He would rather die himself, but no one, except one equal with God, could atone for man's disobedience.

---

16   White, E., Patriarch and Prophets, p. 68

Sanctuary History in Old Testament Times.

The years rolled by, and the great hand of time marked off the centuries. The family of Adam multiplied rapidly and spread throughout the earth, and the prince of this world worked overtime with marvellous cunning and deceit to steal man's affections away from God. Before long most of mankind was brought under his control, and the world was now divided into two camps - the minority who worshiped God and obeyed His commandments, and the majority who refused Him both worship and obedience. Wickedness increased to such a fearful extent that man's thoughts were continually evil, and the earth was filled with violence (Gen 6:5-7, 11). After approximately 2,000 years, the inhabitants of this world passed the point of no return and God sent a worldwide flood to destroy them.

Through righteous Noah and his family, God kept a knowledge of truth alive on the earth. After the flood Noah reinstated the sacrificial system. His first act upon leaving the ark was to sacrifice one of each of the clean animals. It was an act of faith in a world now devastated by flood. God's response was to stretch a beautiful rainbow across the sky - a visible sign of His presence, protection, and love.

As Noah's family grew and populated the earth, wickedness once again took possession of the people, but God's plans and purposes are never defeated. The patriarchs, Noah, Abraham, Isaac, and Jacob, continued to perform the simple system of sacrifices instituted by God. These men possessed powerful intellects and understood perfectly that the lamb represented Christ's sacrifice on man's behalf. They lived close to God and did not need many forms and ceremonies. They passed on to their descendants their knowledge of God, His law, and His requirements. As they journeyed from place to place, they raised up their altars and God drew near, often showing His acceptance of their offering by sending down fire from heaven to consume it.

Abraham, the father of the faithful, was born twenty-five years before the death of Shem - Noah's son and father of the Messianic line. Near the end of Abraham's long and fruitful life, God called upon him to act a part in a great drama depicting Calvary. This was to impress upon Abraham's mind the terrible cost of Calvary, and to leave for future generations a vivid illustration of what the sacrifices were designed to teach.

One night God spoke to Abraham and commanded him to sacrifice his son Isaac upon Mt Moriah. Appalled and horrified by such a request Abraham could have refused - he had that choice. But over the years he had learned to trust God in all things. God had never failed him, and so in quiet obedience he went.

The father's heart was heavy with pain and grief as he trudged the three days to Mt Moriah with his beloved son by his side. He did not understand the command. It caused him much anguish. It did not make sense to kill this son, the one through whose line the promised Messiah was to come. But Abraham trusted God, even in pain and darkness. The belief that God would resurrect his son was the only hope that gleamed in his tortured mind.

As they climbed the mountain together, the innocent Isaac, with the wood for the sacrifice tied to his back, suddenly asked, *"My father, Behold the fire and the wood; but where is the lamb? And Abraham replied, 'My son, God will provide Himself a lamb.'"* Abraham hardly understood the significance of his own words.

When it came time to tell Isaac what God required, the son, like Christ, was a willing sacrifice. Though alarmed and frightened, he submitted to his father's request and allowed himself to be bound upon the altar. Isaac had also learned to trust God - in life as well as in death. As Abraham lifted his trembling arm with the knife clutched tightly in a bloodless hand, God called to him, *"Abraham, Abraham . . . Lay not your hand upon the lad, don't do anything to him. For now I know that you fear God, seeing you have not withheld your son, your only son, from Me* (Genesis 22:1-19)."

Then the eyes of Abraham were opened, and he saw the lamb which God had provided in Isaac's place. A ram caught in a thicket - a crown of thorns around its head. This ram, a mature male, prefigured Christ - the One who would be offered in our stead, so that we, like Isaac, may go free.

What a moving illustration of the pain our Heavenly Father would endure when His Son carried *"the wood"* on His back up the hill to Calvary! But for God there would be no one to stay the knife. The ram with the crown of thorns was His Son. God's Son must die so that Abraham's son might live. Such is the price of love; the love God has for His wayward children. To bring them back into fellowship with Himself there was only one way - the way of the cross.

Isaac's inquiry, *"My Father . . . Where is the lamb"* was answered centuries later by John the Baptist who, when seeing Jesus by the Jordan River, exclaimed, ***"Behold the Lamb of God!"*** (John 1:29).

Again the years rolled by. Isaac's son, Jacob, married and twelve sons were born to him. During a time of great famine, he moved his sons and grandchildren to Egypt where there was plenty of feed for their large herds of sheep and cattle. The family grew and prospered until they numbered many thousands and alarmed the Egyptians.

To crush any potential threat to their national security, and to provide an economic boost to the Egyptian economy, they forced the children of Jacob (Israel) to become their slaves. As time passed, they were subjected to greater and still greater cruelty. With their days consumed by incessant toil, and surrounded by heathen darkness, they soon lost sight of the significance of their simple sacrifices and drifted toward Egyptian idolatry. Was a knowledge of the true God about to be extinguished from this earth at last?

Once more God intervened for the saving of mankind and for the preservation of truth. Using Moses as His general, He delivered the people from Egypt, and restored to them a knowledge of His law and the sacrificial system. However, after many years of slavery they could no longer grasp the truths of salvation without simple illustrations, so God gave them the sanctuary. It was the plan of salvation in kindergarten form, a pictorial representation of His entire plan to restore in man the image of God. *"A wonderful art gallery; where, by the hand of a master artist, the different parts of the marvellous plan of redemption are portrayed."*[17]

The command given to Moses was, *"And let them make me a sanctuary that I may dwell among them"* (Exodus 25:8). How God longs to be with His children! The very first picture we have of God after Adam and Eve sinned is that of Him walking in the garden, seeking for, and calling to His wayward children (Genesis 3:8, 9). They have disobeyed Him and are hiding, but He has not forsaken them.

The sanctuary was a miniature model of the one already existing in heaven, *"the true tabernacle, which the Lord pitched, and not man...the more perfect tabernacle, not made with hands"* (Hebrews 8:1,2 and 9:11). All the work connected with it was a representation of the work that Jesus would do, on earth and in heaven, for the redemption of the lost race. It was the most wonderful object lesson ever given, a living parable, a masterpiece of true education.

When Jesus walked this earth, He taught the people by means of parables. He illustrated the unknown by the known, the unseen by the seen. Divine truths were connected to familiar objects and scenes. For example, picture in your mind a day by the Sea of Galilee. A large, eager crowd is gathered on the shore to hear the Lord teach. Beside the sea lies the beautiful plain of Gennesaret, and beyond the plain rise the Galilean hills. Upon both hillside

---

17   Haskell, S., *The Cross and Its Shadow*, p. 24

and plain famers are busy casting seed into the ploughed ground. Looking upon the scene before Him, Jesus begins His object lesson with the immortal words: *"Behold a Sower went forth to sow . . ."* (Matthew 13:1-9). In the future, whenever the people saw a farmer casting seed into the ground, they would recall the Saviour's words.

Jesus Himself was an object lesson. By knowing Him, hearing Him, seeing Him, touching Him, the people learned about God. The invisible glory of God was revealed in the visible human form of Jesus of Nazareth.

Likewise, the great purpose of the sanctuary was to teach complex truths about the position and work of Christ which would be difficult to understand without it. It would be the key that would unlock the treasure house of God's Word, and reveal to man the grand, central theme of the Bible. It would be an arena to present the great drama of the ages - acted out by sinner and priest and directed by God Himself.

> *"All the doctrines of salvation through Christ are symbolized in the sanctuary - the gift of God's only begotten Son to the world, His crucifixion, burial, resurrection, and ascension. His work as High Priest, as Judge, and as King Eternal. And the work of the angels and of the Holy Spirit."* [18]

Let us now take a brief journey through time as we look at the history of this sanctuary before it was finally destroyed in 70 AD.

a. The Sanctuary at Sinai

God's first 'classroom' was built at the base of Mt Sinai. To show Moses what He required in the building of this project, God called him up onto the mountain where He communed with him for forty days and forty nights. During this time Moses was shown a miniature model, or a *'pattern,'* of the sanctuary already existing in heaven - *"a greater and*

---

18   Smith, U., *Looking Unto Jesus*, p. 21

more perfect tabernacle, not made with hands" (Hebrews 9:11). The Divine Architect required exactness of detail - and skill, wisdom, and perfection in the execution of the work, because the services of the sanctuary illustrated the work of Christ in saving mankind.

Exodus chapters 25-31 give the complete list of details presented to Moses. This description occupies more space in the Bible than any other subject and gives us a clue as to the importance God attaches to this study.

Eight times in the Bible reference is made to the *'pattern'* of the heavenly sanctuary which was given to Moses on Mount Sinai.[19] He was shown the blueprint, if you like, of that wonderful structure in heaven, the dwelling place of God,[20] so that he could more intelligently build a model of it on earth.

What did it look like? The Bible gives many details, of which we will give just a brief summary.

It was so constructed that it could be taken apart and carried by the children of Israel during their forty years of wandering in the wilderness. It was

---

19   See Exodus 25:9, 40; 26:30; 27 :8; Numbers 8:4;
     1 Chronicles 28:11,12,18,19; Acts 7:44; Hebrews 8:5

20   Psalm 11:4, 102:19, Habakkuk 2:20, Isaiah 6:1,
     Jeremiah 17:12, John 2:13-16, Revelation 11:19

therefore small, not more than 16.8 m x 5.5 m, yet it was a structure of extraordinary magnificence.

The walls consisted of upright boards of acacia wood overlaid with gold and set in silver sockets. These were held in place by pillars and connecting bars, also overlaid with gold. The roof consisted of four different coverings designed for beauty and protection. The inner covering, the one forming the ceiling of the sanctuary; was composed of fine linen exquisitely embroidered with figures of angels in blue, purple, and scarlet thread. It presented a picture of outstanding beauty and splendour – a faint representation of the canopy of glory above the throne of God, where He sits surrounded by myriads of angels ready to fulfill His commands.

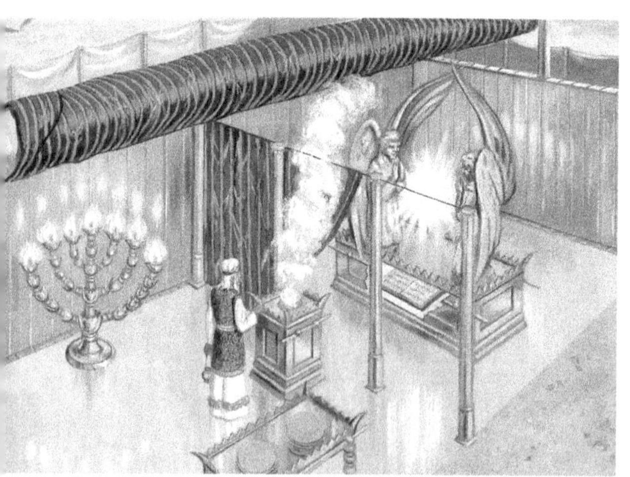

A richly embroidered curtain suspended from five pillars overlaid with gold formed the entrance to the tabernacle and faced towards the east.

The sacred tent was divided into two apartments by a rich and beautiful curtain hanging from gold-plated pillars. This curtain, like the "door" and the ceiling, was of the most gorgeous colours - blue, purple, and scarlet - and was decorated with cherubim embroidered with threads of silver and gold. These figures represented the angels and their work in the plan of redemption.

In the first apartment, or Holy Place, were three articles of furniture. The table of shew bread and the altar of incense were beautiful pieces of furniture made from acacia wood and overlaid with gold. The seven-branched candlestick was made from one solid piece of gold and decorated with exquisitely wrought flowers resembling lilies. As there were no windows in the sanctuary, the lamps were never all extinguished at one time, but shed their light by day and night.

In the next apartment, the Most Holy Place, was a single piece of furniture called the Ark of the Covenant. It was a chest of acacia wood, overlaid within and without with pure gold, and decorated with a golden crown. In this chest was kept the Ten Commandment law which had been inscribed on tables of stone by God Himself, and presented to Moses on Mt Sinai (Deuteronomy 10:1-5). This was the law which the children of Israel had lost sight of during their years of slavery in Egypt.

The cover of the ark was called the Mercy Seat and was made from one solid piece of gold. Mounted on either end of the Mercy Seat and facing each other, were two golden angels with their heads turned reverently downward toward the ark. Between the angels, and over the Mercy Seat, shone the visible manifestation of God's glory, called the Shekinah. When God was present, this glorious light shone over the curtain between the two apartments, flooding them both with light.

"No language can describe the glory of the scene presented within the sanctuary—the gold-plated walls reflecting the light from the golden candlestick, the brilliant hues of the richly embroidered curtains with their shining angels, the table and the altar of incense, glittering with gold. Beyond the second veil the sacred ark with its mystic cherubim, and above it the holy Shekinah, the visible manifestation of Jehovah's presence; all but dim reflection of the glories of the temple of God in heaven, the great centre of the work for

man's redemption." [21]

This wonderful structure was enclosed by an open space called the court, which was surrounded by screens of fine white linen suspended from pillars of shining brass. These hangings, which enclosed the court, were only about one half as high as the walls of the tabernacle, and so the building could be plainly seen by the people without.

The entrance to the court faced toward the east. It was composed of costly and beautiful curtains embroidered in a similar manner to the ones which formed part of the sanctuary itself.

In the court, nearest the entrance, stood the brazen altar of burnt offering. Upon this were consumed all the sacrifices made unto the Lord. Between this altar and the door to the sanctuary stood the laver, a large, shining, basin-like structure made from the brass mirrors donated by the women of Israel. It was here that the priests were required to wash their hands and feet before entering the tabernacle.

This tent-like structure was carried by the Israelites during their forty years of wandering in the wilderness. During these years, it was taken down and erected some fifty times. When it came time to break camp, the Shekinah cloud of glory, the pillar of light, went before the people to search out a new resting place. Where it came to a halt, those chosen by God to carry the sacred ark placed it directly below the cloud. The tabernacle was then erected around the ark by those especially appointed to this work by God Himself.

Thus, in this "*waste howling wilderness*" (Deuteronomy 32:10), the people could travel confidently, knowing that God Himself was watching

---

21   White, E., Patriarchs and Prophets, p. 349

over them and leading them safely to the Promised Land (Exodus 40:36-38).

b. Solomon's Temple

In the Promised Land, the wilderness sanctuary continued to be the centre of worship until Solomon's temple replaced it. This magnificent structure, commissioned by King David, and built by his son King Solomon, was one of the wonders of the ancient world.

"It has been calculated that this famous building contained 86 tons of gold, and 126 tons of silver . . . The splendour of Solomon's Temple defied comprehension. Nowhere on the face of this planet did a structure of such size and beauty command the awe of man. People from many lands travelled great distances just to set eyes on this temple, never to be disappointed. Its array of shining metals and precious stones was dazzling beyond belief. This enormous temple featured planks of cedar and cypress – fir trees hand-crafted to expose their elegant grains. The entire structure was overlaid on the inside with gold. Precious stones of onyx and marble were seen in abundance. Silver, brass,

and iron were used. Outer courtyard and inner chambers were adorned with high-reaching palm trees and colourful flowers." [22]

The history of Solomon's temple became the history of the religious experience of the children of Israel. When they departed from God, it was neglected and started to fall into disrepair. Several kings stripped it of its treasures to procure treaties with foreign kings, and at times it was even polluted by idolatrous worship as the Israelites fell further and further away from God. Several good kings, notably Hezekiah and Josiah, attempted to halt this process of spiritual decline by repairing the building and restoring true worship, but it was all in vain. [23]

God sent prophet after prophet to warn His people, but they would not listen. [24] After centuries of disobedience, warnings despised, and prophets abused, God at last allowed this magnificent temple to be destroyed by the Babylonians. In 586 B.C. Nebuchadnezzar, king of Babylon, swept down upon Jerusalem, looted and destroyed the temple, and took many of the people captive.

"Among the righteous still in Jerusalem, to whom had been made plain the divine purpose, were some who determined to place beyond the reach of ruthless hands the sacred ark containing the tables of stone on which had been traced the precepts of the Decalogue. This they did. With mourning and sadness, they secreted the ark in a cave, where it was to be hidden from the people of Israel and Judah because of their sins and was to be no more

---

22   Gray, J., The Ark of the Covenant, p. 123

23   2 Kings 21:4-7; 2 Chronicles 29:3-35; 2 Kings 22:3-7

24   2 Chronicles 36:14-20; Jeremiah 11:11,12

restored to them. That sacred ark is yet hidden. It has never been disturbed since it was secreted." [25]

c. Zerubbabel's Temple

After spending seventy years in captivity, the Jews were given permission to return to their native land. Most, by this time, had become so comfortable in Babylon that they decided to stay on, but a faithful remnant returned. With Zerubbabel in charge, they began the arduous task of rebuilding the temple (Ezra 6:14-22). The older men in the company, those who still remembered the first house of God, wept *"with a loud voice"* when they saw the foundations of the new (Ezra 3:12). They recalled the magnificence of Solomon's temple, and saw that this new structure would in no way compare with that splendid building. Worse still, the Ark of the Covenant had not been located, and a large stone, called "The Foundation Stone", was put in its place.

d. Herod's Temple

Zerubbabel's temple continued to serve as Israel's center of worship until near the time of Christ. Then Herod's temple took its place. In 20 B.C., King Herod began the work of repairing and remodelling the older structure. There was no furniture in the Most Holy Place, only the stone left over from Zerubbabel's temple. The other furnishings were probably the same as in Solomon's temple.

---

25   Prophets and Kings, 453 (published in 1917)

By the time of Christ, building operations had been in progress for forty-six years. The temple was not actually completed until A.D 66 – just four years before it was destroyed by the Romans.

It was a beautiful marble and gold structure set on a hill, with steps leading up from every direction in a series of terraces four hundred feet above the valley. The Jewish historian, Josephus, likened the temple to a snow-covered mountain.

Viewed from the Mount of Olives where Jesus foretold its destruction, it was a thing of beauty, an object to inspire awe and worship.

"This stately and grand structure was the pride and glory of the Jewish nation."

"While the westering sun was tinting and gilding the heavens, its resplendent glory lighted up the pure white marble of the temple walls and sparkled on its gold-capped pillars. From the crest of the hill where Jesus and His followers stood, it had the appearance of a massive structure of snow, set with golden pinnacles. At the entrance to the temple was a vine of gold and silver, with green leaves and massive clusters of grapes executed by the most skilful artists. This design represented Israel as a prosperous vine. The gold, silver, and living green were combined with rare taste and exquisite workmanship. As it twined gracefully about the white and glistening pillars, clinging with shining tendrils to their golden ornaments, it caught the splendour of the setting sun, shining as if with a glory borrowed from heaven." [26]

This stately and grand structure was the pride and glory of the Jewish nation.

e. A Saviour is Born

Day after day, year after year, the round of sacrifices and services which pointed to the coming of the Saviour con-

---

26   White, E., The Desire of Ages, p. 575

tinued, until they became mere dimly understood rituals. Even the prophecies which pointed so clearly to the birth, life, and death of Christ were misunderstood and misinterpreted. Priests and rulers looked not for a Saviour who would give His life as a ransom for mankind, but for a mighty king who would deliver them from the yoke of Rome, and exalt Israel to a position of pre-eminence among the nations. As the true spiritual meaning of the sanctuary and its services was lost, *"darkness covered the earth, and gross darkness the people"* (Isaiah 60:2).

Into this darkness stepped the Light of the world.   It was time to sweep back the tide of formalism and ignorance and bring back a knowledge of true religion. The Son of God laid aside His divine glory and power and took upon Himself weak human flesh[27]. As the great clock of time struck the hour, the Lamb of God was born in a stable in Bethlehem. The King of glory in a manger!

All heaven watched to see how their beloved Commander would be received by those He had come to save. Would there be a royal reception for the King of the universe? They watched in vain, for He *"came unto His own, and His own received Him not"* (John 1:11).

Was there an excuse for such neglect on the part of God's people? No! The prophets plainly foretold His birth, His work, His life, His betrayal, His death - even the time of His coming to this earth. His resurrection and ascension were also clearly portrayed in the Old Testament writings. Heaven had done everything possible to prepare the people for this significant event. The sanctuary service itself dramatized Christ's plan to save man, especially making plain His role as the Lamb of God. Even Gabriel, the mighty angel from the throne of God, came to the temple to inform Zacharias the priest that the Messiah's coming was at hand (Luke 1:5-17). But not a single preparation to welcome Him was made by the priests and religious leaders.

---

27   Philippians 2:5-8; Hebrews 2:14, 16-18

The angels determined that Jesus was not to be left without a reception. In the fields outside Bethlehem, some simple-hearted but godly shepherds were watching over their sheep the night Jesus was born. As they waited out the silent hours, they discussed the prophecies which pointed to a soon coming Redeemer. Suddenly a glorious light shone around them, and Gabriel stood before them. He had bypassed the haughty priests and rulers, to joyfully announce to these simple shepherds the good news. *"Behold"* he declared, *"I bring you good tidings of great joy . . .for unto you is born this day in the city of David, a Saviour, which is Christ the Lord"* (Luke 2:9-11).

"He had bypassed the haughty priests and rulers, to joyfully announce to these simple shepherds the good news."

The accompanying host of angels could no longer remain silent or hidden from view. Suddenly the sky seemed full of angelic beings and the whole field was illuminated with their glory. *"Earth was hushed, and heaven stopped to listen"* as beautiful celestial music echoed and re echoed around the surrounding hills.

> *"Glory to God in the highest, And on earth peace, and good will toward men"* (Luke 2:13, 14).

The heavenly music gradually died away, and the glorious light faded as the angels withdrew. Once more darkness covered the Bethlehem hills. With hearts overflowing with joy and wonder, the shepherds forgot their sheep and ran to find a Babe lying in a manger.

f. The End of the Sanctuary System

For approximately thirty-three and a half years, Jesus fulfilled to the letter all the prophecies concerning Himself. He plainly declared by word and by deed that He was Israel's Messiah - the One whom the sanctuary symbolized. But stubborn unbelief controlled the minds of the Jewish leaders. They refused to see in Jesus the long hoped for Messiah. They wanted a temporal king, and Jesus did not offer them an earthly kingdom, so they rejected Him.

When Jesus died as the substitute for man's sins, the significance of the sacrificial system came to an end. It was now time for God's classroom on earth to be shut down. The attention of Christ's followers was now to be directed to the heavenly temple where Jesus, after His resurrection, would minister as mankind's High Priest and Advocate.

On the cross, as Jesus cried out with a loud voice, *'It is finished,'* the thickly woven temple curtain separating the Holy from the Most Holy Place, was suddenly *"rent in twain"* (John 19:30; Matthew 27:51). A mysterious hand had taken hold of that heavy curtain and effortlessly ripped it in half. It was the time of the evening sacrifice. Tradition holds that as the priest was about to take the life of the lamb, the sound of the ripping curtain transfixed and terrified him. The knife dropped from his nerveless hand, and the lamb escaped!

The Jewish nation sealed its rejection of Christ by putting Him to death, and by this act they brought an end to the sacrificial system. God now left His sanctuary on earth for good. Its sacredness had departed. It was doomed to destruction. To continue its services now would be a hollow mockery.

g. The Destruction of the Temple

Herod's temple remained standing until A.D. 70. It was then destroyed by the Roman armies, just as Jesus had prophesied it would be. With a breaking heart He had sorrowfully announced from the Mount of Olives, *"Verily I say unto you, there shall not be left here one stone upon another; that shall not be thrown down"* (Matthew 24:1-2).

Approximately thirty-nine years after the death of Jesus, Titus and his armies besieged Jerusalem. In the general destruction of the city, Titus determined to save the beautiful temple. However, Jewish rebels hid in the sanctuary, and from behind its protective walls attacked the Roman

soldiers. This infuriated them.

At last Titus decided to take the temple by storm, though still hoping to save the building if possible.

> "But his command to preserve the temple was disregarded. In the struggle a firebrand was flung by a soldier through an opening in the porch, and immediately the cedar-lined chambers about the holy house were ablaze. Titus rushed to the place, followed by his generals and legionaries, and commanded the soldiers to quench the flames. His words went unheeded. In their fury the soldiers hurled blazing brands into the chambers adjoining the temple, and then with their swords they slaughtered in great numbers those who had found shelter there. Blood flowed down the temple steps like water. Thousands upon thousands of Jews perished. Above the sound of the battle, voices were heard shouting : 'Ichabod!' - the glory is departed.

> "Titus found it impossible to check the rage of his soldiers. He entered with his officers and surveyed the interior of the sacred edifice. The splendour filled them with wonder. As the flames had not yet penetrated to the Holy Place, he made a last effort to save it . . . However, furious animosity against

the Jews, the fierce excitement of battle, and the insatiable hope of plunder, overruled even the orders of Titus. The soldiers saw everything around them radiant with gold, which shone dazzlingly in the wild light of the flames . . . Unperceived, one of the soldiers thrust a lighted torch between the hinges of the door, and in an instant, the whole building was in flames.

"It was an appalling spectacle to the Romans - what was it like to the Jews? The whole summit of the hill which commanded the city, blazed like a volcano. One after another the buildings fell in with a tremendous crash and were swallowed up in the fiery abyss. The roofs of cedar were like sheets of flame. The gilded pinnacles shone like spikes of red light; the gate towers sent up tall columns of flame and smoke. The neighbouring hills were lighted up. Dark groups of people were seen watching in horrible anxiety the progress of destruction. The walls and heights of the upper city were crowded with faces, some pale with the agony of despair, others scowling unavailing vengeance . . . Both the city and the temple were razed to the foundations, and the ground upon which the holy house had stood was 'ploughed like a field' (Jeremiah 26:18). . . In the siege and the slaughter that followed, more than a million of the people perished." [28]

"O Jerusalem, Jerusalem, you that killed the prophets, and stoned them which are sent to you, how

---

28   White, E., The Great Controversy, pp.33,34 .
Selected from the writings of Jewish historian, Josephus.

often would I have gathered your children together, even as a hen gathers her chickens under her wings, and you would not! Behold, your house is left unto you desolate" (Matthew 23:37, 38).

And so ended the history of the sanctuary of the Old Testament - the sanctuary of the first covenant whose services began at the gate of Eden. The sacrificial system dominated the worship of God's people for approximately 4,000 years - from the fall of man until Calvary. Now it was no longer needed because the significance of the sacrifices was fulfilled by the death of Jesus Christ.

Today this ancient sacred site on Mt Moriah, the scene of Abraham's great test, is covered by an Islamic Mosque, the Dome of the Rock. For almost 2,000 years devout Jews have wailed over the destruction of their temple. Some extremists hope to destroy the Dome of the Rock and rebuild the temple, but it would be a futile exercise. Jesus is now ministering in the heavenly temple, of which the earthly was just an elaborate, scaled-down model. They need to lift their eyes heavenward.

h. The Heavenly Temple

Is there a sanctuary of the New Testament, of the new covenant, or has God abandoned His sanctuary model? No, His ways are perfect and never need to be altered. *"I am the Lord, I change not"* (Malachi 3:6).

God still has a sanctuary; the one Moses saw in vision when he was shown a miniature model of it on Mount Sinai. This is the sanctuary Paul writes so extensively about in the book of Hebrews, and which the apostle John saw in vision. It is the *"great powerhouse of Jehovah, the source of all the help necessary to overcome every temptation of*

Satan." [29]

When Christ returned to heaven, God gave His apostles great light regarding the heavenly sanctuary, especially now that the earthly model had been destroyed. Paul, in the book of Hebrews, clearly teaches that the sacrificial services of the temple were fulfilled in Christ and reveals His present position and work in the heavenly temple.

> *"We have such a High Priest, who is set on the right hand of the throne of the Majesty in the heavens. A Minister of the sanctuary, and of the true taber-nacle, which the Lord pitched, and not man"* (Hebrews 8:1, 2).

Christ is now High Priest of the *"more perfect tabernacle, not made with hands. . . For Christ is not now entered into the holy places made with hands, which are figures* (patterns) *of the true; but into heaven itself, now to ap-pear in the presence of God for us"* (Hebrews 9:11, 24).

In chapter four of the book of Revelation, the apostle John describes a vision he received of the heavenly tem-ple. A door in heaven is opened and he is privileged to look right into the very heart of the throne room of God. Here he sees *"seven lamps of fire"* burning before His throne. In chapter eight, John describes an angel standing by a gold-en altar holding a golden censer full of incense. In chapter eleven, he sees into the Most Holy Place – *"And the temple of God was opened in heaven, and there was seen in His temple the ark of His testament"* (Revelation 11:19). These items, - a golden candlestick, a golden altar, a golden cen-ser and the ark of His testament - are all sanctuary items.

The language of Revelation is rich in sanctuary symbolism:

> *"Therefore they* (the 144,000), *are before the throne of God, and serve Him day and night <u>in His temple</u>. And He that sits on the throne shall dwell among them"* (7:15).

---

29   Haskell, S., The Cross and Its Shadow, p. 22

"And he opened his mouth in blasphemy against God, to blaspheme His name, and His tabernacle, and them that dwell in heaven" (13:6).

"And another angel came out of the temple, crying with a loud voice to Him that sat on the cloud, Thrust in Thy sickle, and reap: for the time is come for Thee to reap; for the harvest of the earth is ripe" (14:15, 17).

"And there came a great voice out of the temple of heaven, from the throne, saying, 'It is done'" (16:16).

Down through the centuries God's faithful children have always understood that when they sought the Lord *"their prayers came up to His holy dwelling place, even unto heaven"* (2 Chronicles 30:27). King David certainly believed this. *"In my distress I called upon the Lord and cried unto my God. He heard my voice out of His temple, and my cry came before Him even into His ears"* (Psalm 18:6; 2 Samuel 22:7).

The temple in heaven is the throne room of the universe, the dwelling place of God. Before the earthly temple was forsaken by the Lord, Jesus referred to it as *"My Father's house"* (John 2:16).

"The Lord is in His holy temple; let all the earth keep silence before Him" (Habakkuk 2:20).

"Be silent . . . before the Lord: for He is raised up out of His holy habitation" (Zechariah 2:13).

"The Lord is in His holy temple, the Lord's throne is in heaven" (Psalm 11:4).

"I saw the Lord sitting upon a throne, high and lifted up, and His train (glory), filled the temple" (Isaiah 6:1).

"The Lord shall roar from on high, and utter his voice from His holy habitation" (Jeremiah 25:30).

"There came a great voice out of the temple of

heaven, from the throne, saying, 'It is done"' (Revelation 16:17).

"A glorious high throne from the beginning is the place of our sanctuary" (Jeremiah 17:12).

The early Christian church understood that Christ was even then ministering on their behalf in the sanctuary in heaven. To Christ above they presented their prayers and requests. But as the centuries passed, a knowledge of salvation as taught by the sanctuary was gradually lost to view - especially when the Bible was taken from the people during the Dark Ages. At this time a man made system of salvation was instituted to take the place of Christ's ministry. True Christians were persecuted and killed by the millions for daring to worship God according to their conscience. The beautiful work of Christ on man's behalf, the only true salvation, was again largely lost sight of.

But God will never allow truth to die. People everywhere are rediscovering sanctuary truth as we move into the last days of this earth's history. A correct understanding of the sanctuary will shed a flood of light upon the mysteries of the Bible and will vitalize Christian experience and strengthen our faith in the closing work of God.

"The earthly sanctuary with its types and symbols is like the powerful lenses of the telescope that make it possible to view heavenly bodies which otherwise would be invisible. To the eye of the ignorant these wonderful lenses appear like ordinary glass. But the astronomer, who longs to know more of the wonders of the heavens, is filled with rapture as he gazes through them." [30]

---

30   Haskell, S., The Cross and Its Shadow, pp. 22-24

Chapter 5

To Build a Sanctuary

The Three Essentials

1) Obedience to God's Requirements

On earth the sanctuary story begins with God's people in servitude in the land of Egypt. As already noted, famine forced Jacob, his twelve sons, their families, flocks, and herds, to move into Egypt. They settled in the land of Goshen in the fertile Nile delta. Here they prospered until pharaohs arose who knew not the God of Jacob and Joseph. Concerned for national security, and greedy for cheap labour; these pharaohs forced the Israelites into slavery. For over 200 years the descendants of Abraham endured a servitude that became increasingly severe and cruel as the years rolled by. In their distress they cried out to God. God heard their cry and delivered them by a series of mighty miracles which destroyed Egypt's prosperity and caused Pharoah to release them.

At the Red Sea the children of Israel faced total annihilation, but once again God delivered them. Despite His awesome power God was like a gentle, caring father to the Israelites. With His glory hidden in a cloud, He personally led them through the *"waste howling wilderness"* of the Sinai desert (Exodus 40:38). He fed them manna from heaven when they were hungry and gave them water from a rock when they were thirsty. Now it was time for them to build a house of worship, the sanctuary; but first they must be instructed in His ways for God had a high and holy purpose for His people. As a great Christian author once expressed it, *"Higher than the highest human thought can reach is God's ideal for His children."* [31]

To Israel was granted the great privilege of not only being incorporated into a church, but also a nation under the personal administration of the God of the universe! They were to be God's 'showcase' to the world, *"a peculiar treasure . . . above all nations . . . a kingdom of priests and a holy nation"* (Exodus 19:4-6).

But before they could become a *"holy nation,"* the attention of the people must be directed to God's great moral law which formed the foundation of His government. This law, known and obeyed by the patriarchs, had been largely forgotten during the long years of Egyptian slavery. It was God's purpose to make the children of Israel the guardians of this law so that they might hold it in trust for the whole world. By living out its principles they were to have the high honour of being God's light to a world enshrouded in darkness. If they were true to their trust, God would make them a power in the world and would exalt them above all other nations. Under His wise and holy rule, they would demonstrate the superiority of the worship of the true God above that of every other god.

To achieve this purpose, God led Israel by a pillar of cloud from the Red Sea to a quiet, yet majestic place in the wilderness. Here He planned that they should rest for almost twelve months while He personally instructed them in the way of righteousness. At the foot of Mount Sinai, they spread out their tents in an orderly fashion according to God's command. Above them on the mountain top, a cloud veiled the presence of their invisible Leader. From a rock

---

31   White, E,. The Desire of Ages, p. 311

God caused a river of water to gush forth to provide for their personal needs and for the needs of their flocks and herds. At night, a pillar of fire assured them of divine protection, and while they slept, the bread of heaven fell gently upon the ground.

Each morning the rays of the rising sun gilded the dark ridges which encircled the camp and filled the valley with sunshine, reminding these weary people of God's constant love and care. Surrounding them like a protective wall, the vast, rugged heights in their solitary grandeur seemed to speak to the heart of God, of His strength, His majesty, and His love. It was a scene to inspire awe and worship, and it was here that Israel was to receive the most wonderful revelation ever given by God to man. He had gathered His people to this special place to impress upon them the sacredness of His requirements, and to instil in them the need for great and radical change.

The Giving of the Law

To impress the Israelites with the sacredness of their trust, God proposed to speak the law Himself from the heights of Sinai. Following directions given by God, Moses instructed the people to spend three days preparing themselves physically and spiritually for this momentous event, then with reverent solemnity he led them to the base of the mountain. The mount itself was fenced off to prevent any person or animal from accidently intruding upon sacred ground. At the foot of the mountain were assembled at least 603,550 men aged twenty years and over. The women were also gathered there, as well as children less than twenty years of age. Some authorities estimate that approximately three million people assembled to hear God speak that day (Numbers 1:45,46). It was a holy Sabbath day, the 5th day of the month of Sivan, the day of Pentecost.[32]

Upon the heights a thick dark cloud rested, almost engulf-

---

32   See Jewish Calendar p. 84

ing the entire mountain, and from this cloud vivid flash-es of lightning pierced the darkness, and peals of thunder echoed and re-echoed from the surrounding peaks. *"And Mount Sinai was altogether on a smoke because the Lord descended upon it in fire. And the smoke thereof ascended as the smoke of a furnace, and the whole mountain quaked greatly." "And the glory of the Lord was like a devouring fire." "The voice of the trumpet sounded long, and waxed louder and louder,"* so that all the people trembled (Exodus 19:16-19; 24:17).

Suddenly the thunder ceased. The sound of the trumpet was quieted, and all was still. A period of solemn silence followed, and then the voice of God was heard proclaiming His divine law, the Ten Commandment (Exodus 20:1-17). His voice, rich and melodious, like the sound of many wa-ters, rolled down from the mountain heights, and engulfed the valley. He paused after each precept, and then that voice, richer than the most sublime music, pronounced the next command. The people, with their faces to the ground, listened with trembling awe.

> *"This was the only time that with audible voice, God ever addressed His assembled people on earth, an event well calculated to inspire in man the solemni-ty and sacredness of the law of God, His eternal law that governs the entire universe."* [33]

Both Father and Son, together with myriads of angels, came to the mount that day (Deuteronomy 33:2; Psalm 68:17). So awesome was the scene of God's grandeur and majesty that the people fell upon their faces before the Lord, and even the intrepid Moses exclaimed, *"I fear exceedingly and quake"* (Hebrews 12:21).

God's sermon that memorable Sabbath morning was brief but emphatic and was certainly the most important ser-mon ever preached. He had more to say to the people but withheld further instruction as the Israelites were over-

---

33   Peck, S., The Path to the Throne of God, p. 36

whelmed with terror. The fiery display on the mountain, the roaring of thunder, the sound of the mysterious trumpet, and the unspeakable power of God's voice so terrified the people that they urgently begged Moses, *"speak thou with us and we will hear, but let not God speak to us lest we die"* (Exodus 20:19).

God heard their cry of distress and understood. He always understands the fears of His children, and in His compassion and tender mercy He did not reprove them. Instead, He called Moses up alone into the mountain so that He could give him the rest of His instructions for Israel.

God's first requirement was the building of an altar at the base of the mountain, so that the sacrificial system could be continued (Exodus 20:24). Next, He outlined for Israel a series of civil laws, called judgments, which illustrated and applied the principles of the Ten Commandments. These judgments are recorded in Exodus chapters 21 to 23.

Early the next morning, while the glory and majesty of God's presence rested on the heights above them, an altar was built as directed, and the covenant between the Lord and His people duly ratified (Exodus 24:3-7). Now Moses, together with seventy elders, was called back into the cloud to await further communications from God. While waiting, the men searched their hearts for secret, unconfessed sins, and meditated and prayed. There on the mountainside they beheld the glory of God above them, and under His feet there appeared to be *"a paved work of a sapphire stone."* It was as *"the body of heaven* (sky blue) *in its clearness"* (Exodus 24:10).

For six days they waited. Then *"on the seventh day"* Moses was summoned by God to enter alone into the midst of the cloud (Exodus 24:16-18). There he remained for the next forty days and nights, and during this time he was given instructions for building the sanctuary and received the Ten Commandment law, engraved by God Himself on tables of stone. God did not trust His precepts to the memory of a people who were so prone to forget, so He engraved them into stone to show that they cannot be erased or changed. The Holy Scriptures record that they were *"written with the finger of God"* (Exodus 31:18).

The law and the sanctuary always go together. The law tells us what God requires, and the sanctuary teaches us how God has made it possible for us to obey. The law without the sanctuary is dead works. The sanctuary without the law is a round of meaningless ceremonies.

It is interesting to conjecture as to what kind of stone God wrote His Ten Commandments on. The only stone mentioned in the description of His presence on Mount Sinai is the precious *"sapphire stone,"* a lustrous clear blue stone, *"as the body of heaven in its clearness"* (Exodus 24:10). The prophet Ezekiel was later given a vision of God's throne which he said appeared to be made of sapphire (Ezekiel 1:26). How fitting it would be for God to write the Ten Commandment law on the same precious stone on which His feet rested while He spoke His law from Mount Sinai - the same stone which forms the very throne of God! His law and His throne carved from the same blue sapphire - unmistakably symbolizing the law as the foundation of His government! And how fitting it should be a blue stone, a colour representing obedience to law. God required the people to sew a blue band around the borders of their garments, so that they might *"look upon it, and remember all the commandments of the Lord, and do them"* (Numbers 15:37-41). Maybe for this same reason God has placed a blue sky over our heads!

Soon afterwards, because of the golden calf apostasy, these precious tables of stone were broken. Moses then cut two more tables from ordinary stone, and upon these God once again wrote His law (Exodus 34:1,4,28). Is this not a marvellous picture of the long-suffering, mercy, and patience of God toward those who break His law?

Instructions Regarding the Sanctuary

While on the mountain with God, Moses received incredibly detailed instructions regarding the building of the sanctuary. Eighteen times in Exodus chapters 39 and 40 it is stated that even the smallest details were to be *"as the Lord commanded Moses."* And eight times in the Scriptures reference is made to the "pattern," or model, shown Moses on the Mount, emphasizing the fact that in no respect, however minute, was the 'blueprint' to be disregarded.[34]   It is impossible to account for God giving such minute details except to emphasize the spiritual meaning of the building itself in all its varied parts.

God does not multiply words without a purpose, as *"every word of God is pure"* (Proverbs 30:5). If God repeats anything it is *"because the thing is established by God"* (Genesis 41:32)

The description of the structure and furnishings of the tabernacle, together with the services connected with it, occupies more space in the Bible than any other subject in either the Old or the New Testaments. Surely this should indicate to us the importance of its study. We must dig, and dig deep, to find the treasures it contains.

2) Willing and Sacrificial Giving

When the time came to build the tabernacle, Moses' first words to the people were God's last words to him on the subject: *"These are the words which the Lord hath commanded, that ye should do them. Six days shall work be done, but on the seventh day there shall be to you a holy day, a Sabbath of rest to the Lord. Whoever does work therein shall be put to death"* (Exodus 35:1,2).

After making it abundantly clear that the people should honour God's holy day of rest, Moses announced that he was now going to take up a collection for the building of

---

34   Exodus 25:9,40; 26:30; 27:8; Numbers 8:4; Acts 7:44; Hebrews 8:5; 1Chronicles 28:11-12,18-19.

the sanctuary, for God had said, *"Of every man that giveth it willingly with his heart ye shall take My offerings"* (Exodus 25:2; 35:4,5).

A large amount of the most precious and costly materials was required, yet God would only accept freewill offerings. Only a willing gift, a gift of love, could fitly represent God's gift to man. In giving His Son, God gave all (John 3:16; Galatians 2:20). The spirit of self-sacrifice purchased salvation for us, and the same spirit will be in the hearts of all God's children. The Lord asked for generous donations and the people gave freely. Today the donation would be valued in the millions of dollars.

> *"They came, both men and women, as many as were willing hearted, and brought bracelets, earrings, and rings, and necklaces, all jewels of gold . . . And offerings of gold."* They also brought *"blue, and purple, and scarlet, and fine linen, and goats' hair, and red skins of rams, and badgers' skins . . . Silver and brass . . . and acacia wood . . . And all the women that were wise hearted did spin with their hands, and brought that which they had spun, both of blue, and of purple, and of scarlet, and of fine linen. And all the women whose hearts stirred them up in wisdom spun goats' hair. And the rulers brought onyx stones, and stones to be set for the ephod, and for the breastplate. And spice, and oil for the light, and oil for the anointing, and for the sweet incense . . . A willing offering unto the Lord . . . for all manner of work, which the Lord had commanded"* (Exodus 35:22-29).

"Gold or goats" hair! God will use the least as well as the most expensive gift if it is brought with a willing heart. From this great variety of gifts one tabernacle was to be built - unity in diversity. How wonderfully God works with our willing gifts - and with us!" [35]

---

35   Peck, S., The Path to the Throne of God, p. 49

Some may be asking, where did all these gifts come from? Before God delivered the Israelites *"at midnight,"* He instructed them to visit their Egyptian taskmasters and request wages for their many years of servitude. By this time the Egyptians were anxious to be rid of the Hebrews because of the plagues which had devastated their land. They were also very much in awe of the Israelites' God, and so gave the people large amounts of silver and gold, and other precious things. The amount collected was so great that it is recorded, *"they spoiled the Egyptians,"* (Exodus 11:2-3; 12:35-36). When Pharaoh issued his command for the immediate departure of the Israelites, they went forth laden with the wealth of their oppressors. This was the fulfillment of God's promise to Abraham, that at the end of 400 years in Egypt, the people would come out *"with great substance"* (Genesis 15:13-14).

God gave so they could give. This is how God works. *"Give and it shall be given unto you. Good measure, pressed down, shaken together, and running over . . . for with the same measure that you use, it will be measured back to you"* (Luke 6:38).

As the sanctuary was in the process of being constructed, the people continued to bring their offerings until those in charge of the work found they had enough - more than enough. Moses commanded, *"Let not man or woman make any more work for the offering of the sanctuary. So, the people were restrained from bringing,"* (Exodus 36:5-7).

3) The Inspiration of the Holy Spirit

The sanctuary was not built by skillful craftsmen relying on natural ability. Men and women were inspired and enabled by the Spirit of God. As Jesus has truly said, *"Without Me you can do nothing"* (John 15:5). Men and women chosen by God were filled, *"with the Spirit of God in wisdom, and in understanding, and in knowledge, and in all manner of workmanship"* (Exodus 35:31).

"There is no limit to the usefulness of one who, putting self aside, makes room for the working of the Holy Spirit upon his heart, and lives a life wholly consecrated to God. All who consecrate body, soul, and spirit to His service will be constantly receiving a new endowment of physical, mental, and spiritual power." [36]

36   White, E., Ministry of Healing, p. 159

Jewish Calendar

ABIB

Sun	Mon	Tue	Wed	Thu	Fri	Sab
						1
2	3	4	5	6	7	8
9	10	11	12	13	(14)	15
16	17	18	19	20	21	22
23	24	25	26	27	28	29
30						

ZIF

Sun	Mon	Tue	Wed	Thu	Fri	Sab
	1	2	3	4	5	6
7	8	9	10	11	12	13
14	15	16	17	18	19	20
21	22	23	24	25	26	27
28	29					

SIVAN

Sun	Mon	Tue	Wed	Thu	Fri	Sab
		1	2	(3)	4	(5)
6	7	8	9	10	11	(12)
13	14	15	16	17	18	19
20	21	22	23	24	25	26
27	28	29	30			

Abib 14 - Passover: Ex.12:2; 13:4

Sivan 3 - Sinai Encampment: Ex.19:1

Sivan 5 - Law Given: Ex.19:10,11,16; 20:1-17

Sivan 12 - Moses called into cloud after six days of preparation: Ex. 24:12-18.

Chapter 6

"Behold the Lamb"[37]

Jesus in the Court of this Earth

With Chapters 4 and 5 as background, it is now time to begin an exciting journey through the sanctuary and discover what the plan of salvation means to us personally.

Jesus is the great Pioneer who has blazed salvation's trail for us through new, untried, and dangerous territory. By His life and death on planet Earth, He has prepared a way by which we may be reconciled to God and receive again the gift of immortality. By following in the footsteps of Jesus, by keeping to His rules, we cannot fail. We fail only as we refuse to listen to His voice. We fail when we make up our own rules and try to blaze our own trail. We fail when we follow man instead of Christ and turn a deaf ear to the Holy

---

37   "After the descendants of Abraham became the nation of Israel, God instituted the sacrificial system as recorded in Leviticus. This sacrificial system did not, could not, and was not meant to abolish sin (Hebrews 10:4), because only Christs death on the cross can do that (1 John 3:5) . . . The animal sacrifices were meant to demonstrate the meaning and necessity of the future death of Christ the Messiah, as *the Lamb of God who takes away the sin of the world*" (John 1:29; cf. Isaiah 53:6; Hebrews 9:11-14).

Grigg, Russell, How to have a right relationship with God, Creation Magazine, Vol. 44, No. 2, 2022.

Spirit. There is only one way back to God, and this is portrayed in symbolic form by the sanctuary and its services. *"Thy way* O God *is in the sanctuary"* (Psalm 77:13).

I am reminded of a story I heard while living in the States about a group of pioneers on their way to the Californian gold fields from their homes in the Midwest. A tried-and-true trail had already been laid. It was long and hard, but it got the travellers to their destination. By following this trail they reached the Sierras in time to cross over before winter snows blocked the way.

One group of travellers however, impatient to get to their destination sooner, listened to the voice of one who promised an easier, quicker route. They were warned by a local farmer of the dangers that lay ahead and urged to turn back, but stubbornly they refused. They had faith in their new guide. However, by following his directions they soon found themselves lost on an unmarked trail. They tried one route and then another, and in the process lost valuable time and resources. Tempers frayed and unity between fellow travellers deteriorated.

After many dangers and frustrations, they at last came upon a large, dry, salt lake. Their false guide had gone on ahead with another party, but he left a note saying the lake was only forty miles across. This information proved incorrect. The lake was at least twice that distance. Without water in that dreadful summer heat many of the livestock, including the valuable oxen, perished. Wagons had to be abandoned, and possessions littered the desert. On the other side of that trackless waste, the weary pioneers at last reached the junction where the true and tried road to the west met their unmarked trail. They saw that the travellers who had taken the longer route had passed that way several weeks before. Now well behind schedule, and with winter soon to descend upon them, they hurried on. But it was too late! Bitter winter snows trapped them in a mountain pass, and approximately half the party perished.

There is only one true Guide on the journey of life. As we press on the upward way, there will be many false guides to direct our feet onto unsafe paths. We need to keep our eyes on the One who has walked this way before us. He tells us *"I am the Way, the Truth, and the Life. No man cometh unto the Father except through Me"* (John 14:6). We can trust Him. His way is found in the Holy Bible. If the way presented, no matter how enticing it may appear, is not the way of the Guidebook, leave it alone. Remember to *Follow the Lamb!*

1) THE SANCTUARY GATE - God's Amazing Gift

As every part of the sanctuary depicts our Saviour and His mission in some unique way, it is not surprising to find that even the gate to the sanctuary court represents Jesus, especially His invitation, *"Come unto Me"* (Matthew 11:28). Our spiritual walk begins and ends with Jesus. He is represented by the gate to the sheep fold (John 10:7,9), and by the ladder Jacob saw in a dream stretching from earth to heaven (Genesis 28:12). *"Strait is the gate and narrow is the way"* that leads to eternal life, but it is a glorious way, consecrated by the footprints of Christ Himself (Matthew 7:13,14).

By using the special sanctuary cubit of 1.8 feet or 0.5 m. (Ezekiel 43:13), we find that the court surrounding the sanctuary measured approximately ninety by one hundred eighty feet, or 54.9 x 27.4 m (Exodus 27:18). This space was divided into two squares, each ninety-by-ninety feet.

The walls of the court were composed of hangings of fine white linen, representing the robe of Christ's righteousness surrounding and covering His *'born-again'* children, as they pass through the sanctuary experience on their way back to God (compare Exodus 38:16 and Revelation 19:8).

The entrance gate was twenty cubits (36 feet or 11m) wide and was in the centre of the eastern wall. The curtains forming the door were composed of purple, blue, and scarlet woollen threads woven into a beautiful veil and embroidered with fine wires of pure gold (Exodus 27:16; 39:3). *"When completed it was a gorgeous piece of exquisite and durable tapestry reflecting the rainbow colours and, especially in the sunshine, brilliantly illuminated with the inwrought gold."* [38]

A similar, though more luxuriously embroidered veil led into the Holy Place, and still another into the Most Holy Place. Each represented Jesus, the only *"name under heaven given among men, whereby we must be saved"* (Acts 4:12). Each veil represents a new and vital step forward in the Christian's experience as he advances toward the throne of God.

- In the courtyard *justification* is pictured, and the only way to obtain it is through the veil - Jesus Christ.

- In the Holy Place *sanctification* [39] is illustrated, and the only way to obtain it is through the veil - Jesus Christ.

- In the Most Holy Place *glorification* is the goal, and the only way to obtain it is through the veil - Jesus Christ.

"Jesus is the gateway to every stage of Christian growth." [40]

Each veil was embroidered with golden cherubim, illustrating the important part angels must play in the plan of redemption (Exodus 26:31).

---

38   Peck, S., The Path to the Throne of God, p. 64

39   These terms will be explained in greater detail later in the book

40   Hardinge, L., Shadows of His Sacrifice, p. 12

A Symphony of Colour

As already noted, all features of the sanctuary service, including the construction of the building itself, taught an important lesson about Christ and His work. Even the exquisite colours used in each of the veils taught a spiritual lesson. They represent the lovely character and self- sacrificing mission of Christ. This cascade of colour summarizes who Jesus is.

Purple symbolizes His kingship and authority. It reminds us that Jesus is *"King of kings, and Lord of lords"* (Revelation 19:16).

Scarlet represents His self-sacrificing love. It reminds us of One who was *"despised and rejected of men, a Man of sorrows and acquainted with grief."* The One by *"whose stripes we are healed"* (see Revelation 19:13; Isaiah 53, Psalm 22). It speaks of the cross.

Blue symbolizes His obedience to the law of God. Of Himself Christ could triumphantly exclaim through His servant David, *"I delight to do Thy will O My God, yea Thy law is within My heart,"* and on the eve of His crucifixion He could proclaim with full assurance, *"I have kept My Father's commandments"* (Psalm 40:8; John 15:10).

Gold, the chief of metals, represents the divinity of Christ (Revelation 14:14; 21:18, 21). It reminds us of God's promise to make His children, through the sanctuary experience, more precious than fine gold, even more precious than the *"golden wedge of Ophir"* (Isaiah 13:12).

White is the symbol of purity and represents the righteous character of Christ. It reminds us of God's promise to the sinner - *"Though your sins are as scarlet, they shall be as white as snow. Though they are red like crimson, they shall be as wool"* (Isaiah 1:18; Revelation 19:8).

Together these colours produce a life-saving formula for all of God's children to follow.

Those faithful ones who remain loyal to Jesus will, when He comes again, be clothed in sparkling white robes, and will wear glittering golden crowns upon their heads (Revelation 7:9,13,14; 19:8; 2 Timothy 4:8). We can't afford to miss this wonderful destiny. Let us take heed to the words of Jesus, *"Hold that fast which thou hast, that no man take thy crown"* (Revelation 3:11).

Obedience to law +	Sacrifice and self-denial =	Royal children of King Jesus
(Blue)	(Scarlet)	(Purple)

The lovely entrance curtain was hung on four brass pillars trimmed with silver, the symbol of redemption through suffering. Let us never forget that Jesus was betrayed for thirty pieces of silver - the price of a slave. The four pillars represent the four gospels which together tell the story of Jesus. Each gospel, or pillar, holds up before our wondering gaze one of the four colours which form the tapestry of Jesus' earthly life and ministry.

Matthew	His kingship (purple).
Mark	His service and sacrifice (scarlet).
Luke	His humanity and perfect obedience (blue)
John	His divinity (gold)

The Courtyard

As noted previously, the court was divided into two squares, each ninety-by-ninety feet. The brazen altar stood in the centre of the first square, while the ark of the Most Holy Place stood in the centre of the second square.

The first square illustrates the work of Christ on earth for the salvation of man. The second square illustrates the work of Christ in heaven for us. The centres of these squares, the altar, and the ark, are significant. The altar represents the cross of Christ - the cost of a broken law.

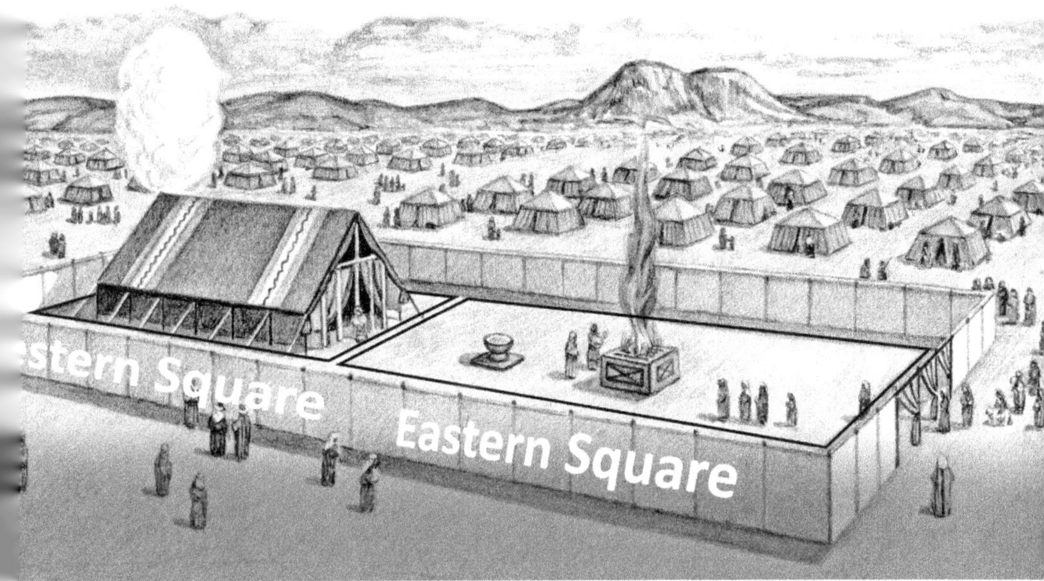

The ark contained the law and lay beneath a golden 'mercy seat.' It represents the mercy of God in forgiving and restoring the sinner.

2) THE BRAZEN ALTAR - God's Amazing Love

The beautiful entrance gate represents Christ's character and draws us to Him. As we look upon Him, we begin to see the ugliness of sin and long to be set free from its power. This awakening of spiritual intelligence, like the first rays of the early morning sun, signals to us the beginning of our spiritual journey.

As we step through the gate of our new understanding, we are immediately confronted by a large brazen, or brass, altar. It is constructed from acacia wood and overlaid with brass. Encircling the altar is the "compass," a narrow platform on which the priest could walk while attending the fire and arranging the sacrifice (Exodus 27:5; 38:4).

Tied near the altar we see a beautiful little white lamb, and on the altar is another lamb in the process of being consumed by the flames. What did this mean to the ancient Israelite? What did it mean to Christ Himself? What does it mean to someone living in the 21st Century? After all, these things happened many, many years ago.

To understand the significance of the altar to modern day readers, we must come face to face with the solemn fact that there is no other way for man to be saved but by the blood of Jesus Christ. Regarding mankind God has declared three indisputable facts:

How can our small minds grasp the enormity of the sacrifice? What did the brazen altar mean personally to the world's Redeemer? The sufferings of Christ did not begin or end with His visit to this world.

1. *"All have sinned,"* (Romans 3:23).

2. *"The wages of sin is death,"* (Romans 6:23).

3. *"Without the shedding of blood there is no remission* (forgiveness) *for sin,"* (Hebrews 9:22).

No silver, gold, or penance can purchase salvation. All the money in the world, all the good deeds a man can possibly do, cannot purchase forgiveness for a single sin. *"You know that you were not redeemed with corruptible things as silver and gold . . . but with the precious blood of Christ"* (1 Peter 1:18,19). Any teaching that denies the atonement of Christ has no pardon or salvation to offer its adherents.

The altar of sacrifice was composed of brass which is made by smelting together copper and zinc in a furnace. The furnace represents the fires of affliction through which Christ would pass in the courtyard of this world. Brass signifies strength, stability, endurance, and victory through suffering.

When in vision the apostle John saw Christ officiating as our High Priest in the heavenly sanctuary, His feet appeared *"like unto fine brass, as if they burned in a furnace"* (Revelation 1:15). Fine brass is of such superior quality that its value at one time was even greater than that of gold.   This is a very fitting symbol of the feet of Him who walked through the fires of affliction to redeem us. Isaiah 53 and Psalm 22 both vividly portray the sufferings of Christ for our redemption. He was a *"Man of sorrows . . . acquainted with grief "* He was *"brought as a lamb to the slaughter;"* and *"for the transgression of His people was stricken"* (*Isaiah 53:3, 8*).

How can our small minds grasp the enormity of the sacrifice? What did the brazen altar mean personally to the world's Redeemer? The sufferings of Christ did not begin or end with His visit to this world. When Jesus offered to pay the redemptive price and this offer was accepted by the Father, He entered the shadow of the cross, and His crucifixion sufferings began. This is what the apostle John meant when he declared that Jesus is *"the Lamb slain from the foundation of the world"* (Revelation 13:8).

The cross of Calvary is but a revelation to our dull senses of the awful suffering that sin, from its very inception, has brought to the heart of God. The shadow of the cross reaches both ways, to the beginning and to the end of sin. Not until sin is finally eradicated from the universe will the Son of God fully escape from the shadow of this emblem of humiliation, shame, and suffering.

His death did not make the law of no effect as some will tell us or lessen its holy claims. Instead, the cross proves the unchanging nature of the law of God. If the holy law of God could have been abolished, changed, or set aside in any way, Jesus need not have died.

The cross of Calvary stands as proof positive that God cannot change His law in any way, not even to save His Beloved Son from a shameful and agonizing death. The cross magnifies the law and makes it honourable. From Christ's own divine lips are heard the words: *"Think not that I am come to destroy the law, or the prophets. I am not come to destroy but to fulfill"* (Matthew 5:17). He is the law personified.

a) Christ and the Brazen Altar

The final scenes of the events leading to Calvary began soon after sunset on the 14th day of Nisan,[41] in an *"upper room,"* probably in the home of John Mark and his mother Mary (Acts 12:12).

After His farewell address to His disciples,[42] Jesus led them out into the darkness of that tragic night toward the Garden of Gethsemane, nestled at the foot of the Mount of Olives. *"Gethsemane"* means in Hebrew to *"crush out the oil."* It was here that Jesus took upon Himself all of mankind's sins. Here the separation from the Father began. The Holy Spirit was crushed, or squeezed out of His life, as the sins and guilt of the whole world were placed upon Him.

"Leaving His disciples within hearing of His voice, Jesus went a little distance from them and fell on His face and prayed. His soul was agonized, and He pleaded: "O My Father; if it is possible let this cup pass from Me: nevertheless not as I will, but as Thou wilt" (Matthew 26:39).

---

41   According to the best available astronomical information, 14th Nisan fell on Friday, April 27, AD 31." Raymond E Cottrell - RH, June 9, 1955. (Friday began at sunset on what we know as Thursday evening)

42   See John 13:31-38, and chapters 14-16.

"The divine light of God was receding from His vision, and He was passing into the hands of the powers of darkness. In His soul anguish He lay prostrate on the cold earth. He had taken the cup of suffering from the lips of guilty man, and proposed to drink it Himself, and in its place give to man the cup of blessing. The sins of a lost world were upon Him and overwhelming Him. He was suffering in man's stead as a transgressor of His Father's law. The wrath that would have fallen upon man was now falling upon Christ. It was here that the mysterious cup trembled in His hand. It was the sense of His Father's frown, in consequence of sin, which rent His heart with such piercing agony and forced from His brow great drops of blood, which, rolling down His pale cheeks, fell to the ground, moistening the earth...

"We have but a faint conception of the inexpressible anguish of God's dear Son in Gethsemane, as He realized His separation from His Father in consequence of bearing man's sins. He became sin for the fallen race. The sense of the withdrawal of His Father's love pressed from His anguished soul these mournful words: 'My soul is exceeding sorrowful, even unto death . . . If it is possible, let this cup pass from Me.' Then with entire submission to His Father's will, He adds: 'Nevertheless not as I will, but as Thou wilt,' (Matthew 26:38,39).

"The divine Son of God fell fainting, dying to the ground. The Father sent a mes-

senger from His presence to strengthen the divine Sufferer and brace Him to tread His bloodstained path. Could mortals have viewed the amazement and the sorrow of the angelic host as they watched in silent grief the Father separating His beams of light, love, and glory from the beloved Son, they would better understand how offensive sin is in His sight.

"He was betrayed with a kiss into the hands of His enemies and hurried to the judgment hall of an earthly court, there to be derided and condemned to death by sinful mortals. There the glorious Son of God was 'wounded for our transgressions. He was bruised for our iniquities.' He bore insult, mockery, and torture, until 'His visage was so marred more than any man, and His form more than the sons of men,' (Isaiah 53:5; 52:14).

"Who can comprehend the love here displayed! The angelic hosts behold with wonder and with grief Him who had been the Majesty of heaven, and who had worn the crown of glory, now wearing the crown of thorns, a bleeding victim to the rage of an infuriated mob, fired to insane madness by the wrath of Satan. Behold the patient Sufferer! Upon His head is the thorny crown. His lifeblood flows from every lacerated vein. All this in consequence of sin! Nothing could have induced Christ to leave His honour and majesty in heaven, and come to a sinful world, to be neglected, despised, and rejected by those He came to save, and finally to suffer upon the cross, but eternal, redeeming love, which will ever remain a mystery.

"Wonder, O heavens, and be astonished, O earth! Behold the oppressor and the oppressed! A vast *multitude enclose the Saviour of the world. Mockings and jeerings are mingled with the coarse oaths of blasphemy. His lowly birth and humble life is commented upon by unfeeling wretches. His claim to be the Son of God is ridiculed by the chief priests and elders, and vulgar jests and insulting derision are passed from lip to lip. Satan has full control of his servants.*

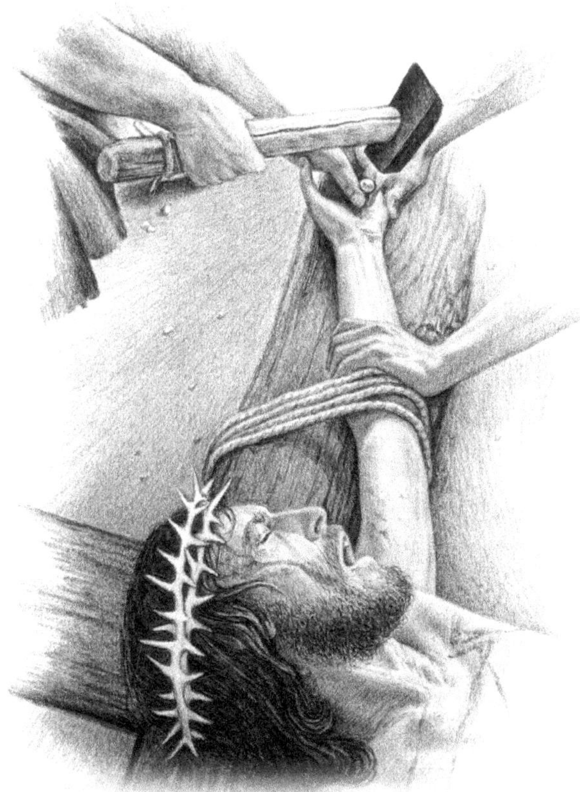

"In order to work more effectually, he commences with the chief priests and elders, and imbues them with religious frenzy. They are actuated by the same satanic spirit which moves the most vile and hardened wretches. There is a corrupt harmony in the feeling of all, from the hypocritical priests and elders to the most debased.

"Christ, the precious Son of God, is led forth, and the cross in laid upon His shoulders. Every step leaves in its place pools of blood which flow from His lacerated back and head. Thronged by an immense crowd of bitter enemies and unfeeling spectators, He is led away to the crucifixion. 'He was oppressed, and He was afflicted, yet He opened not His mouth. He is brought as a lamb to the slaughter, and as a sheep be-

fore her shearer is dumb, so He opened not His mouth' (Isaiah 53:7).

"Upon arriving at the place of execution, the condemned are bound to the instruments of torture . . . And now the hammer and nails are brought, and as the spikes are driven through the tender flesh and fastened to the cross, the heart-stricken disciples bear away from the cruel scene the fainting form of the mother of Christ.

"Jesus makes no murmur of complaint. His face remains pale and serene, but great drops of sweat stand upon His brow. There is no pitying hand to wipe the death dew from His face, nor words of sympathy and unchanging fidelity to stay His human heart. He is treading the winepress all alone, and of the people there are none with Him (Isaiah 63:3). While the soldiers are doing their fearful work, and He is enduring the most acute agony, Jesus prays for His enemies - 'Father, forgive them; for they know not what they do' (Luke 23:34). That prayer of Christ for His enemies embraces the whole world, taking in every sinner who ever lived, until the end of time.

"After Jesus is nailed to the cross, it is lifted by several powerful men and thrust with great violence into the place prepared for it, causing the most excruciating agony to the Son of God. And now a terrible scene is enacted. Priests, rulers, and scribes forget the dignity of their sacred office, and join with the rabble in mocking and jeering the dying Son of God, saying, 'If Thou be the King of the Jews, save Thy-

self' (Luke 23:37). And some deriding-ly repeat among themselves, 'He saved others; Himself He cannot save (Mark 15:31). The dignitaries of the temple, the hardened soldiers, the vile thief upon the cross, and the base and cruel among the multitude - all unite in their abuse of Christ.

"The chief priests and elders revile God's dear Son while in His expiring agonies. Yet inanimate nature groans in sympathy with her bleeding, dying Author. The earth trembles. The sun refuses to behold the scene. The heavens gather blackness, and darkness descends for three full hours.

Angels have witnessed the scene of suffering until they can look no longer and hide their faces from the horrid sight. Christ is dying! He is in despair, and they cannot come to Him to lighten the gloom of that terrible hour!

"Doubts assail the dying Son of God. He cannot see through the portals of the tomb. Bright hope does not present to Him His coming forth from the tomb as a conqueror and His Father's accep-tance of His sacrifice. The sin of the world, with all its terribleness, is felt to the utmost by the Son of God. The displeasure of the Father for sin, and its penalty which is death, is all that He can realize through this amazing darkness. He is tempted to fear that sin is so offensive in the sight of His Father that He cannot be reconciled to His Son. The fierce temptation that His own Father has forever left Him causes that piercing cry from the cross, 'My God, My God, why hast Thou forsaken Me?' (Matthew 27:46).

"In silence the people watch for the end of this fearful scene. Again, the sun shines forth, but the cross is enveloped in darkness. Suddenly the

> *gloom is lifted from the cross, and in clear trumpet tones that seem to resound throughout creation, Jesus cries, 'It is finished.' 'Father, into Thy hands I commend My spirit' (Luke 23:46). A light encircles the cross, and the face of the Saviour shines with a glory like unto the sun. He then bows His head upon His breast and dies."* [43]

This is what the brazen altar meant to the Son of God.

b) The Israelite and the Brazen Altar

Even though the sinner is now free from sin and guilt, a record of his covered and forgiven sin remains on the books of heaven until the Day of Atonement

When an Israelite committed sin, he broke the Ten Commandment law contained in the ark, and only faith in the Redeemer to come could save him from eternal separation from God. To show his faith, he must bring a perfect offering to the sanctuary, *"a lamb without blemish and without spot,"* a fitting symbol for Christ, the spotless Lamb of God (1 Peter 1:19). He was then required to place his hands upon the head of the lamb and confess his sins, symbolically transferring his sin and guilt to the innocent victim.

The laying on of hands is an old Hebrew custom by which something possessed is symbolically transferred to someone else. The ancient patriarchs passed on the birthright blessing to the eldest son in this manner (Genesis 48:14,16). Jesus blessed the children by placing His hands upon them (Mark 10:16). He transferred healing the same way (Mark 6:5). Paul received his sight by the laying on of hands, and likewise believers received the Holy Spirit (Acts 9:12; 19:6).

The sinner possesses only one thing - sin - and by laying his hands on the animal's head he transfers his sin to a substitute. The transfer complete, the sinner must now kill the lamb with his own hand. The animal dies because sin is placed upon it. Technically it has become the "sinner," and is therefore under the condemnation of the law, while the

---

43   Selected from Testimonies Vol. 2, pp 200-215, & The Story of Redemption, pp 221-226, by E. White

lawbreaker walks away a free man.

The ministration of the priest, also a figure of Christ, now begins. He dips his finger in the blood and imprints it upon the horns of the brazen altar. This symbolizes the making of a record of the transfer of sin from a wicked, polluted life to a pure, sinless life. This transaction can occur only because of Calvary (2 Corinthians 5:21). *"The sin of Judah is written with a pen of iron; with the point of a diamond, it is engraved on the tablet of their heart, **and on the horns of your altars**"* (Jeremiah 17:1).

The priest then takes more of the blood into the Holy Place of the sanctuary and sprinkles it before the veil, and with his finger imprints it upon the horns of the golden altar. This portrays the keeping of a record of the sin in the *'books'* of the heavenly sanctuary, and fulfills the Saviour's promise to remove our sins far from us. *"As the heaven is high above the earth . . .As far as the east is from the west, so far has He removed our trans-gressions from us"* (Psalm 103:10-12).

Even though the sinner is now free from sin and guilt, a record of his covered and forgiven sin remains on the books of heaven until the Day of Atonement (Judgment). On that day, the heavenly register will be cleansed of de-filement by the removal of all the sins of the truly penitent recorded there (Revelation 3:5). [44]

The Hebrews looked upon sin as something tangible, something that could be physically moved from the sin-ner to the victim, and then, via the blood, to the sanctuary. Clifford Goldstein, a Christian Jewish writer, compares sin to a deadly virus which is transported in the blood by a special carrier, the priest, to a place of quarantine, the sanctuary.[45] Here it is kept until finally destroyed by the only One who can eradicate sin-Jesus Christ Himself.

----

44   The Day of Atonement is covered in detail in chapters 8 and 10.

45   Goldstein, C., False Balances, p. 109

Another offering of deep significance to the Israelites was the whole burnt offering. This sacrifice originated at the gate of Eden and was offered by the patriarchs down through the centuries. Every morning and evening a lamb without blemish was chosen to be entirely consumed upon the altar - representing Christ who gave all for our salvation. The fire which burnt this offering was kindled by God showing that He not only accepted but shared the sacrifice. This fire burned day and night, symbolizing the continual availability of Christ's righteousness and forgiveness for the sinner, even on the day of judgment.

Morning and evening all Israel bowed in prayer before the sanctuary as the whole burnt offering was placed upon the altar. It was at this time each day that the captive Daniel in the court of Babylon, turned his face toward Jerusalem and presented his petitions to God.

Today the custom of morning and evening worship is still carried on in many Christian families. The whole burnt offering represents the consecration of self. It symbolizes complete surrender to God and wholehearted dedication to His service. It means putting all that we possess on the altar to be used as God directs. It was to the whole burnt offering which Paul referred when he wrote, *"I beseech*

you therefore brethren, by the mercies of God, that you present your bodies a living sacrifice, holy, acceptable unto God, which is your reasonable service" (Romans 12:1).

c) The Christian and the Brazen Altar

The transfer of sin from sinner to victim to priest, and then finally to the sanctuary, is a vivid portrayal of what happens when anyone, ancient Israelite or 21st century Christian, comes to Jesus asking for forgiveness and cleansing. The only difference is the ancient Israelite looked forward in faith to the sacrifice of God's dear Son on Calvary, while the Christian today looks back in faith to that same momentous event.

When the sinner repents and is forgiven a legal transfer occurs in heaven. Because of the cross our sins are placed on Christ (the Lamb), and His righteousness transferred to us. This process is called **justification.** It means that we are legally declared forgiven and reconciled to God. It means we are covered with the robe of Christ's righteousness. *"For He* (God) *made Him* (Jesus) *who knew no sin to be sin for us, that we might become the righteousness of God in Him"* (2 Corinthians 5:21).

This transfer can be illustrated by a simple diagram.

What Jesus does in the sanctuary is wonderfully illus-

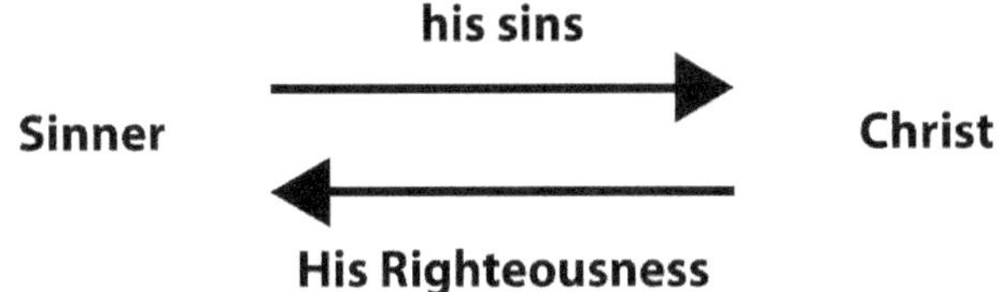

trated in Zechariah chapter 3. Here we see Joshua, representing God's people, standing before the King of the universe clad in filthy garments while Satan, the *"accuser of the brethren"* (Revelation 12:10), stands ready to charge Joshua with all the sins he (Satan) tempted him to commit. (As one preacher described it, Satan is like the school bully who entices you to do something wrong, and then runs to tell the teacher!)

Joshua cannot defend himself because he knows that Satan's charges are correct. He kneels before God, humble and repentant, depending on the sin pardoning Saviour to defend him. The Angel of the Lord, who is Jesus, silences Satan with the words, *"The Lord rebuke thee, O Satan . . . Is this not a branch plucked out of the fire?"* Jesus then commands one of the attending angels, *"Take away the filthy garments from him."* And to Joshua, who represents you and me, He says, *"Behold, I have caused thine iniquity to pass from thee, and I will clothe thee with change of raiment"* (Zechariah 3:1-4).

> *"The iniquity is transferred to the innocent, the pure, the holy Son of God. And man, all undeserving, stands before the Lord cleansed from all unrighteousness, and clothed with the righteousness of Christ. Oh, what a change of raiment is this!"* [46]

Is this all that the altar means to the Christian today? Do we simply transfer our sins to Christ by heartfelt repentance and confession, and then walk away completely free from all guilt and condemnation?

'Yes,' because this is God's gift to us at the brazen altar of forgiveness, and if this truth is received by faith, it becomes a reality for us. However, we must never forget we have an enemy who is doing all in his power to turn us away from our new allegiance and keep us in bondage to him.

When one of Satan's subjects comes to Jesus desiring freedom from sin, he immediately does all he can to discourage such a soul from his purpose. He will use friends, family members, actual or threatened loss of income, sickness, accidents, or of whatever means he can avail himself, to

---

46   White, E., "That I May Know Him," p. 108

turn the new believer away from Christ. At such a time as this the new Christian must press closer and closer to Christ, trusting in His promises and in the protection of holy angels - *"For He shall give His angels charge over thee to keep thee in all thy ways"* (Psalm 91:11).

> *"Because He hath set his love upon Me, therefore I will deliver him. I will set him on high because he hath known My name. He will call upon Me and I will answer him. I will be with him in trouble, I will deliver him, and honour him. With long life I will satisfy him and show him my salvation"* (Psalm 91:14-16).

> *"The angel of the Lord encamps round about them that fear Him and delivers them. O taste and see that the Lord is good: Blessed is the man that trusts in Him"* (Psalm 34:7, 8).

Throughout the Holy Scriptures are scattered hundreds of such precious promises for the sons and daughters of God. Seek these out, believe them, and pray for the blessings God promises to those who put their trust in Him. He will never leave us nor forsake us. It is true that trials will be permitted to come upon us to refine us  and ennoble our characters. Like fire purifies gold, these experiences are designed to burn up the dross in our lives and develop what is pure and good. As the grand old hymn proclaims:

> *"Must Jesus bear the cross alone,*
> *and all the world go free?*
> *No, there's a cross for everyone,*
> *and there's a cross for me."*

So, what does the brazen altar mean to us? It means that Jesus has obtained salvation for us at the price of infinite suffering. It also means that we too will experience the fires of affliction, especially as we turn from this world and begin our walk with the Lord. But Jesus will be by our side, we will never walk alone.

While everyone's testimony will be different, perhaps an illustration from my own experience will suffice to demonstrate this point. When I made the decision to follow Jesus, Satan saw that he was losing one of his subjects and his enmity was aroused. This is always the case and can be expected. My marriage became the special target for his attacks. Like a ship caught on rocks and pounded by heavy seas, our relationship slowly but surely began to disintegrate. Ridicule and scorn became a daily occurrence as I tried to bring my life practices into harmony with God's will. Communion with God through prayer and Bible study was impossible in the home. This had to be done secretly in the peaceful seclusion of a nearby wooded area. I dared not attend church, any church. I was just a struggling, lonely, and sometimes frightened 'baby' Christian, but Christ did not leave me to battle the enemy alone.

Morning by morning He assured me of His presence, protection, and love in a remarkable way. Some will say this was purely my imagination, but I know in my heart it was not, and I know of others who have had similar experiences. As I sought the Lord in prayer in my secluded spot, I soon became aware of a ray of sunlight which broke through the clouds and treetops and covered me with its gentle radiance morning by morning. This occurred regardless of weather conditions, even on those days when heavy dark clouds filled the heavens. At such times Jesus seemed very close. I came to look for and expect this phenomenon.

Soon afterwards we moved to another town where there were no nearby woods in which to commune with my Saviour. Did God now forget this lonely, struggling child of His? Never! He has engraved us upon the palms of His hands. It would be easier for a mother to forget her newborn baby than for God to forget His own (Isaiah 49:15,16). My place of prayer, when alone, was now a central room in the house with no windows, apart from two narrow openings under the ceiling. But once again the dear Saviour gave tangible evidence of His abiding presence by sending through those tiny openings a bright ray of light, morning by morning - as if from the very throne of God! Our Lord has numerous ways, tailor-made to meet each particular need, to bring comfort and strength to our sinking hearts.

Following close on the heels of verbal and emotional abuse came adultery. Once more I sought comfort in the great outdoors. From a cabin in the mountains, I pulled on my hiking boots day by day, and roamed the high, rugged trails for hours at a time. Is happiness possible during great pain? Let me give an unequivocal 'yes.' Only our Saviour can turn the most heartbreaking situations into occasions for gratitude and praise. Here, alone in the mountains, I experienced some of my happiest days.

One particular day will ever stay in my memory. I determined to climb the highest peak in the area. From the top I found myself gazing with awe and reverence at the beautiful scene before me. The tree line was far below. Before me stretched range after range of blue-grey mountains marching away into some distant eternity. The sky was a vivid blue canopy overhead. Patches of snow lay upon the ground, and scraggly little plants clung to the alpine slopes. Flitting from rock to rock were gorgeous, red-breasted robins with brilliant black and white coats. The breeze was crisp, clean, and heavenly. Overwhelmed by all this grandeur, and with a grateful heart, I knelt to thank God for bringing me to this beautiful spot. While in prayer I felt God draw near, so near I dared not open my eyes. I thought, 'If I just reach out my hand, I will be able to touch you, Lord.' The cares of this life drained away at that moment, and my cup of joy was full.

> *"Thou anointest my head with oil, my cup runneth over. Surely goodness and mercy shall follow me all the days of my life: and I will dwell in the house of the Lord forever!"* (Psalm 23:5,6).

No, it was not over yet! Down from the mountain top valleys of despair were waiting. But I had met with my Lord, and I knew who held the future. I could afford to rest in His care and wait patiently for Him to bring me through this trial. It took six more years.

The experience was very maturing for me. I had much to learn, and much rubbish in my own soul to be forgiven and forsaken. Therefore, the Lord has to permit His children to pass through these experiences to refine us and to teach us what it means to be a Christian.

Yes, there is a cross, but never forget the One who went to the cross before us. We never have to be without the assurance of our heavenly Father's presence. He prepares us for each new trial, strengthens us to pass through it, and blesses us for our faithfulness to Him. As one man of God exclaimed, 'After each new trial I stand as it were on tiptoe reaching out for the blessing I know God has in store for me.'

Whatever we may be called upon to give up for His sake He promises to replace it with something better. Yes, Satan is going about like a *"roaring lion seeking whom he may devour"* (1 Peter 5:8), but always remember, *"the Lord is good"* (Psalm 34:8).

> *"Beloved, think it not strange concerning the fiery trial, which is to try you, as though some strange thing happened unto you. But rejoice, inasmuch as ye are partakers of Christ's sufferings, that when His glory shall be revealed, ye may be glad also with exceeding joy"* (1 Peter 4:12,13).

The Encampment of Angels

They are camping round about me,
Perish every doubt and fear.
For the campfires of the angels
From the glory land are near.
Hedged about like the mountains
Round Jerusalem of old,
I am compassed by the angels
From the shining streets of gold.

I can see their white tents gleaming
'Mid the radiant glory bright,
And I hear the faithful tramping
Of the Sentinel at night.
For my Watcher sleepeth never,
And His eye is never dim,
He will keep my soul forever
If I only trust in Him.

They are camping round about me,
'Mid the busy cares of life,
'Mid its trials and temptations,
'Mid its bustle and its strife.
They will leave me never, never!
They are guardians true and tried.
See! They pitch their white tents
closer,
And they'll never leave my side.
- L.D. Avery-Stuttle

> *"The fact that we are called upon to endure trial shows that the Lord Jesus sees in us something precious which He desires to develop. If He saw in us nothing whereby He might glorify His name, He would not spend time in refining us. He does not cast worthless stones into His furnace. It is valuable ore that He refines."* [47]

> *"The trials of life are God's workmen to remove the impurities and roughness from our character . . . Upon no useless material does the Master bestow such careful, thorough work. Only His precious stones are polished after the similitude of a palace."* [48]

> *"Those who surrender their lives to His guidance and to His service will never be placed in a position for which He has not made provision. Whatever our situation, if we are doers of His word, we have a Guide to direct our way. Whatever our perplexity, we have a sure Counsellor. Whatever our sorrow, our bereavement, or loneliness, we have a sympathizing Friend."* [49]

Wonderful Saviour! Amazing grace! He will never turn away any trembling soul who comes to Him for healing from the disease of sin. Though our sins are as scarlet, He will make them as white as snow.

The following story provides a fitting note on which to close this section on the brazen altar. It was written more than one hundred years ago and describes what God can do for the most hopeless, degraded sinner.

"The Man That Died for Me."

For many years I wanted to go as a foreign missionary, but my way seemed hedged about. At Last I went to live in

---

47   White, E., Ministry of Healing, p. 471

48   White, E., Mount of Blessing, p. 10

49   White, E., Ministry of Healing, pp. 248-249

California. Life was rough in the mining country where I lived with my husband and little boys.

While there I heard about a man who lived over the hills and was dying of tuberculosis. The men said, "He is so vile that no one can stay with him. So, we place some food near him, and leave him for twenty-four hours. We will find him dead one day and the sooner the better. Never had a relative, I guess."

This pitiful story haunted me as I went about my work. For three days I tried to get someone to go and see him to find out if he needed better care. As I turned from the last man, vexed with his indifference, the thought came to me, "Why not go yourself? Here is missionary work if you want it." I will not tell how I weighed the probable uselessness of my going, nor how I shrank from one so vile as he. It was not the kind of work I wanted.

But at last, one day I went over the hills to his little hut. It was a mud cabin, containing but one room. The door stood open. In one corner on some straw and coloured blankets, I found the dying man. Sin had left awful marks on his face, and if I had not been told that he could not move, I would have retreated. As my shadow fell over the floor he looked up and greeted me with an oath. I stepped forward a little, and again he swore.

"Don't speak so, my friend," I said.

"I ain't your friend. I ain't got no friends," he said.

"Well, I am your friend, and . . ."

But the oaths came quickly, and he said, *"You ain't my friend. I never had any friends, and I don't want any now."*

I reached out, at arms' length, the fruit I had brought for him, and stepping back to the doorway asked if he remembered his mother hoping to find a tender place in his heart. But he cursed her. I spoke of God, and he cursed Him. I tried to speak of Jesus and his death for us, but he stopped me with his oaths, and said, "That's all a lie. Nobody ever died for others."

I went away discouraged, saying to myself that I knew it was useless. But the next day I went again, and every day for two weeks. He did not show the gratitude of a dog, and at the end of that time I said that I was not going any more. That night as I was putting my little boy to bed, I did not pray for the miner. My little boy noticed it and said: -

"Mama, you did not pray for the bad man."

"No," I answered, with a sigh.

"Have you given him up, Mama?"

"Yes, I guess so."

"Has God given him up Mama? Ought you to give him up till God does?"

I could not sleep that night. I thought of the dying man, so vile, and with no one to care! I rose and went away by myself to pray; but the moment I knelt, I was overpowered by the sense of how little meaning there had been to my prayers. I had no faith, and I had not really cared, beyond a kind of half-hearted sentiment. I had not claimed his soul for God. O, the shame of such missionary zeal! I fell on my face literally as I cried, *"O Christ, give me a little glimpse of the worth of a human soul!"* Do not pray this way unless you are willing to give up ease and selfish pleasure; for life will take on a different meaning after this revelation.

I remained on my knees until Calvary became a reality to me. I cannot describe those hours.

They came and went unheeded; but I learned that night what I had never known before, what it was to travail for a human soul. I saw my Lord as I had never seen Him before. I knelt there till the answer came. As I went back to my room, my husband said: -

"How about your miner?"

"He is going to be saved."

"How are you going to do it?" he asked.

"The Lord is going to save him. I do not know that I will do anything about it," I replied.

The next morning brought a lesson in Christian work that I had never learned before. On other days I had waited until afternoon, and then when my work was over, I would change my dress and take a walk while the shadows were on the hillsides. That day the moment my little boys went to school, I left my work and hurried over the hills, not to see *"that vile wretch,"* but to win a soul. I thought the man might die.

As I passed on, a neighbour came out of her cabin and said, *"I will go over the hills with you."*

I did not want her to go, but it was another lesson for me. God could plan better than I could. She had her little daughter with her and as we reached the cabin, she said, *"I will wait out here."*

I do not know what I expected, but the man greeted me with an awful oath. Still, it did not hurt, for I was behind Christ, and I stayed there. I could bear what struck Him first. While I was changing the basin of water and towel for him, things which I had done every day but which he had never thanked me for, the clear laugh of the little girl rang out upon the air.

"What's that?" said the man eagerly.

"It's a little girl outside waiting for me."

"Would you mind letting her come in?" he said, in a different tone from any I had heard before.

Stepping to the door I beckoned to her; then, taking her hand, said, *"Come in and see the sick man, Lucy."* She shrank back as she saw his face, but I assured her with, *"Poor sick man! He can't get up. He wants to see you."*

She looked like an angel, her bright face framed in golden curls and her eyes tender and full of pity. In her hands she held the flowers she had picked from the purple sage, and bending toward him said, *"I'm sorry you are so sick. Do you want my flowers?"*

He laid his great, bony hand beyond the flowers, onto the plump hand of the child, and tears came to his eyes as he said, *"I had a little girl once. Her name was Lucy. She cared for me. Nobody else did. Guess I'd been different if she'd lived. I've hated everybody since she died."*

I knew at once that I had the key to the man's heart. The thought came quickly born of that midnight prayer service, and I said, *"When I spoke of your mother and your wife, you cursed them. I know now that they were not good women, or you could not have done so."*

"Good women! O, you don't know nothin' bout that kind of woman! You can't think what they was!"

"Well, if your little girl had lived and grown up with them, wouldn't she have been like them? Would you have liked to have her live for that?"

He evidently had never thought of that, and his great eyes looked off for a full minute. As they came back to mine, he cried, *"O God, no! I'd killed her first. I'm glad she died."*

Reaching out and taking the poor hand, I said, *"The dear Lord didn't want her to be like them. He loved her even more than you did, so He took her away. He is keeping her for you. Don't you want to see her again?'*

"O, I'd be willing to be burned alive a thousand times over if I could just see my little girl once more!"

O friends, you know what a blessed story I had to tell that hour. I had been so close to Calvary that night that I could tell it in earnest! The poor face grew ashy pale as I talked, and the man threw up his arms as if his agony was mastering him. Two or three times he gasped, as if losing his breath. Then, clutching me, he said, *"What's that you said t'other day 'bout talkin 'to someone out o'sight?"*

"It is praying. I tell Him what I want."

"Pray now, quick. Tell him I want my little girl again. Tell Him anything you want to."

I took the hands of the child and placed them on the trembling hands of the man. Then dropping on my knees with the child in front of me, I bade her pray for the man who had lost his little Lucy and wanted to see her again. As nearly as I remember this was Lucy's prayer: -

"Dear Jesus, this man is very sick. He has lost his little girl, and he feels bad about it. I'm so sorry for him, and he's sorry, too. Won't You help him, and show him how to find his little girl again? Please do. Amen."

Heaven seemed to open before us, and there stood One with the prints of the nails in His hands and the wound in His side.

Lucy slipped away but the man kept saying, *"tell Him more about it. Tell Him everything. But, O, you don't know!"* Then he poured out such a torrent of confession that I could not have borne it but for One who was close to us at that hour.

By and by the poor man grasped the strong hand. It was three days later that the poor tired soul turned from everything to Him, the Mighty to save, *"the Man that died for me."*

He lived on for weeks, as if God would show how real was the change. I was telling him one day about a meeting, when he said, *"I'd like to go to a meetin' once."*

So, we planned a meeting, and the men from the mills and the mines came and filled the room. *"Now, boys,"* said he, *"get down on your knees while she tells about that Man that died for me."*

I had been brought up to believe that a woman should not speak in meeting, but I found myself talking, and I tried to tell the simple story of the cross. After a while he said: -

"Boys, you don't half believe it, or you'd cry. You couldn't help it. Raise me up. I'd like to tell it once."

So they raised him, and between his short breathing and coughing, he told the story. He had to use the language he knew.

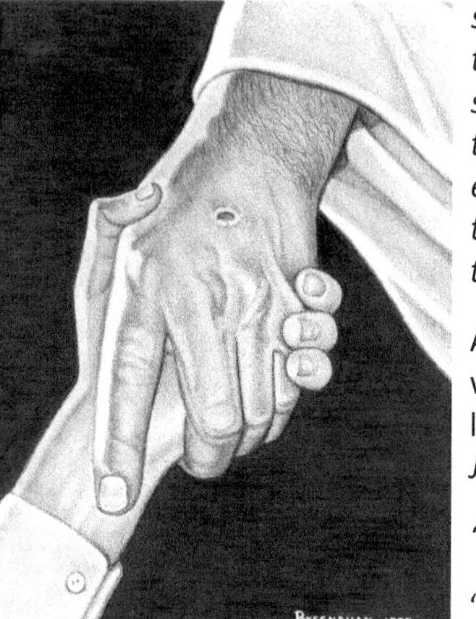

"Boys," he said, *"you know how the water runs down the sluice-boxes and carries off the dirt and leaves the gold behind. Well, the blood of that Man she tells about went right over me just like that. It carried off about everything, but it left enough for me to see Lucy, and to see the Man that died for me. O boys, can't you love Him too?"*

A few days later there came a look into his face which told that the end had come. I had to leave him, so I said, *"What shall say tonight, Jack?"*

"Just good night," he said.

"What will you say to me when we meet again?"

"I'll say 'Good morning,' over there."

The next morning the door was closed, and I found two men inside sitting silently by a board stretched across two stools. They turned back the sheet from the dead, and I looked on the face which seemed to have come back nearer to the image of God.

"I wish you could have seen him when he went," they said.

"Tell me about it."

"Well, all at once he brightened up, bout midnight, an'

smilin' said, I'm goin' boys. Tell her I'm going to see the Man that died for me." And he was gone.

Kneeling there with my hands over those poor cold ones, which had been stained with human blood, I asked that I might understand more and more the worth of a human soul, and be drawn into a deeper sympathy with Christ's yearning compassion, *"not willing that any should perish."*

From *"Stories Worth Reading"* pp 304-310

AMAZING GRACE

Amazing Grace! How sweet the sound,
That saved a wretch like me!
I once was lost, but now am found,
Was blind, but now I see!

'Twas grace that taught my heart to fear,
And grace my fears relieved.
How precious did that grace appear
The hour I first believed!

The Lord has promised good to me,
His word my hope secures.
He will my shield and portion be
As long as life endures.

Through many dangers, toils, and snares,
I have already come.
'Tis grace hath brought me safe thus far,
And grace will lead me home.

When we've been there ten thousand years,
Bright shining as the sun,
We've no less days to sing God's praise
Then when we'd first begun.

John Newton

3) THE LAVER - God's Amazing Grace

There was another piece of furniture in the court-yard which is also of great significance to the Christian. It was called the *'laver,'* a large round shaped bowl containing water (Exodus 30:17-21).

The laver was located in the first square of the court between the altar and the entrance to the Holy Place. The Word of God identifies two distinct parts to the laver. Whenever it is mentioned, a *'foot'* is also referred to. The *'foot'* probably received the water used by the priests for washing before entering the sanctuary building.

The laver, like the Altar of Sacrifice and its utensils, was made of brass. But unlike these, it was fashioned from polished brass mirrors, or *"the looking glasses of the women,"* who, *"assembled at the door of the tabernacle"* (Exodus 38:8). These were very devout women, like the prophetess Anna of Jesus' time (Luke 2:36,37).

From these polished mirrors the laver was made. The function of a mirror is to reveal what the natural face looks like with its imperfections and uncleanliness. Therefore, the Bible likens the law of God to a mirror. *"Whosoever looks into the perfect law of liberty . . . is like a man beholding his natural face in a glass"* (James 1:25,23).

In the law the sinner beholds his sins and imperfections of character. He sees his uncleanness, his filthy garments, and his need of a Saviour. Paul likens the law to a schoolmaster who brings us to Christ (Galatians 3:24). While the law has no power to save us, it can and does show us our need, and points us to the Saviour as the only One who can deliver us from our condition.

The altar and the laver are closely linked and represent justification - that which Christ accomplished for us while in the courtyard of this earth.

- The **brazen altar** makes the first step on the journey back to God possible. The apostle John describes our first step and God's response this way, *"If we confess our sins, He is faithful and just to forgive us our sins."*

- However, this is only half the verse, half the formula. The rest of the verse reveals to us the second half of the justification process - *"and to cleanse us from all unrighteousness"* (1 John 1:9). This cleansing is represented by the **laver.**

The Brazen Altar + the Laver = Justification

Forgiveness + Cleansing = Salvation

John, who was an eyewitness to the death of Christ, records that when one of the soldiers pierced the side of Jesus with a spear, *"blood and water"* flowed from the wound (John 19:34). The blood represents the brazen altar of forgiveness, the water represents the laver of cleansing - both made possible by the death of Christ (1 John 5:6). This cleansing process is symbolized for us today by the rite of baptism.

Christian baptism by immersion was ordained by Christ and carried out by John the Baptist, who baptized Jesus in the river Jordan as an example for us to follow. This rite was continued by the apostles and formed part of the teachings of the New Testament Church (Acts 22:16).

Here again is an example of God using something tangible to illustrate a spiritual truth. No other form of baptism, other than that by immersion, can illustrate the wonderful miracle of cleansing which the laver represents. The whole body is lowered beneath the water. The breath temporarily ceases, representing death to the past life of sin.

The new Christian is raised out of the water, representing the resurrection power of Christ to make a new man or woman of the believer. This transformation is called the *'new birth.'* Baptism is a memorial, established by our Lord Himself, of His power to forgive us and to recreate us in the image of God.

> *"Know you not, that as many of us as were baptized into Jesus Christ were baptized into His death? Therefore, we are buried with Him by baptism into death; that like as Christ was raised from the dead by the glory of the Father, even so we also should walk in newness of life . . . Now if we are dead with Christ, we believe we will also live with Him,"* (Romans 6:3-12).

> *"For as many of you as have been baptized into Christ have put on Christ"* (Galatians 3:27).

> *"Then Peter said unto them, 'Repent, and be baptized every one of you in the name of Jesus Christ for the remission of sins, and ye will receive the gift of the Holy Spirit"* (Acts 2:38).

> *'And now why do you tarry? Arise, and be baptized, and wash away your sins, calling on the name of the Lord,"* (Acts 22:16).

> *"Go ye therefore, and teach all nations, baptizing them in the name of the Father, and of the Son, and of the Holy Ghost"* (Matthew 28:19).

How Can I Know That I have been 'Born Again'?

"Not by works of righteousness which we have done, but according to His mercy He saved us, by the washing of regeneration and the renewing of the Holy Spirit" (Titus 3:5).

"Regeneration" means 're-creation,' 'revival,' or 'reformation,' (Webster's Dictionary). To receive the *"washing of regeneration"* signifies the beginning of a new life for the believer. Jesus described this new life as analogous to be-

ing *"born again"* (John 3:3).

Baptism is the adoption ceremony for 'born again' Christians, by which they become sons and daughters of the Heavenly King - royal children belonging to the household of God.[50] At baptism, the Father, Son, and Holy Spirit are present to receive the new believer into the family of God, and his or her name is written in God's family register, the Lamb's Book of Life (Exodus 32:32; Revelation 21:27).

With this new relationship come new responsibilities. We become, *"ambassadors for Christ,"* and by our life, words, and acts, we encourage others, *"in Christ's stead, "*to also become *"reconciled to* God" (2 Corinthians 5:18-20).

Thus, from the very beginning of our Christian walk, we have the privilege of becoming *"labourers together with God"* (1 Corinthians 3:9).

What does it mean to us personally to be 'born again'? It was several years after I had accepted Christ that I began to understand. The revelation came to me suddenly and unexpectedly. At the time I was flying high above the Pacific Ocean between the United States and Australia. As we crossed the International Date Line, I began to ponder on this unique opportunity to live through the same day twice. This thought led to others, and before long I lapsed into an old familiar pattern of negative thinking - *"I have made such a mess of my life. I am too great a sinner for the Lord to have any use for me now. I have made too many mistakes. If only I had the opportunity to begin all over again, knowing what I know now."*

It was then that the Lord broke into my thoughts and spoke to my mind so clearly and forcefully that I involuntarily turned to see who was speaking, *"You do have a second chance. It is called the 'new birth.'"*

---

50   1 John 3:1,2; John 1:12,13; Romans 8:15,16.

Suddenly light began to penetrate the darkness, and new, fresh, and this time positive thoughts, crowded my mind. My first, or physical birth, delivered me into this world as a member of the family of the first Adam. I inherited the spiritual deformities of my ancestors. My natural desires were selfish. I loved this world and the things of this world - its fashions, its entertainments, its amusements.

But one day the cross of Calvary was laid across my path, and I began to desire that *"Better Land."* By the grace and power of God I turned around and began to walk in a different direction. The pleasures of sin and the attractions of this world began to fade. I now found myself hating the things I once loved and loving the things I once hated. Though I did not know it at the time, I was experiencing that *"enmity"* against Satan and his ways which God, back in Eden, had promised to put into the hearts of all His children (Genesis 3:15).

I once enjoyed sleeping late, rising at the last possible moment to get dressed, grab some food, and be on my way to work. Now I loved to get up early to spend time with the Lord in Bible study and prayer.

Other changes occurred almost imperceptibly. The books I once enjoyed reading, the television I once enjoyed watching, friends whose company I once enjoyed, slowly lost their appeal. Like a butterfly emerging from its cocoon, I could hardly recognize my former self. This is resurrection power. This is the 'new birth.' My old self and my old ways have been laid in the grave. My sins are forgiven, and my name recorded in the Lamb's Book of Life. And I did not know this until that moment far above the Pacific Ocean! What a wonderful and patient God we serve! What a privilege to be part of heaven's royal family. This is what is means to be 'born again.'

> *"Therefore, if any man be in Christ, he is a new creature. Old things are passed away. Behold, all things are become new"* (2 Corinthians 5:17).

Chapter 7

"Go and Sin No More"

The Holy Place Experience

As the sun began to sink on the evening of Abib 14, the body of Jesus was tenderly taken down from the cross and laid in Joseph's new tomb (Luke 23:52-54; John 19:38-42). Here He quietly rested during the sacred Sabbath hours while His murderers and persecutors celebrated a 'high day' - a Passover service which had lost its significance and had now become obsolete.

In heaven a different celebration was in order. As Jesus bowed His head in total submission to His Father's will and yielded up His life, a shout of triumph rang through the portals of heaven. *"The Lord hath triumphed gloriously,"* sang the angels, and songs of praise echoed and re-echoed throughout the universe of God. With His own blood Jesus had signed the emancipation papers of all humanity, and the death knell of Satan was sounded. The kingdom of grace had triumphed, and now all who accepted the sacrifice of Jesus on their behalf could enter in (Matthew 3:1,2).

Meanwhile, early Sunday morning (Abib 16) *"while it was yet dark"*, the women came to the tomb with sweet-smelling spices to anoint the body of Jesus. To their great sorrow and surprise, He was not there. While they pondered what to do next, two angels *"in shining garments"* suddenly appeared beside them (Luke 24:4). They told the astonished women that Jesus had risen and instructed them to carry the good news to the sorrowing disciples. The guards, who *"shook with fear and became like dead men"* (Matt 28:4), were nowhere to be seen. After recovering their wits, they ran to tell the chief priests and elders what had happened. As these religious leaders listened, they began to tremble. Hur-

riedly they consulted together. Then bringing from their treasury large sums of money they urged the soldiers to proclaim throughout Jerusalem that *"the disciples came by night and stole Him away while we slept"* (Matthew 28:11-15).

Early on the morning of His resurrection, Jesus ascended to heaven to present His sacrifice to the Father (John 20:16,17). He had fulfilled His pledge to give His life as a ransom for the fallen race, and God accepted the sacrifice and ratified the covenant. Jesus now returned to His followers on earth to encourage them and to strengthen their faith. Soon after His return He met with Cleopas on the road to Emmaus.

Jesus proved His resurrection to the disciples *"by many infallible proofs"*, and repeated to them *"the things pertaining to the kingdom of God"* (Acts 1:3).

He then commanded His disciples to wait in Jerusalem until they received the power of the Holy Spirit. This would enable them to take the gospel message to the world. Not only to the Jews but also to the Gentiles.

The same promise God gave to Israel at its inception, was now given to the infant Christian church. *"You are a chosen generation, a royal priesthood, a holy nation, a peculiar* (special) *people: that ye should show forth the praises of Him who hath called you out of darkness into His marvelous light."* [51]   In Christ's absence the Comforter, the Holy Spirit, would be His representative.

His work on earth now finished, Christ ascended to heaven once more to begin the second phase of His redemptive work - that of High Priest and Intercessor in the heavenly sanctuary.[52] As His disciples watched in awe, Jesus slowly ascended until a cloud of angels *"received Him out of their sight"* (Acts 1:9).[53] With songs of joy they escorted Him to the throne of God while two remained behind to comfort the sorrowing disciples with the assuring words, *"this same Jesus who is taken up from you into heaven, will so come in like manner as you have seen Him go into heaven,"* (Acts 1:11; John 14:1-3).

1) Jesus In The Holy Place.

Let us now join Jesus as He ascends to heaven to continue His work for the salvation of man. The Bible gives us sufficient detail so our imagination can safely fill the gaps without doing despite to the Word of God.

As the dazzling cloud of angels with Jesus in its midst approaches the gates of Paradise, they sing in rapturous joy to the angels within:

> *"Lift up your heads, O ye gates, and be ye lifted up,*

---

51   Compare 1Peter 2:9 with Exodus 19:5,6.

52   Hebrews 4:14; 6:20; 8:1,2; 9:11,24.

53   Revelation 1:7; Matthew 24:30,31; 2 Thessalonians 1:7.

ye everlasting doors: and the KING OF GLORY shall come in."

The angels within jubilantly inquire:

"Who is this KING OF GLORY?"

Back comes the triumphant answer:

"The Lord strong and mighty, The LORD mighty in battle. Lift up your heads, O ye gates, Even lift them up, ye everlasting doors, And the KING OF GLORY shall come in!"

Once again, the angels from within joyfully inquire:

"Who is this KING OF GLORY?"

And the answer comes ringing back in a burst of adoration and praise:

"The LORD of hosts, He is the KING OF GLORY! Selah" (Psalm 24:7-10).

As if never tiring of singing praises to the King of Glory, the song echoes back and forth until the very courts of heaven resonate with joyful melody.

Suddenly the *"portals of the city of God are opened wide, and the angelic throng sweeps through the gates amid a burst of rapturous music."* [54] What a reception awaits the meek and lowly One! Not only is there *"an innumerable company of angels"* (Hebrews 12:22), but also representatives from unfallen worlds, all eager to welcome the Redeemer and to celebrate His victory. The Father Himself is there to welcome His beloved Son. Seated upon His magnificent throne of indescribable glory, and surrounded by cherubim and seraphim, He eagerly awaits the arrival of the Conqueror.

No human language can portray the marvelous intricacy

____

54   White, E., The Desire of Ages, p. 835

and glory of the throne of God.[55] When the apostle Paul was given a vision of Paradise, he said the things he saw and heard there were *"not lawful for a man to utter."* Or as Moffat translates it, *"no human lips can repeat"* (2 Corinthians 12:4).

Surrounding this glorious throne is a rainbow, more beautiful and resplendent than mortal eye has ever seen (Revelation 4:3). To this magnificent throne the angels escort the Son of God. Only a short time before He has worn the shameful crown of thorns, the symbol of the curse of sin, but now He is seated at the right hand of the Father and *"crowned with glory and honour"* (Mark 16:19; Ephesians 1:20; Hebrews 2:9).

God the Father now gives the command, *"Let all the angels of God worship Him!"* (Hebrews 1:6). This is the signal the angels have been eagerly waiting for. In joyful adoration the vast angelic throng prostrates itself before Jesus, and all heaven rings as their voices unite in lofty strains proclaiming, *"Blessing and honour, and glory, and power be unto Him that sitteth upon the throne, and unto the Lamb forever and ever"* (Revelation 5:13; John 17:5).

This wonderful coronation ceremony climaxes with the anointing of Jesus as High Priest of the heavenly sanctuary. As this anointing ceremony takes place, the Holy Spirit overflows in rich currents onto the waiting disciples below, giving them power to establish the Christian church *"in Jerusalem, and in Judea, and in Samaria, and unto the*

---

55   See Jeremiah 17:12; Isaiah 6:1-4; Ezekiel 1:26-28.

uttermost parts of the earth" (Acts 1:5,8). This is the day of Pentecost.

Before the second coming of Christ there will be another outpouring of the Holy Spirit similar to Pentecost, but with even greater power. The outpouring of the Holy Spirit on the day of Pentecost was the *"early"* or *"former rain"* which watered the gospel seed causing it to germinate and grow. The *"latter rain"* will be more abundant and will ripen the harvest in preparation for Christ's return (Joel 2:23; Hosea 6:3). The latter rain is represented by *"another angel come down from heaven, having great power, and the earth was lightened with his glory"* (Revelation 18:1).

Once more the church around the circle of the globe will give the *"everlasting gospel"* with *"tongues of fire"*, and thousands will be converted in one day. May the Lord hasten that day!

The anointing of Jesus in the heavenly sanctuary is pictured graphically for us by the anointing of the high priest, Aaron, in the earthly sanctuary before its services began. [56]   As the sanctuary services on earth were but *"shadows,"* or illustrations, of what takes place in heaven, we can know that the work of redemption was fully transferred to the sanctuary above after the resurrection of Christ. The ripping of the temple veil by an unseen hand at the very moment Jesus died signaled the end of the Jewish ceremonial system - which vividly portrayed the courtyard phase of the plan of redemption. The sacrifices and offerings of the Jewish system were no longer divinely recognized.

Now Jesus was about to begin the second phase of His plan to redeem mankind. This phase must be conducted in the Holy Place of the heavenly sanctuary.

---

56   See Exodus 30:25-30 and Leviticus 8:10-12.

2) The Christian in The Holy Place

As the Christian passes through the courtyard experience, he is forgiven, cleansed of all past sins and mistakes, and adopted into the family of God. The gospel seed has been planted in his heart, he has received the *"early rain,"* and the seed has germinated and is now beginning to grow. Do we move on from this experience and nourish the gospel seed, or do we stay in the courtyard continually sinning, repenting, and bringing lambs to be slaughtered? - as did the ancient Jews.

There are some today who still teach that this is all there is to salvation. However, it is obvious that the Lord does not want us to remain immature Christians, just as a parent does not want his baby to stay a baby forever. He encourages him to sit, crawl, walk, and run. In a similar manner our heavenly Father wants us to grow and mature spiritually. He wants the seed in our hearts to flourish and bring forth fruit for the kingdom of God. For this reason, He has given us the Holy Place, a 'sandbox model' illustrating Christian growth and maturity. This is a lifelong process and is called 'sanctification'. Sanctification means to be 'made holy,' or as Webster's dictionary defines it, *"the act or process of God's grace by which the affections are purified, or alienated from sin, and exalted to a supreme love for God and righteousness."* Holiness is a Bible principle:

- *"Let us go on to perfection* (holiness), *not laying again the foundation of repentance from dead works . . .,"* the courtyard experience (Hebrews 6:1).

- *"The very God of peace sanctify you wholly. I pray God your whole spirit, and soul, and body be preserved blameless unto the coming of our Lord Jesus Christ"* (1Thessalonians 5:23).

- *"Follow peace with all men, and holiness, without which no man will see the Lord"* (Hebrews 12:14).

- *"For this is the will of God, even your sanctification"*

(1Thessalonians 4:3).

- *"Be ye therefore perfect, even as your Father in heaven is perfect "* (Matthew 5:48).

- *"As He which hath called you is holy, so be ye holy in all manner of conversation* (conduct), *because it is written, Be ye holy, for I am holy"* (1 Peter 1:15,16).

- *"And in their mouth was found no guile* (deceit). *For they are without fault before the throne of God"* (Revelation 14:5).

- Therefore, *''forgetting those things which are behind, and reaching forth unto those things which are before,"* let us *"press toward the mark for the prize of the high calling of God in Christ Jesus"* (Philippians 3:13,14).

How can the Christian possibly attain to such a high standard? He cannot! Once again Christ is our substitute. As we received forgiveness by faith, so must we also receive righteousness by faith. And as we cannot 'see' that we are forgiven, so we cannot always 'see' our growth toward holiness. We accept by faith that *"He which hath begun a good work in us will perform it until the day of Jesus Christ"* (Philippians 1:6).

Sanctification is the second half of the salvation formula. The whole process was summed up succinctly by Jesus Christ when He said to the woman caught in the very act of adultery, *"Neither do I condemn thee, go and sin no more."* This poor woman was dragged before Jesus with the demand that she be stoned to death according to Jewish law. Jesus made no reply. Instead, He stooped down and quietly began to write the sins of her accusers in the dust of the ground. Mortified to be thus exposed, they sullenly withdrew one by one, leaving the woman alone with Jesus. It was then that He spoke those immortal words of forgiveness to the trembling woman. She left forgiven and cleansed, with the words *"Go and sin no more"* ringing in her ears. This is what the Lord says to the forgiven and cleansed child of God today. *"Go and sin no more"* - this is the Holy Place experience.

Why is it necessary for us to go on to holiness? Why should not forgiveness alone suffice for salvation? Let me explain with a simple illustration. You have bought an old house. The weeds have grown up around it, several windows are broken, the paint is peeling, the plumbing needs repair, and the foundations are shaky. However, you look beyond its dilapidated state and visualize what it may become, so contracts are exchanged, and you are now the legal owner. Do you leave the house as it is? No, you want to live in it one day; but cannot in its present condition. So, over time you carefully repair and renew the old, neglected house, exchanging broken parts for new, making changes inside and out until it begins to resemble your ideal. As you work, it more and more reflects your character. It begins to carry your impress. People who know you well immediately recognize the house as your property.

So, it is with Christ. We are His property. He bought us at Calvary; His blood is the purchase price. He wants to dwell in us, but our characters are defective. We are controlled by bad habits and selfishness, and by inherited and cultivated tendencies to evil. In short, we are not a fit dwelling place for our Heavenly King. Jesus wants to change all that. He wants us to reflect His image, to carry His impress. He wants the world to know that we have *"been with Jesus"* and learned of Him (Acts 4:13). He wants to dwell in our hearts, and use us as instruments for His glory. *"For we are His workmanship, created in Christ Jesus unto good works . . . a habitation of God through the Holy Spirit "* (Ephesians 2:10, 22). As we were once created by the power of God but ruined by sin, so He now wants to recreate us by that same power. This is sanctification.

Let me give another illustration. You have found a child living on the streets. He is filthy, ragged, and uninviting in every way. But your heart of compassion yearns for this child, and you decide to adopt the homeless waif. Your first work is to take off his filthy clothing and give him a good bath. Next you clothe him in clean, sweet-smelling garments, and invite him to eat at your table.

The child has undergone a complete transformation on the outside, but what about the inside! You soon discover that he has acquired some nasty, anti-social 'street' habits which make him unfit company for your family. He lies without a second thought, steals whenever your back is turned, has a violent temper, is a glutton at the table, and has absolutely no manners. Obviously, you cannot leave him in this condition. So now begins the slow, firm, but loving re-education process during which he is made to see that he must abide by the rules of your home to live there. He understands that he can return to the streets at any time if he so desires. No strong, coercive measures are used in this home - only those principles which are in harmony with free-will, love, and compassion.

The child has a choice. He can either cooperate with his adoptive parents, accept the rules of the home, and learn how to bring his life into conformity to their standards, or he can return to the streets. Or he may take a third route, that unfortunately taken by many Christians. He may outwardly comply but remain a street kid at heart. Under a clean, smooth exterior, he may still be a liar, a glutton, and a thief, and at the opportune moment these characteristics will resurface. Jesus calls such 'Christians' who are guilty of taking His name in vain, *"white-washed sepulchers, which indeed appear beautiful outwardly, but are within full of dead men's bones and all uncleanness . . .ye outwardly appear righteous unto men, but within ye are full of hypocrisy and iniquity"* (Read Matthew 23 for a full description).

The justified Christian is like a disabled ship that has been towed to port for repairs. It is 'safe' but not sound. Likewise, the new Christian is 'saved' but not free from weaknesses and defects. He needs reconstruction and restoration. This is the work Jesus entered the Holy Place in heaven to perform on our behalf, but He needs our willing consent and active cooperation. He carefully and lovingly examines every case and outlines a program of discipline and reform tailor-made to suit the needs of every Christian. The Holy Place experience will ensure that we are clean inwardly as well as outwardly, and not just *"white washed sepulchers."*

While on this earth our Lord perfected a holy, righteous character while subject to the same temptations, evil influences, and trials we face. *"For we have not a High Priest who cannot be touched with the feeling of our infirmities but was in all points tempted like as we are, yet without sin"* (Hebrews 4:15). We are invited by Jesus to confess our sins directly to Him, and as our High Priest, He will forgive us, grant us power to overcome sin, and work out in us His own righteous character.

> *"Let us therefore come boldly unto the throne of grace, that we may obtain mercy, and find grace to help in time of need"* (Hebrews 4:16).

Jesus is only a prayer away. He nourishes tenderly the tiny seed of truth which has been planted in our hearts. *"A bruised reed shall He not break, and the smoking flax shall He not quench"* (Isaiah 42:3). In the Holy Place He gives us His Word as food on which to grow. He gives us His Holy Spirit as gentle rain to refresh the soul. He surrounds us with the sunshine of His love, and we are invited to breathe the atmosphere of heaven, which is prayer, the breath of the soul. With a heart open to these influences, the 'baby' Christian cannot help but grow into *"a perfect man, unto the measure of the stature of the fulness of Christ"* (Ephesians 4:13).

> *"The righteous will flourish like the palm tree. He will grow like the cedar in Lebanon. Those that are planted in the house of the Lord will flourish in the courts of our God"* (Psalm 92:12).

The following diagram illustrates Christian growth as described in 2 Peter 1:4-8. As we climb Peter's ladder Christ's righteous robe will cover us, and while thus covered we are perfect in God's sight though still immature Christians. Jesus will be by our side uniting His power to our human weakness, so that together we may move steadily upward toward the throne of grace, while ever keeping in mind the warning words of Jesus, *"No man, having put his hand to the plow, and looking back, is fit for the kingdom of God"* (Luke 9:62).

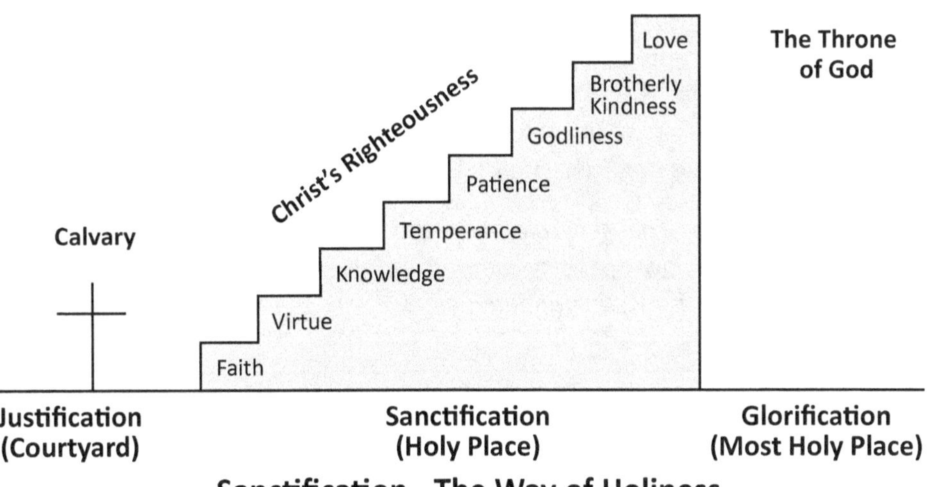

Three Essentials to Winning the Prize

As the new Christian cannot pass through the beautifully embroidered curtain into the Holy Place in person, he must accept the experience by faith. In the earthly sanctuary the priests were the only ones who could enter this sacred precinct, so the ancient Israelite also en-

tered by faith - the first step on Peter's ladder.

The Holy Place was a room ten cubits wide by twenty cubits long, or eighteen ft (5.5 m.) by thirty-six ft (11m.). In our imaginations let us step inside this holy room. All around is pure gold. At the far end is a veil suspended from five gold-plated pillars, which separates this room from the Most Holy Place. Like the other two curtains, it is also woven from blue, purple, and scarlet woolen thread and richly embroidered with golden cherubim. The ceiling is of the same color and design. Along both sides are boards covered with glittering gold and engraved with angel figures. We are literally surrounded by 'angels', even as Christ is surrounded by angels in the sanctuary above. These figures represent the *"innumerable company"* of angels connected with the work of the sanctuary. They are *"ministering spirits sent forth to minister for them who shall be heirs of salvation"* (Hebrews 12:22; 1:14).

"The rich colours in the veils, reflected in the yellow of the golden walls, give the effect of a rainbow surrounding us, similar to the rainbow around God's throne." [57]

To our right, on the northern wall, is the golden table with its ornate crown and twelve loaves of bread. To our left, toward the southern wall, stands the seven branched candlestick, exquisitely wrought with lilies, and made from one solid piece of gold. Its soft light enhances the atmosphere of reverence and awe which fills this sacred place like a living presence.

Just before the veil separating the two apartments stands a golden altar fragrant with sweet-smelling incense. The fire upon this altar is kindled by God and is sacredly cherished.

The articles of furniture in the Holy Place represent the three essentials for Christian growth and maturity.

---

57   Peck, S., The Path to the Throne of God, p. 146

- The bread on the golden table symbolizes the study of God's Word. It is given so that we may *"grow in grace and in the knowledge of our Lord and Saviour Jesus Christ"* (2 Peter 3:18).

- At the golden altar, the sweet incense typifies prayer, *"the breath of the soul."*

- The golden candlestick symbolizes Christ who said, *"I Am the light of the world. He that follows me shall not walk in darkness, but shall have the light of life"* (John 8:12). It is also a symbol of Christ reflected in the life of a true follower of Jesus.

- The gold in the sanctuary amounted to approximately 2,631 kgs (5,800 lbs), worth many tens of millions of dollars in today's currency. Sanctification is indeed a priceless experience. Our Saviour's promise to us is, *"I will make you more precious than fine gold, even more than the golden wedge of Ophir"* (Isaiah 13:12).

  "Holiness is not rapture. It is an entire surrender of the will to God. It is living by every word that proceeds from the mouth of God. It is doing the will of our heavenly Father. It is trusting God in trial, in darkness as well as in the light. It is walking by faith and not by sight. It is relying on God with unquestioning confidence and resting in His love." [58]

a) The Golden Table Experience
(Exodus 25:23-30)

The golden table represents the first step in sanctification - the daily study of the Word of God. The table itself was made from acacia wood overlaid with pure gold symbolizing the humanity of man combined with the divinity of Christ. This combination will always bring success in the Christian warfare. In the lesson book of the sanctuary, this truth is foundational to the development of a Christlike character. Jesus tells us plainly, *"Without Me you can*

---

58 White, E., The Acts of the Apostles, p. 51

do nothing," but with Me *"you can do all things"* (John 15:5; Philippians 4:13). The Bible itself is an example of the human and the divine working in cooperation. It was inspired by God but written by man.

The Crowns

From the description of the table given in the Scriptures it appears to have had a lower shelf upon which were kept the golden dishes, spoons, bowls, and chalices for the bread and wine. Both the upper and lower shelves were decorated with a crown of pure gold, thus forming a double crown (Exodus 37:10-16).

A crown worn by a king represents his power and authority. Similarly, this double crown on the golden table represents the power and authority of the Word of God. Received into the life of the Christian it has power to change

him. *"For the Word of God is quick* (living) *and powerful, and sharper than any two-edged sword, piercing even to the dividing asunder of soul and spirit . . . and is a discerner of the thoughts and intents of the heart"* (Hebrews 4:12).

The Word of God has *authority.* It brought the worlds into existence. *"By the word of the Lord were the heavens made; and all the hosts of them by the breath of His mouth"* (Psalm 33:6). When God speaks, *"let all the earth keep silence before Him"* (Habakkuk 2:20). *"It is His to speak. It is ours to obey".* [59]

The Word of God makes the proud humble, the rebellious meek and contrite, the disobedient obedient. It cuts away the *"fleshly lusts which war against the soul,"* and takes self out of the heart (1 Peter 2:11).

The golden crown also represents the crown of life promised to the overcomer.

"Behold, I come quickly. Hold fast that which thou

---

59   Peck, S., The Path to the Throne of God, p. 169

hast, that no man take thy crown."

"Be thou faithful unto death, and I will give thee a crown of life" (Revelation 2:10; 3:11; 4:4).

The Bread

At the beginning of each Sabbath, the Kohathites, a division of the tribe of Levi, made twelve large, round, flat loaves of unleavened bread. Some scholars estimate that these loaves were between two and five inches thick, and from eighteen to twenty-two inches across. These were placed hot on the table in two piles of six. On top of these loaves was placed pure frankincense - a dry, resinous, aromatic gum from a tree which grows in Arabia.

The bread lay on the table for one week, being replaced the next Sabbath with another batch of freshly baked bread. The week-old loaves were then eaten by the priests.

The old loaves were not removed until the freshly baked ones were ready to take their place, as bread must always be present on the table. For this reason, it was sometimes referred to as the *"Bread of the Presence."* Similarly, the Word of God should always be present in our homes and in our hearts (Psalm 16:8). The bread was an ever-present reminder that Israel depended upon God for sustenance - both physical and spiritual, and a constant promise from Him that He would provide for their every need.

Christ, the Bread of Life

The bread also symbolizes Jesus who was born in Bethlehem, the *'house of bread.'* Jesus said, *"I Am the Bread of Life . . . I Am the Living Bread which came down from heaven. If any man eat of this Bread, he shall live forever . . . The words that I speak unto you, they are spirit, and they are life"* (John 6:48-63).

A careful study of John 6:31-65 will reveal that the *"bread*

of life" refers to both the body of Jesus and His Word, the Holy Bible. The expression *"eating His flesh"* symbolizes devouring the Word of God in earnest, prayerful study. As the priests ate daily of the sacred sanctuary bread, so we need also to eat daily of the Bread of Life by carefully studying the Bible, until its message, like the food we eat, becomes part of the very fibre of our being. This is the first essential to *'growing'* in Christ. God has the following promises for the faithful student of His Word:

- *"Sanctify them through Thy truth. Thy Word is truth"* (John 17:17).

- There are *"given unto us exceeding great and precious promises, that by these ye might be partakers of the divine nature"* (2 Peter 1:4).

- *"All Scripture is given by inspiration of God, and is profitable for doctrine, for reproof, for correction, for instruction in righteousness, that the man of God may be perfect, thoroughly furnished unto all good works"* (2 Timothy 3:16,17).

- *"Thy Word have I hid in my heart that I might not sin against Thee"* (Psalm 119:11).

- *"How shall a young man cleanse his ways? By taking heed according to Thy Word"* (Psalm 119:9).

- *"Now ye are clean through the Word I have spoken unto you"* (John 15:3).

There is no substitute for the study of the Scriptures. It is as essential for the nourishment of the soul as physical food is for the nourishment of the body.

> *"The Word of God is the living bread, giving refinement, wisdom, cleansing, spiritual strength and endurance, and finally sanctification and eternal life."* [60]

> *"Obedience to the Word of God cleanses, refines and ennobles our lives. It enables us to be true servants of God."* [61]

Frankincense

Frankincense was placed on the bread during the week and burned on the golden altar daily. The sweet smelling incense rising heavenward represents our prayers mingling with the incense of Christ's righteousness.

By being placed on the bread, it reminds us that never should the Bible be studied without prayer. We should always ask for the enlightenment of the Holy Spirit before beginning our studies. If we forget to pray, Satan stands ready to implant error and confuse our minds. *"The Spirit of truth is the only effectual teacher of divine truth."* [62]

The study of the Bible is our safeguard through times of trouble. We should dig deep into the Word, comparing scripture with scripture, and discover its truths for ourselves. Satan knows that the earnest, sincere, and prayerful study of God's Word is our only safety during the perils of these last days, therefore it is his constant study to keep men's minds distracted and occupied with other things to prevent them from obtaining a knowledge of God. But if we hunger and thirst after righteousness, God's promise is sure, we will be filled! (Matthew 5:6). His Holy Spirit will guide us in our studies and protect us from deception – our greatest danger. See Matthew 24.

As we daily feed upon the Word, we will become more and more like our Redeemer. Through faith we will see the face of Him who is invisible, and one day soon *"when He shall appear, we shall be like Him, for we shall see Him as He is"* (1 John 3:2).

> *"And they shall see His face, and His name shall be in their foreheads"* (Revelation 22:4)

---

61   Peck, S., The Path to the Throne of God, p. 171

62   White, E., Steps to Christ, p. 44

As we daily feed upon the Word, we will become more and more like our Redeemer.

"With the Word of God in his hands, every human being, wherever his lot in life may be, may have such companionship as he shall choose. In its pages he may hold converse with the noblest and best of the human race and may listen to the voice of the Eternal as He speaks with men. As he studies and meditates upon the themes into which "angels desire to look," he may have their companionship. He may follow the steps of the heavenly Teacher and listen to His words as when He taught on mountain and plain and sea. He may dwell in this world in the atmosphere of heaven, imparting to earth's sorrowing and tempted ones thoughts of hope and longings for holiness; himself coming closer and still closer into fellowship with the Unseen. Like Enoch of old who walked with God, he may draw nearer and nearer the threshold of the eternal world, until the portals shall open, and he shall enter there. He will find himself no stranger. The voices that will greet him are the voices of the holy ones, who, unseen were on earth his companions - voices that here he learned to distinguish and to love. He who through the Word of God has lived in fellowship with heaven will find himself at home in heaven's companionship." [63]

b) The Golden Altar Experience
(Exodus 30:1-10)

The golden altar, or the altar of incense, represents another essential to gaining the prize. This altar was also called the *'altar of prayer.'* Like the table, the altar of incense was made of acacia wood overlaid with pure gold. It was positioned in front of the ark of the covenant with its mercy seat (symbolizing the throne of God) but hidden from it by a beautiful curtain. From each corner of the altar were projections called *'horns'* and around the top was a beau-

---

63   White, E., *Education*, p. 127

tiful crown of gold.

Holy fire was kept continually burning on the altar, and from it ascended the fragrance of the incense which was placed upon it morning and evening. This sweet-smelling perfume pervaded the whole sanctuary by day and night and was wafted by the breezes over the whole camp of Israel.

This incense was composed of equal amounts of four fragrant gums and resins and was prepared according to directions given by God. It was considered very sacred, and the recipe therefore was not to be copied by the people for personal use or for monetary gain. To do so would result in the offender being *"cut off from among the people"* (Exodus 30:34-38). 

Fresh incense was placed upon the altar by the high priest at the time of the morning and evening sacrifice. During this special time, called the *"time of incense,"* the people gathered about the sanctuary for prayer and worship (Luke 1:10).

It was a time for the Israelites to present their petitions to God, and to rededicate themselves to Him. As their prayers ascended to the throne of God, they mingled with the sweet perfume of the rising incense. The incense represented the righteousness of Christ which must accompany our prayers for them to be acceptable to God. Passing as they do through the corrupt and selfish channels of humanity, they are unacceptable to God unless purified by the righteousness of our great High Priest, Jesus Christ. He places, as it were, His signature upon our prayers, and presents them to the Father as His own desire on the sinner's behalf.

The practice of morning and evening prayer should be adopted by every Christian. To those families who observe this time of daily worship, God has given one of His most precious promises - *"there I will meet with thee"* (Exodus 30:6).

God looks with pleasure upon those who love Him, bowing morning and evening to seek forgiveness for sins and mistakes, and to present their petitions to Him. Such homes will diffuse the sweet fragrance of Christlike love, not only within their own border, but also out into the neighbourhood beyond.

While family and public prayer are very important, it is our personal time spent alone with God which sustains and nourishes the soul. Jesus is our example in prayer. He was often in prayer, seeking from His Father fresh supplies of strength that He might be fortified each day for life's duties and trials. *"His humanity made prayer a necessity and a privilege. He found comfort and joy in communion with His Father. And if the Saviour of men, the Son of God, felt the need of prayer, how much more should feeble, sinful mortals feel the necessity of fervent, constant prayer."* [64]

Prayer, like the all-pervading incense, should become part of our daily experience for it is impossible for the soul to grow and prosper while prayer is neglected. There are times when we should draw apart to a quiet retreat for meditation and prayer. However, it is important to keep in mind that we can pray at all times and in all places - while we go about our daily work, in the crowded streets, or in the middle of a business meeting: anywhere, any place, any time, we can send up our silent petitions to God. It is our privilege to keep so near to God that in *"every unexpected trial our thoughts will turn to Him as naturally as the flower turns toward the sun."* [65]

Why Some Prayers are not Answered?

- <u>Unbelief Hinders God</u>. We must ask, believing that God hears us. Unless we ask in faith, it is written, *"Let not that man think that he will receive anything of the Lord"* (James 1:7).

"He who comes to God must believe that He is, and

---

64 White, E., Steps to Christ, p. 45

65 White, E., Steps to Christ, p. 4

that He is a rewarder of those who diligently seek Him" (Hebrews 11:6).

Jesus said to His disciples, *"Whatever things you ask when you pray, believe that you receive them and you will have them"* (Mark 11:24).

Do we really believe these promises? If not, we need to pray, *"Lord, help Thou my unbelief"* (Mark 9:24). We need to talk faith, to practice faith, and to say in our hearts, *"I choose to believe the promises of God."*

- <u>Selfishness Hinders God</u>. *"Ye ask, and receive not, because ye ask amiss, that ye may consume it upon your lusts"* (James 4:3).

Often, in our blindness, we pray selfishly for things which would not be a blessing to us, but rather a curse. God in His mercy and wisdom will not give us that which will take us further away from Him, and result in eternal loss. Wise parents likewise will not give their children all the things they ask for, knowing from their vantage point of greater experience and wisdom, that such things will harm the child.

The artist Raphael is said to have worn a candle attached to his cap while painting so that his shadow would not fall across his work. Many a prayer is spoiled by our own shadow. Too often we pray for that which will bring glory to us, rather than for what will bring glory to God.

- <u>Willful Disobedience Hinders God</u>. *"He who turns away his ear from hearing the law, even his prayer will be an abomination"* (Proverbs 28:9). If we know what God requires of us and refuse Him obedience, we cannot expect Him to answer our prayers.

- <u>An Evil Heart Hinders God</u>. *"If I regard iniquity in my heart, the Lord will not hear me"* (Psalm 66:18).

The thought implied in the word "regard," is the cherishing of secret sin with no serious attempt to put it away. This was Judas's problem. He secretly cherished

the sin of covetousness, and continually resisted the promptings of his conscience until covetousness became a consuming passion, and he could betray his Lord for thirty pieces of silver. When the Lord convicts us that something in our lives needs to be dealt with, we should not turn a deaf ear to His pleadings but cooperate with Him in the removing of it from our lives. We must clear the King's highway, so that Jesus can present our petitions to God perfumed with the incense of His righteousness.

• <u>Irreverence Hinders God</u>.   When we come into the presence of God we should remember that He is the King of kings, the Ruler of the universe, the great Creator of all things. Even the angels veil their faces when they approach Him. We should keep the *"fear of the Lord"* in our hearts and not address Him as we would an equal. Is it any wonder that many of our prayers never reach the throne of God?

• <u>An Unforgiving Spirit Hinders God</u>. *"If you do not forgive men their trespasses, neither will your Father forgive your trespasses"* (Matthew 6:12,15).

If we expect our prayers to be heard, we must forgive others to the same extent as we hope to be forgiven. Peter was troubled on this point. *"Lord,"* he asked, *"how often shall my brother sin against me, and I forgive him? Until seven times?"* Jesus answered, *"Not until seven times, but until seventy times seven."*

He then proceeded to illustrate further by telling the parable of the unmerciful servant whose Lord had forgiven him a debt of 10,000 talents. But when a fellow servant who owed him a mere 100 pence could not pay his debt, he angrily cast him into prison, *"Likewise will My heavenly Father do also to you"* (Matthew 18:21-35).

• <u>Prayer with Thanksgiving Pleases God.</u> *"Be anxious for nothing, but in everything by prayer and supplication with thanksgiving let your requests be made known unto God"* (Philippians 4:6).

"Continue in prayer . . . with thanksgiving" (Colossians 4:2).

Our prayers should not consist wholly in asking. We should not always be thinking of our own wants and forget the benefits we receive. Our appreciation for Christ will add sweet incense to our prayers.

"Keep your wants, your joys, your sorrows, your cares, and your fears before God. You cannot burden Him. You cannot weary Him. He who numbers the hairs of your head is not indifferent to the wants of His children. "The Lord is very compassionate and of tender mercy" (James 5:11).

"His heart of love is touched by our sorrows, and even by our utterances of them. Take to Him everything that perplexes the mind. Nothing is too great for Him to bear, for He holds up worlds, He rules over the affairs of the universe. Nothing that in any way concerns our peace is too small for Him to notice.

"There is no chapter in our experience too dark for Him to read. There is no perplexity too difficult for Him to unravel. No calamity can befall the least of His children, no anxiety harass the soul, no joy cheer, no sincere prayer escape the lips, of which our heavenly Father is unobservant, or in which He takes no immediate interest. "He heals the brokenhearted and binds up their wounds" (Psalm 147:3). The relations between God and each soul are as distinct and full as though there were not another soul for whom He gave His beloved Son."

- White, E., Steps to Christ, p. 100

A FRIEND IN JESUS

What a friend we have in Jesus,
All our sins and griefs to bear!
What a privilege to carry
Everything to God in prayer!
O what peace we often forfeit,
O what needless pain we bear,
All because we do not carry
Everything to God in prayer.

Have we trials and temptations?
Is there trouble anywhere?
We should never be discouraged,
Take it to the Lord in prayer.
Can we find a Friend so faithful,
Who will all our sorrows share?
Jesus knows our every weakness,
Take it to the Lord in prayer.

Are we weak and heavy laden,
Cumbered with a load of care?
Precious Saviour, still our refuge,
Take it to the Lord in prayer.
Do thy friends despise, forsake thee?
Take it to the Lord in prayer,
In His arms He'll take and shield thee,
Thou will find a solace there.
- John M. Scriven

c) The Golden Candlestick Experience
(Exodus 25:31-40)

The candlestick with its seven golden lamps was located on the south side of the Holy Place. Unlike the table and the altar, which were made of wood overlaid with gold, the candlestick was made from one solid piece of gold weighing a talent, or about 120 pounds (54 kg). From a central shaft three branches projected from either side, creating seven lamps in all. These branches were decorated with exquisitely hand carved ornaments resembling lilies, buds, and almonds. Altogether seventy ornaments adorned this magnificent piece of craftsmanship. The Bible gives a very detailed description, and adds this caution for the workman, *"Look that thou make them after their pattern, which was showed thee in the mount"* (Exodus 25:40). Any variation from God's exact plan would mar the spiritual lessons He wished to teach.

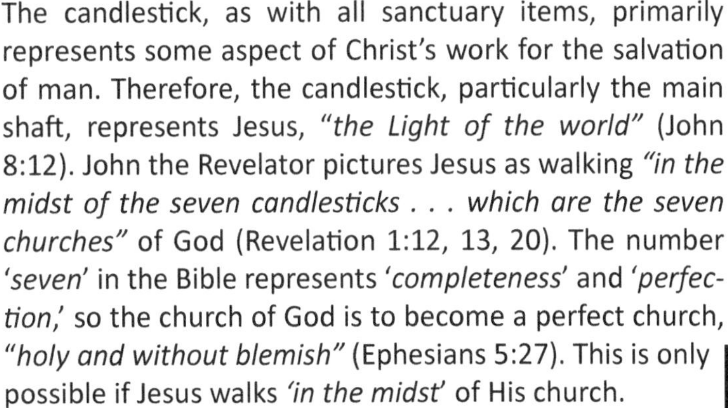

The candlestick, as with all sanctuary items, primarily represents some aspect of Christ's work for the salvation of man. Therefore, the candlestick, particularly the main shaft, represents Jesus, *"the Light of the world"* (John 8:12). John the Revelator pictures Jesus as walking *"in the midst of the seven candlesticks . . . which are the seven churches"* of God (Revelation 1:12, 13, 20). The number 'seven' in the Bible represents 'completeness' and 'perfection,' so the church of God is to become a perfect church, *"holy and without blemish"* (Ephesians 5:27). This is only possible if Jesus walks *'in the midst'* of His church.

Pure Gold

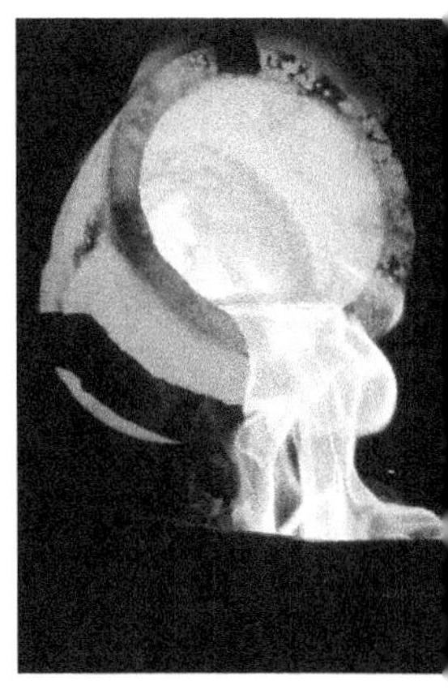

The first thing we notice about the candlestick is that it was beaten into shape from one piece of solid gold. Each of the beautiful ornaments was skilfully shaped with blows from the workman's hammer. It is easy to see how these blows represent the sufferings of our Lord who was *"wounded for our transgression"* and *"bruised for our in-*

iquities." But here also is illustrated the purifying of the church. Of this process it is written, *"He will sit as a refiner and purifier of the sons of Levi, and purge them as gold and silver, that they may offer unto the Lord an offering in righteousness"* (Malachi 3:3).

The individuals who form part of the church of God will often feel the workman's hammer, *''for we are His workmanship, created by Christ Jesus unto good works"* (Ephesians 2:10). Then *''beloved, think it not strange concerning the fiery trial which is to try you, as if some strange thing happened unto you"* (1 Peter 4:12).

God permits the fires of affliction, like the fires which soften gold, to consume the dross of pride and selfishness from our hearts. When instead of self we reflect the image of Jesus, our light will shine for Him.

The second thing we notice about the candlestick is its great value. The candlestick was the most elaborate as well as the most valuable of all the sanctuary vessels and represents the high value that Jesus places on service which comes from the heart. *"Let your light so shine before men, that they may see your good works, and glorify your Father which is in heaven"* (Matthew 5:16).

Almond Ornaments

Some of the ornaments were fashioned to resemble almonds, the Hebrew word for which means *"to hasten,"* because the almond tree is one of the first to blossom each spring. It is a welcome indication of the beginning of new life; of the new life received by the *'born-again'* child of God.

"The King's business requires haste" (1 Samuel 21:8). A sense of urgency will be in the hearts of all who proclaim to the world a crucified and risen Saviour. *"The word of the Lord came unto me saying, Jeremiah, what seest thou? And I said, I see a rod of an almond tree. Then said the Lord unto me, Thou hast well seen, for I will hasten My word to perform it"* (Jeremiah 1:11, 12).

Pure Olive Oil

"Command the children of Israel that they bring unto thee <u>*pure*</u> *olive oil,* <u>*beaten*</u> *for the light, to cause the lamps to* <u>*burn continually*</u>*"* (Leviticus 24:2; Exodus 27:20).

1. <u>The Pure Oil</u>. In the vision of the candlestick which the Lord gave to the prophet Zechariah, we learn what the pure oil represents. It was a time of trouble for Israel. King Cyrus of Persia had given the exiled Israelites permission to return to their native land and rebuild their temple; destroyed 70 years earlier by King Nebuchadnezzar of Babylon. But continuing and relentless attacks from enemies had discouraged Zerubbabel. Difficulties arose like a mountain before him, and progress was slow and uncertain. It was at this time that the Lord sent a message to Zerubbabel through His servant, Zechariah. Zechariah explains what he saw in vision:

   "And (the angel) *said unto me, What seest thou? And I said . . . I behold a candlestick all of pure gold, with a bowl upon the top of it, and seven lamps thereon . . . And two olive trees by it, one upon the right side of the bowl, and the other upon the left side. So I spoke to the angel that talked with me, saying, What are these my Lord? The angel answered . . . Know thou not what these are? And I said, No, my Lord. Then he replied...This is the word of the Lord unto Zerubbabel, saying, Not by might, nor by power, but by My Spirit, saith the Lord of hosts. Who art thou, O great mountain? Before Zerubbabel thou shall become a plain,"* (Zechariah 4:1-7).

The pure oil is the Holy Spirit working in us so that we may accomplish God's purpose. In Zerubbabel's case it meant that he was to go forward in faith, and the mountains of difficulties would become like a plain for the accomplishment of his work. The oil was the assurance to him that, by the power of the Holy Spirit, he would surely finish the task God had given him. *"Faithful is He that calleth you, who also will do it"* (1Thessalonians 5:24).

Without the *'pure oil'* of the Holy Spirit, it is impossible for the followers of Jesus to accomplish God's purpose for them. The oil is God's assurance to us that He *"which hath begun a good work in us will perform it until the day of Jesus Christ"* (Philippians 1:6).

2. <u>The Beaten Oil</u>. Just as the gold was beaten to form the candlestick, so the olive was crushed to extract the oil for the lamps. As the oil represents the Holy Spirit, we have here illustrated the truth that the Holy Spirit shares in the sufferings which our salvation has cost heaven. The oil was beaten to *"cause the lamps to burn continually."*

Jesus' last promise to His disciples before He returned to heaven was, *"I will send unto you the Comforter, which is the Holy Spirit, "* and *"He will teach you all things"* (John 16:7; 14:26). It is the role of the Holy Spirit to reveal truth to every sincere believer, and to bestow spiritual power upon him. His work is to search all the dark corners of this world seeking to win lost souls to Jesus. In this role it is written that He *''pleads in our behalf with unspeakable yearning and groanings too deep for utterance"* (Romans 8:26, Amp .)

We are warned, *"grieve not the Holy Spirit of God"* by being indifferent to His pleadings (Ephesians 4:30; 1:13). To continue to resist Him is to commit the unpardonable sin - the only sin God cannot forgive because the sinner can no longer be reached. He has placed himself beyond heaven's grasp.

> *"Whosoever will speak a word against the Son of man, it will be forgiven him. But unto him that blasphemes against the Holy Spirit it will not be forgiven"* (Luke 12:10).

His conscience has become seared as with a hot iron, and he will no longer listen to the voice of God to his soul. The command which was once given to one of the tribes of

Israel will be repeated in the case of such a one, *"Ephraim is joined to idols, leave him alone"* (Hosea 4:17).

3. <u>Burn Continually</u>. The oil in the lamps burned continually giving light by day and night. By a daily, prayerful study of the Word of God, fresh supplies of oil will flow into our lives so that our lamps of witness may burn continually.

As the sole purpose of a candle is to give light, so the sole purpose of the church is to give light. A lamp that does not shine, or shines only dimly, is of little value. A church that does not shine may have a *'form of godliness,'* but denies God the right, through the power of the Holy Spirit, to transform the life (2 Timothy 3:5).

Our efforts to bless others will react in blessing upon ourselves. This is God's purpose in giving us a part to play in the plan of redemption. Through unselfish service for others, we share in the blessing, the joy, and the spiritual uplift which results.

> *"No more surely is a place prepared for us in the heavenly mansions, than is there a special place designated on earth where we are to work for God."* [66]

Who Lit the Lamps?

Only the high priest could perform the sacred work of lighting the lamps in the earthly sanctuary, and only Christ, our High Priest, can light our lamps. In the evening the high priest put a fresh supply of oil in the lamps, and in the morning, he trimmed them so that they would shine brilliantly all through the day. This was also the time when incense was burned on the golden altar, clearly revealing the link between prayer and service. Without prayer, our work for others will avail little. As we kneel for morning and evening prayer, our High Priest will give us a fresh supply of His Spirit. He connects us with Himself, the source

---

66   White, E., Christs Object Lessons, p. 327

of power, so that we may be light bearers for Him. As a broken electrical circuit cannot pass the power to our household lights, so neither can a broken connection with heaven bring power and victory into our lives.

- *"And God said, 'let there be light, and there was light,'"* (Genesis 1:3)

- *"For God, who commanded the light to shine out of darkness, hath shone in our hearts, to give the light of the knowledge of the glory of God in the face of Jesus Christ"* (2 Corinthians 4:6).

- *"God is light, and in Him is no darkness at all"* (1John 1:5).

- *"Thy Word is a lamp unto my feet, and a light unto my path." "The entrance of Thy Word giveth light. It giveth understanding to the simple"* (Psalm 119:105, 130). [67]

In Conclusion

The Relationship between
Justification and Sanctification

The terms *'justification'* and *'sanctification'* describe two miracles which Christ performs on the sinner's behalf to bring him into right relationship with God. They cannot be separated. Together they make up the experience called *"righteousness by faith."*

Righteousness by faith begins at conversion. The one who is drawn to Christ by the Holy Spirit confesses his sins and

---

[67] What eventually happened to the golden candlestick? In 70 AD Jerusalem was destroyed by Roman armies. The temple was sacked, and its treasures stolen. The golden candlestick was taken by the Roman general Titus as a trophy of his victory. The arch of Titus was built in Rome to commemorate his triumph, and on it was carved a large engraving of the candlestick. Tradition claims that the candlestick now lies at the bottom of the Tiber River where it was thrown by the Vandals when they sacked Rome in 455 AD. When they returned to claim this valuable piece of plunder, it could not be found.

is justified – that is, forgiven and cleansed. However, he soon realizes his total inability to live the Christian life. He is spiritually afflicted with a life-threatening disease called sin and needs the help of the Great Physician. Paul White, an Australian doctor working in Central Africa between the world wars, gives a simple but excellent illustration of God's role as the Great Physician for sin-sick souls. In his book, Jungle Doctor Spots a Leopard, he tells the story of Baruti, a great hunter who has fallen and broken his leg. As Dr. White injects a pain killing drug, Baruti, a Christian, begins to teach a spiritual lesson to the crowd of curious onlookers.

> *"All of you who look," he gestures toward his leg, "You have no doubts that my leg is broken?"*
>
> *"No," came the reply, "we have no doubt that normal legs do not bend in the odd way that yours does!"*
>
> *"Hee!" said Baruti, "and I too have no doubt that my leg is broken. Anyone who said otherwise would be a fool. I am in deep trouble. My leg is useless, and I can do nothing to help myself. By having strong thoughts, I cannot straighten my leg. By having money in my pocket, I cannot take away the pain, neither do charms round my neck nor medicine rubbed into my chest help. To fix this matter, there must be someone who knows how to do it, someone who comes from outside."* [68]

As the doctor gently pulled Baruti's broken leg into position, his assistant Daudi spoke up, *"Isn't that exactly what Jesus came to do?"*

For the helpless sin-sick soul, the Great Physician orders the double cure - the double miracle - justification and sanctification. We are just as dependent upon God for our growth as for our new birth, so there must be two parts to the healing process. Justification deals with the past life.

---

68   White, Paul, Jungle Doctor Spots a Leopard, pp.163-164

(Rom 3:23-26). But what about the present life, the life to be lived forward? This is where sanctification comes in. The *'new-born'* Christian, like a newborn baby, cannot survive alone in this world. He would soon perish spiritually, surrounded as he is with temptations and problems. So, by a miracle of divine grace, the life of Christ is imparted to the new Christian day by day, and thus day by day he grows more and more like Jesus.

Dr. White again takes up the story of Baruti the hunter as he tries to explain this 'double cure' to a young patient from the hospital. Tembo is watching the hunter build a thorn bush trap for a man-eating leopard. Baruti plans to use himself as the bait to entice the leopard to its destruction. Young Tembo wants to know more about Jesus, so as he twists the deadly thorns into place, Baruti explains.

"He was born as you and I are born. He grew, He suffered, He taught people, He healed people. And when He had seen thirty-three harvests, then it was that He suffered greatly for you and me, and everybody everywhere. They whipped Him with a lash that tore His skin. They made a crown of thorns like these, and they pushed it down on His forehead with hands that had no gentleness in them." Tembo shuddered.

Baruti picked up a branch and fingered the two-inch spikes. "You and I know how thorns can hurt . . . but worse was to follow. They drove nails through His hands and His feet, and they nailed Him to a wooden cross. He allowed all these things to happen to Himself, so that He might have the double medicine to offer us for the disease of our soul."

"Double medicine?" said Tembo. "What do you mean?"

"You see, if we ask Him, Jesus will forgive us so that we will not be punished for our sins. This is the first

great medicine of freedom. And the second one stops sin from having power in our lives." [69]

The second great medicine for the soul is sanctification. Unfortunately, too many Christians love their sins and this world more than they love Christ, and so reject the second part of this double cure. They want the salvation offered by the cross, but they do not want to carry a cross themselves. This is because the sanctification process involves crucifying self, that is, our old nature with its carnal desires and passions.

As long as Satan reigns there will be self to subdue and besetting sins to overcome. Our part is to cooperate with the heavenly agencies by guarding well the avenues of the soul from the inroads of Satan. The choices we make day by day will determine the outcome. We must choose to hear that which will uplift the mind, choose to see that which will keep our thoughts pure, choose to read that which will help us grow spiritually, and choose to eat that which will keep our bodies healthy and our minds clear. In other words, we need to feed the spiritual nature and to starve the carnal (See Philippians 4:8). This is what it means to crucify self.

> *"I am crucified with Christ, nevertheless I live. Yet not I, but Christ lives in me. The life which I now live in the flesh I live by the faith of the Son of God who loved me and gave Himself for me"* (Galatians 2:20).

All along life's journey Satan will test our determination with temptations tailor-made to suit our weaknesses, but our heavenly Father keeps constant vigilance and never *"slumbers or sleeps"* (Psalm 121:4).

Victory Through Christ

> *"The Lord Jesus came to our world, not to reveal what a God could do, but what a man could do,*

---

69   Ibid., p. 127

through faith in God's power to help in every emergency . . . Jesus, the world's Redeemer, could only keep the commandments of God in the same way that humanity can keep them." [70]

"As ye have received Christ Jesus the Lord, so walk ye in Him" (Colossians 2:6). By faith we have accepted Christ's forgiveness for all our past sins and mistakes, now by faith we must ask for, and receive, His victory over all sin in our life. *"Salvation is a package deal."*[71] We must accept not only His death on our behalf, but also His life lived on our behalf.

"In this the love of God was manifested toward us, that God hath sent his only begotten Son into the world, that we might live through him" (1 John 4:9).

We are to receive not only His forgiveness, but also His victory! *"The just shall live by faith"*, was the great truth which Martin Luther re-discovered and presented to a world suffering under the deception that by some means they must work their way to heaven (Hebrews 10:38).

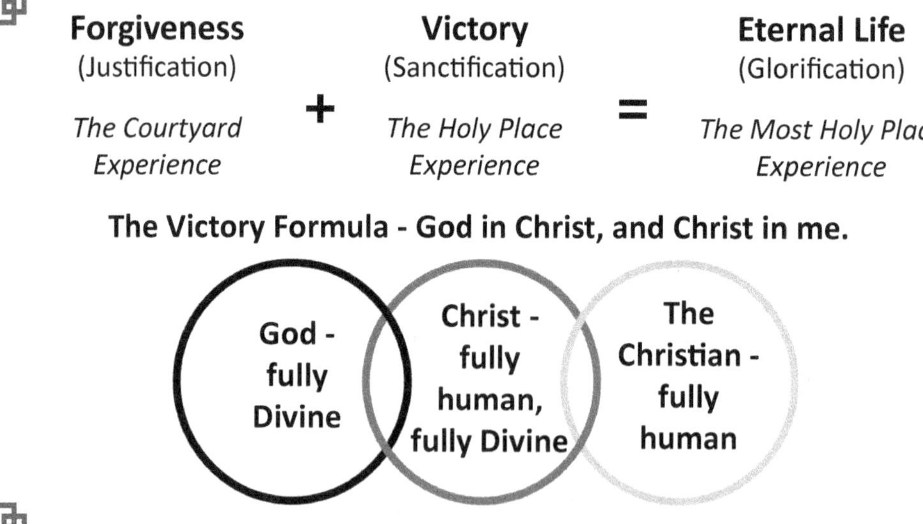

---

70 White, E., Manuscript I, 1892.

71 Goldstein, C., False Balances, p. 175

Faith in the power of an infinite God to enable us to overcome is what the Bible terms *"the faith of Jesus,"* and such faith will characterize God's church in these last days. *"Here is the patience of the saints. Here are they that keep the commandments of God, and the faith of Jesus"* (Revelation 14:12). The only way the saints can keep the commandments of God is by having the faith of Jesus imparted to them day by day.

Christ is the connecting link between God and man. *"Christ in you, the hope of glory"* (Colossians 1:27). What a wonderful Saviour is Jesus our Lord! He is one with God in spirit, and one with man in flesh. With one arm He draws the human family to Himself, and with His other arm He grasps the throne of God, linking man and God together in a saving relationship which only man can sever! Right now, why not invite Jesus and His victories into your heart. He will not enter without an invitation. He will never violate our free will, a freedom He died for rather than take away from us. He stands at the door of your heart and knocks, but you must open the door (Revelation 3:20). *"Ask, and you will receive"* (John 16:24).

> *"He took not on Him the nature of angels, but He took on Him the seed of Abraham. Wherefore in all things it behooved* (was necessary) *for Him to be made like unto His brethren, that He might be a merciful and faithful High Priest in things pertaining to God, to make reconciliation for the sins of the people. For in that He Himself hath suffered being tempted, He is able to succor* (rescue) *them that are tempted."*

> *"For both He that sanctifies, and they that are sanctified, are all one. For this cause He is not ashamed to call them brethren"* (Hebrews 2:16-18, 11).

By surrendering our lives to Christ, by trusting in His promises, we may triumphantly exclaim as we come to the end of life's journey, *"I have fought a good fight. I have finished my course. I have kept the faith. Henceforth there is laid up for me a crown of righteousness, which the Lord, the righteous Judge, will give me at that day"* (2 Timothy 4:7, 8).

> *"God put the offer of salvation in so simple a way that the whole world could grasp it. Everyone can believe. A cripple may not be able to visit the sick, but he can believe. A man who cannot see is unable to do many things, but he can believe. A deaf man cannot hear, but he can believe. Even a dying man can believe. Salvation has been placed within the reach of all, the young and old, the foolish and the brilliant, the rich and the poor, the high and the low. All may have it if they truly believe."* - D.L. Moody, as quoted in Bible Readings for the Home Circle, Vol I, p. 68

Are you now ready to take the last great step? The step that will take you into the Most Holy Place, into the very throne room of the universe, to meet with God. Do not fear. Jesus, your flesh and blood Brother, stands by your side and pleads your case in court. As heaven's Attorney He has never lost a case, and in His hands, He holds your crown of life.

> *"There is therefore now no condemnation to them which are in Christ Jesus, who walk not according to the flesh, but according to the Spirit"* (Romans 8:1).

> *"He is able also to save them to the uttermost that come unto God by Him, seeing He ever lives to make intercession for them"* (Hebrews 9:24).

> *"Behold, I stand at the door and knock. If any man hear My voice, and open the door, I will come into him, and will sup with him, and he with Me. To him that overcometh, will I grant to sit with Me in My throne, even as I also overcame, and am set down with My Father in His throne. He that hath an ear, let him hear what the Spirit saith unto the churches"* (Revelation 3:20-22).

Chapter 8

'Cleansed' or 'Cut-off'?

The Most Holy Place Experience.

The Most Holy Place was a beautiful room. Its dimensions formed a perfect cube, and it occupied the western third of the sanctuary rectangle. Like the Holy Place, it was enclosed by golden boards engraved with angel figures, and the curtains and ceiling were of the same blue, purple, and scarlet weave, upon which were embroidered the mystic figures of golden cherubim. In this apartment was the ark of the covenant.

The Ark of the Covenant
(Exodus 25:10-16)

To Bezaleel, the master workman in precious metals, was committed the sacred and exalted task of constructing the ark, the most important piece of furniture in all the sanctuary (Exodus 37:1). The ark contained the law of God. It was because of man's disobedience that the Lord instituted the sacrificial system and directed Israel to build the sanctuary. It revealed how mankind can once more become reconciled to God through obedience to His law.

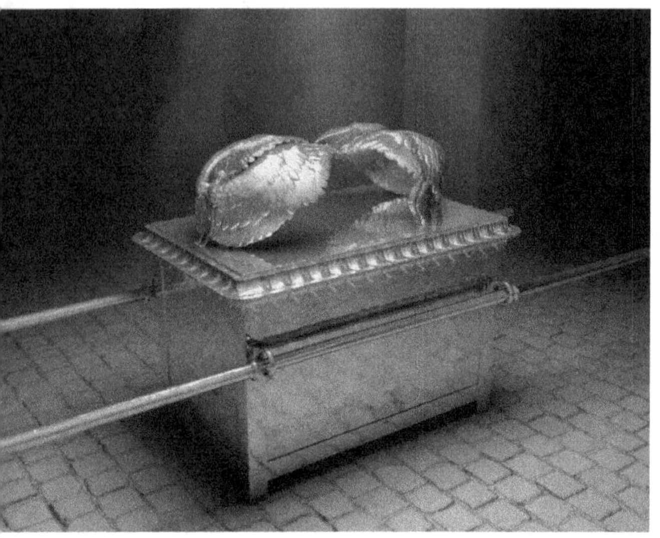

The ark was a chest made from acacia wood, approximately 1.4 m. x 0.8m., and overlaid with pure gold within and without. Like the table of incense and the altar of prayer, the top was decorated with a golden crown. The cover of the ark was fashioned from solid gold and was called the mercy seat. On each end of the mercy seat were mighty winged cherubim of beaten gold. One wing stretched upward, and the other was folded in an attitude of reverence and humility (Ezekiel 1:11). The faces of the cherubim were turned toward each other, and they looked reverently downwards, representing the veneration with which heavenly angels regard the law of God.

Above the mercy seat was the Shekinah, a gloriously bright and dazzling light which represented the visible presence of God. The rays from this light, reflected from the golden walls and furnishings, created a brilliancy too great for human eyes, so God hid His glory within a cloud. On special occasions the glory within the cloud burst forth like the rays of the sun, and the priests ministering in the Holy Place were obliged to retire as dazzling light spilled over the veil and flooded the tabernacle. All this was but a dim reflection of the glories of the temple of God in heaven.

"Thou that dwellest between the cherubim, shine forth" (Psalm 80:1).

"I have looked for Thee in the sanctuary, to see Thy Power

Image: Jeremy Park, Bible-Scenes.com

and Thy glory" (Psalm 63:2).

The Mercy Seat

The Mercy Seat, with its cloud of glory and covering cherubim, represented the throne of God.

> *"The Lord . . . sits between the cherubim"* (Psalm 99:1; 80:1).

> *"The Lord God of Israel dwells between the cherubim. . ."* (2 Kings 19:15).

Here sits the One who is *"**merciful** and gracious, slow to anger and plenteous in **mercy**,"* the One who does not deal with us *"after our sins, nor reward us according to our iniquities. For as heaven is high above the earth, so great is His **mercy** toward them that fear Him"* (Psalm 103:8-12).

The Lord is *"**merciful** and gracious, long-suffering . . . keeping **mercy** for thousands, forgiving iniquity and transgression and sin"* (Exodus 34:6, 7).

*"His throne is upheld in **mercy**"* (Proverbs 20:28).

From the Mercy Seat, above the Ark containing the law of God, every sinner may receive mercy and pardon, because *"righteousness and justice are the foundation of His throne"* (Psalm 97:2 NKJV). Such a blending of justice and mercy only infinite wisdom could devise, and only infinite power accomplish.

The Cherubim

The magnificent angels who were upon the ark were made from beaten gold. As the oil and the flour were *'beaten,'* so were the cherubim. This figure of speech represents

Image: Jeremy Park, Bible-Scenes.com

the sorrow and suffering all heaven has endured because of sin. All heaven suffered in Christ's agony on the cross and in Gethsemane. Not only the Father, the Son, and the Holy Spirit, but also the angels are involved in the infinite sacrifice to redeem man. The news of man's transgression filled heaven with sadness. The angels wept as they heard what sin would cost their beloved Commander. How could they give Him up to a life of humiliation and pain? And from that time forth, *"all through the working out of the plan of salvation, for every temptation suffered, for every trial and persecution endured for Christ's sake, there has been a responsive suffering in heaven"* (Isaiah 63:9).[74]

The cherubim represent two special angels, the most highly exalted of the angel throng. These angels were appointed to be the shining guardians of the law and of God's eternal throne. Before sin, one of these covering cherubim was Lucifer, whose name meant *'the light-bearer.'* He was *"the anointed cherub that covereth,"* who was *"upon the holy mountain of God"* (Ezekiel 28:14).

When Lucifer was cast out of heaven, Gabriel was appointed to take his place. It was Gabriel, *"the angel of the Lord,"* who was sent by God to foretell the birth of John the Baptist, and later, that of Jesus (Luke 1:11, 19). It was Gabriel who came to strengthen Christ in the garden of Gethsemane when the cup of suffering trembled in His hand. It was Gabriel who was sent to the aged apostle John on the Isle of Patmos to reveal to him the future of the Christian church (Revelation 1:1), and it was Gabriel who gave Daniel understanding of his prophetic visions (Daniel 8:16; 9:21). How comforting it is for God's church to know that the one who stands next in honour to the Son of God has been chosen to open His purposes to sinful man!

We are not told the name of the other covering cherub, but it was most likely these two angels who accompanied

---

74   Peck S., Path to the Throne of God, p. 231

Christ throughout His life on earth, and who came to His tomb at His resurrection (John 20:12). In sympathy and love they waited behind at His ascension to reassure the sorrowing disciples that *"this same Jesus, which is taken up from you into heaven, will so come in like manner as ye have seen Him go into heaven"* (Acts 1:11).

The Mercy Seat, the Cherubim, and the Shekinah glory, though unspeakably magnificent, were but a dim reflection of the reality - the Most Holy Place in heaven. The angel figures on the walls, the veils, and the ceiling, represent the myriad of angels who fill the holy places of the heavenly sanctuary. These are the heavenly hosts who *"excel in strength, that do His commandments, hearkening unto the voice of His word. "* These are the Lord's *"ministers... that do His pleasure"* (Psalm 103:20, 21).

In vision, the prophet Daniel saw before the throne of God millions of angelic beings, *"thousand thousands ministered unto Him, and ten thousand times ten thousand stood before Him"* as the judgment scene opened in heaven (Daniel 7:10).

The Law of God

Within the Ark was the Law of God carved into stone by His own finger. Before the world was created, God's law was not written in stone, but upon the hearts of His created beings. The angels had no real sense of any restriction being placed on their freedom. It was natural and pleasant for them to obey, for in doing so they were but carrying out their own impulses. God's law is a *"law of liberty"* to His faithful subjects. Only when we disobey a law do we realise its authority.

We know that Adam and Eve knew of its existence because *"where there is no law, there is no transgression"*

(Romans 4:15). *"Sin is not imputed* (charged to one's account) *when there is no law"* (Romans 5:13). According to His own rules, God could not have expelled Adam and Eve from the Garden of Eden if there was no law, or if they were ignorant of it.

After the fall, man's intellectual and spiritual capacity gradually declined, and God had to define more clearly the principles of His law. Especially was this true after the flood. Those who lived before the flood did not need written records as they possessed great mental and physical vigour, and strong memories. They were able to understand and retain what God gave them and pass this information on uncorrupted to their children and grandchildren for many generations. For nearly one thousand years Adam taught his descendants the law of God. Likewise, Noah passed on this knowledge to his descendants.

When God brought Israel out of Egypt, they were largely ignorant of the law of God. They had spent so many years serving a heathen culture that they no longer recognised the enormity of sin. So, God personally spoke the law to them (Exodus 20:1, 19, 22; Galatians 3:19). The grandeur and power surrounding the speaking of the law from Mt Sinai was designed to impress the people with the true nature of sin, the majesty of the Law Giver, and their need for a Saviour. The law is that *"schoolmaster to bring us to Christ that we may be justified by faith"* (Galatians 3:24).

 When the first copy of God's handwritten law was destroyed, He wrote it for the second time on tables of stone. He then instructed Moses, *"Thou shalt put them into the ark."* And He gave unto Moses *". . . two tables of testimony, tables of stone, written with the finger of God."* *"The writing was the writing of God, graven upon the tables"* (Exodus 25:16; 31:18; 32:16). The law was carved into stone to show that it could never be erased or changed. God's law has always been in existence and forever will be.

*"I delight to do **Thy will**, O My God; yea **Thy law** is within My heart"* (Psalm 40:8).

"I will put My laws into their mind and write them in their hearts. And I will be to them a God, and they will be to Me a people" (Hebrews 8:10).

"The law of his God is in his heart. None of his steps will slide" (Psalm 37:31).

Why is God's law eternal? It is the principle of love defined and it forms the basis for all our relationships. It is the code of Christian conduct. The whole law can be compressed into just two commands - *'Thou shalt love the Lord thy God with all thy heart, and with all thy soul, and with all thy mind. This is the first and great commandment. And the second is like unto it, thou shalt love thy neighbour as thyself. On these two commandments hang all the law and the prophets"* (Matthew 22:35-40).

To meet man's fallen condition, these two foundational laws – love to God and love to man - were expanded and expressed more precisely in the Ten Commandments. (See Exodus 20:1-17). How do we show our love for God? By keeping the first four commands. We do not have any other gods before Him. We do not worship idols or take His name in vain. We keep holy the seventh day as a sign of our loyalty to Him as our Creator and Redeemer.

How do we show our love to our fellow man? By keeping the last 6 commandments. We honour our parents. We do not steal from our neighbour nor covet his goods. We do not lie to him or about him. We do not commit adultery with his or her spouse. We do not destroy his life. By keeping the whole law, we express our love for both man and God. Jesus tells us plainly *"If you love Me, keep My commandments"* (John 14:15). Love is not just an emotion; it is the principle which governs all our dealings with our fellow man.

"This is the love of God that we keep His commandments" (1 John 5:3).

"He who says, 'I know Him,' and keepeth not His commandments, is a liar and the truth is not in him" (1 John 2:4).

Why am I re-emphasizing the law at this point? Because there can be no government without law, and no judgment without law. And God's judgment is already in progress, and His universal government is soon to be established. If we plan to live under His government, we need to abide by His rules today.

'As many as have sinned in the law (knowing the law) *will be <u>judged by the law</u>"* (Romans 2:12).

"So, speak ye, and so do, as they that will be <u>judged by the law</u> of liberty" (James 2:12).

The judgment will determine who have maintained a saving relationship with Jesus. *"For He cometh <u>to judge the earth</u>. <u>He will judge the world with righteousness</u>, and the people with His truth"* (Psalm 96:13).

Paul tells us that God's law is *"holy, and just, and good"* (Romans 7:12). It describes the character of the One who decreed it. Whatever God does is perfect. Therefore, His law is perfect. And yet there are some who say that His universal law of love has been done away with, and still others have even tried to change it! This is almost impossible to believe, but unfortunately it is true. God's law, the foundation of His government, endures forever.

"Consider the glory and majesty attending the broadcast of that law from the flaming mountain top! A vast retinue of holy angels was present. Millions of men and women stood at attention. Lightning flashed. The earth trembled. And amid this signal display of infinite power, the divine Lawgiver announced the precepts that

To meet man's fallen condition, these two foundational laws – love to God and love to man - were expanded and expressed more precisely in the Ten Commandments.

embrace the whole duty of man (Ecclesiastes 12:13). If that law were to be changed, would a faithful all wise God alter or annul it in a less impressive and conspicuous manner than when He proclaimed it from Sinai? Would it be done so secretly and inconspicuously that the church would be left in ignorance and uncertainty? . . . .

A thousand times, No!" [75]

'And do you think any being can change that law? Not till he can break through the bodyguard of angels into the inner temple, dethrone Jehovah, wrench from its position the world's mercy seat of pardon and salvation, and with his would-be omnipotent finger, mutilate the records of the imperishable tables." [76]

Jesus died on the cross of Calvary as proof positive that God's law can never be changed.

"The law of the lord is perfect, converting the soul. The testimony of the Lord is sure, making wise the simple. The statutes of the Lord are right, rejoicing the heart. The commandment of the Lord is pure, enlightening the eyes. The fear of the Lord is clean, enduring forever. The judgments of the Lord are true and righteous altogether. More to be desired are they then gold, yea, then much fine gold. Sweeter also than honey and the honeycomb. Moreover, by them is thy servant warned, and in keeping of them there is great reward" (Psalm 19:7-11).

---

75   Cottrell, R., Our Times, December, 1947

76   Smith, U., Looking Unto Jesus, p. 321

Where is the Ark Now?

When Solomon's temple was built, the ark was taken from its temporary location and placed in the Most Holy Place of this magnificent structure. There it remained until Jerusalem was captured by the Babylonians in 606 B.C. To prevent it from falling into the hands of the invaders, righteous men under the direction of the prophet Jeremiah, took the ark and hid it - perhaps in a cave in the mountains, or in a secret tunnel underneath Jerusalem.

Seventy years later the temple was rebuilt, but the Most Holy Place was destined to remain forever empty. The ark has never been recovered.

In recent years there have been some who have claimed to have found the Ark in a cave under Golgotha, but we cannot take these claims too seriously. One thing we can know for sure though, **God knows** where it is, and in His own time and for His own purposes, He may bring it out for all the world to see.

1) THE ISRAELITE IN THE MOST HOLY PLACE
(Leviticus 16)

We now come to the most solemn and sacred day in the Jewish calendar - Yom Kippur, the Day of Atonement. The year's round of special services and ceremonies have ended, and now only the greatest day in the life of the Israelites remains to be observed. By divine command, the day of Atonement fell each year on the tenth day of the seventh month, the month of Tishri, which corresponds to our September-October (Leviticus 16:29, 30). This date never varied; it was declared to be *"a statute forever"* (v. 29).

Ten days before Yom Kippur, on the first day of the month, there was a special ceremony called the *"blowing of trumpets"* (Leviticus 23:24). Silver trumpets were blown throughout the land proclaiming the approach of the sacred day. This was a signal for all Israel to prepare spiritually and physically before presenting themselves at the temple, for it was *'Yom Hadin,'* the day of judgment. On that day, the case of everyone in Israel would be decided. The sinner would be either separated from his sins or separated from the camp of Israel. Would he be *'cleansed?'* or *'cut off?'* (Leviticus 23:27-30). Even today orthodox Jews in all parts of the world call the ten days prior to the Day of Atonement, *"the ten days of repentance."* These were preparation days for the solemn event.

What did God expect from His people on this special day? God left no one in doubt. Moses was instructed to give to the people four definite assignments: *"It will be a holy convocation unto you. And ye shall afflict your souls and present an offering made by fire unto the Lord. And ye shall do no work* (secular work) *in that day for it is a day of atonement"* (Leviticus 23:27-28). Let us look briefly at each of these four requirements.

1) *"A Holy Convocation."* The people were required to assemble for worship at the sanctuary for prayer, praise, and deep soul searching. All business was laid aside, and the whole congregation of Israel spent the day in solemn humiliation before God. No one could afford to let the day close without confessing every known sin. It was not a day for jesting and joking or frivolous behaviour.

2) *"Ye Shall Afflict Your Souls."* Moffat translates the word 'afflict' as, *'to abstain and fast.'* The people were required to search their hearts and confess every known sin. For this purpose, they were to eat lightly or not at all, so that their minds would be clear and their consciences keen. Daniel gives us a good example of what it means to afflict the soul. When he sought the Lord for understanding of an important matter concerning his people, he wrote, *"I set my face unto the Lord God, to seek by **prayer** and supplications, with **fasting**, and sackcloth and ashes* (**humility**). *And I prayed unto the Lord my God, and made my **confession"*** (Daniel 9:3, 4).

3) *"An Offering Made by Fire."* The regular morning and evening whole burnt offerings formed a part of the services on the Day of Atonement and represented the entire surrender of self and all of one's possessions to God and

to His service. Every idol and every evil thing were to be placed on the altar to be entirely consumed.

4) ***"Ye Shall Do No Work."*** This day was regarded as more sacred than a regular Sabbath. The Hebrew expression, *'shabbath shabbathon'* is translated *"it shall be unto you a Sabbath of rest,"* which literally means *"a Sabbath of Sabbaths,"* - the holiest of rest days.[77] Therefore, all work was laid aside, and thoughts were given over to seeking God and serving Him.

The Preparation of the High Priest

A week before the Day of Atonement, the high priest moved from his home in Jerusalem to a special room attached to the temple. Here he spent the week in meditation and prayer, in heart searching and confession. The night before the great day he did not sleep, but instead rehearsed the ritual to be performed the next day so that there would be no mistake to mar the sacredness of the occasion.

Early on the Day of Atonement all Israel was astir. After a cleansing bath, the first duty of the high priest was to make an atonement for his own sins and the sins of his household. For this purpose, a bullock, the largest and most costly of the sacrifices, was slain, and its blood sprinkled seven times upon the Mercy Seat above the Ark containing the broken law of God.

As the priest was about to enter the Most Holy Place with the blood, *'he paused to place coals of fire from the golden altar into his censer, and sweet-smelling incense upon the coals."* A fragrant cloud of incense, representing the righteousness of Christ, now enveloped him as he appeared in the presence of God. He reverently sprinkled the blood upon and before the Mercy Seat, and then, as he slowly and humbly withdrew from the Most Holy Place, he touched the horns of the golden prayer altar with the blood (Leviticus 16:11-14). Cleansed from all his sins, the high priest was now ready to intercede before God for his

---

77   Jewish Encyclopedia, Vol II, p. 280 (Leviticus 16:31)

people. In this sense he represented Christ, the *"Sinless One,"* who intercedes on our behalf.

The Two Goats

Two goats were now brought to the door of the sanctuary where lots were cast to determine which goat would be the *"Lord's goat, "* and which the scapegoat, or *"Azazel"* (Leviticus 16:7, 8). The Lord's goat, representing Christ *"holy, harmless, and undefiled"* (Hebrews 7:26), was then slain and its blood sprinkled on and before the Mercy Seat and upon the horns of the golden altar in a similar ritual to that performed with the blood of the bullock. The holy places and the golden altar were now declared by God to be cleansed from *"the uncleanness of the children of Israel,* and from *"all their sins"* (Leviticus 16:16, 19).

Why did the holy places of the sanctuary need cleansing? It will be recalled that throughout the year the sins of the people were transferred to the sanctuary via the blood of the innocent sacrifice. This blood was sprinkled *"before the veil,"* and imprinted on the horns of the golden altar (Leviticus 4:6, 17).

 Strong's Hebrew Dictionary translates the expression, *'before the veil,'* as *'on the face of the veil,'* showing that the blood was sprinkled onto the fabric of this beautiful tapestry. The veil and the altar thus preserved a symbolic record of Israel's confessed and forgiven sins. Even though no books were kept in the sanctuary, every drop of blood on the veil and the altar constituted a record of that sin for which the lamb died. The veil, as already shown, represented Jesus as a man carrying the burden of our sins. (See Hebrews 10:19-22.) As these sins marred His precious form, so the blood sprinkled upon the beautiful curtain marred its loveliness. This veil was ripped from top to bottom by an unseen hand the moment Jesus died, symbolizing the torn and bloodied body of Christ dying for our sins upon the cross.

The question may be asked, *'But what happened to that beautiful tapestry and its bloody record of the forgiven and cleansed sins of Israel?'* One Jewish writer, F. C. Gilbert, claims it was *'miraculously restored'* to its original purity on the Day of Atonement.[78] However, other writers claim that the curtain was removed following the completion of the services on the Day of Atonement, and a new one hung in its place. [79]

The record of sins in the sanctuary defiled it and must be removed. As the high priest sprinkled the record of sin with the clean blood of the Lord's goat, he symbolically took the sins of Israel upon himself and carried them out of the sanctuary. This, in effect, removed sin from the sanctuary and cleansed it from its pollution. What was to happen to these sins now? Was the priest to carry them forever?

God commanded Moses: -

> *"And Aaron* (the high priest) *shall lay both his hands upon the head of the live goat and confess over him all the iniquities of the children of Israel, and all their transgressions in all their sins, putting them upon the head of the goat, and shall send him away by the hand of fit man into the wilderness. And the goat shall bear upon him all their iniquities into a land not inhabited, and he shall let go the goat in the wilderness"* (Leviticus 16:21, 22).

It will be recalled that the laying on of hands represented the transferring of something possessed to another. So, as the sun was sinking in the western sky on this sacred day, the high priest laid his hands on the head of Azazel, the scapegoat, and confessed over it the sins of the children of Israel. The animal was then handed to a fit man standing ready for the purpose, and laden with the sins of a forgiven and cleansed people, it was led forth to an isolated region, *'the land of separation,'* and let go - never to return. It was a solemn moment for the people as they saw their

78 Peck, S., The Path to the Throne of God, p. 215

79 Hardinge, L., With Jesus in His Sanctuary, p. 405, 522

sins removed from the camp of Israel and carried away into the land of forgetfulness.

In more recent times, the services of the orthodox Jew on the Day of Atonement have been divided into four parts. At 3:00 p.m. the final exercises begin. Solemn and sacred are the hours and moments until the setting of the sun on that day. In addition to the work of judgment, the penitent soul is reminded that he must be sealed before the day closes. Therefore, during these final hours he prays:

> *"Our Father, our King,*
> *seal our name in the book of life.*
>
> *"Our Father, our King,*
> *seal our name in the book of remembrance.*
>
> *"Our Father, our King, seal our name in the book*
> *of success and prosperity."* [80]

At the end of the day, friends and neighbours, men and women, clasp each other's hand with the glad expression, *"I hope you received a good seal."*

There was now only one more duty to be performed on that sacred day. The bodies of the animals which had been sacrificed were carried out of the camp, and quickly consumed in fiercely burning fires prepared for that purpose. As the sun set, all the sins of Israel had been sent into the *"land of separation,"* and nothing was left but ashes to remind the people of them. The camp of Israel was now wholly clean. It was a wonderful moment for the people. A time of peace and tranquillity and a sense of being *'at one'* with God. This is the meaning of *'atonement.'* This is what is meant by the cleansing of the sanctuary.

---

80   Gilbert, F. C., Messiah in His Sanctuary, p. 69.

Who was Azazel, the Scapegoat?

The term *'the scapegoat'* is used only four times in Scripture - all within Leviticus chapter 16 which details the events of the Day of Atonement. *"The consensus among Hebrew writers and scholars from time immemorial is that Azazel represents the evil one, Satan. This is confirmed by the Book of Enoch, which brings Azazel into connection with the Bible story of the fall of angels . . . Azazel is also represented in that Book as the leader of the rebellious giants in the time preceding the flood. He taught men the art of warfare, of making swords, and knives . . . and revealed to the people the secrets of witchcraft and corrupted their ways, leading them into wickedness and impurity."* [81]

Satan is the instigator of all sin and has a role in every transgression that has ever been committed, from that of the angels who fell, to that of every man who ever lived. It is only fair and just that every sinner should bear the punishment for his sins, but Satan is held responsible for tempting them to sin, for urging them on, for enticing them to ruin. We see this principle of joint responsibility exemplified in the experience of our first parents. Satan tempted them and they fell. They were all guilty, and all were punished according to the extent of their guilt. The serpent was cursed, and Adam and Eve were banished from their garden home. Similarly, as the one who sells alcohol or drugs is partly responsible for the crimes committed by others while under the influence of these poisons, so Satan must be held responsible for his part in every sin. *"Of all the sins that God will punish, none are more grievous in His sight than those that encourage others to do evil."* [82]

"I have set the Lord always before me: because He is at my right hand, I shall not be moved" (Psalm 16:8).

"My help cometh from the Lord, who made heaven

81   Jewish Encyclopedia vol. II, pp. 365, 366. Quoted by F. C. Gilbert, Messiah in His Sanctuary, pp. 63-4

82   White, E., Patriarchs and Prophets, p. 323

and earth. He will not allow thy foot to be moved, He that keepeth you will not slumber. Behold, He that keepeth Israel will neither slumber nor sleep" (Psalm 121:2-4).

"Now unto Him that is able to keep you from falling, and to present you faultless before the presence of His glory with exceeding joy" (Jude 24).

2) CHRIST ENTERS THE MOST HOLY PLACE

The services and ceremonies performed in the earthly sanctuary were but *"examples and shadows of heavenly things"* (Hebrews 8:5). The cleansing of the earthly sanctuary of its record of confessed and forgiven sins by the removal of these sins on the Day of Atonement, was an acted-out drama to help us understand what occurs in heaven. The cleansing of the heavenly sanctuary is the *'blotting out,'* or removal, of the record of the forgiven sins of God's people from the books of heaven.

As the earthly ministration consisted of two parts, the daily and the yearly services, so the ministration in the heavenly sanctuary also consists of two parts. After Jesus left the courtyard of this earth where He was offered as the Lamb of God, He ascended to begin the first phase of His ministry in the heavenly sanctuary - that which took place in the Holy Place. The final phase of His ministry began when He entered the Most Holy Place to cleanse the sanctuary of its record of sin, and to determine who would be among the future subjects of His kingdom. This work is presently going on (see Chapter 9).

When the great clock of heaven struck the hour for Christ to begin His work of judgment, God moved His throne from the Holy Place into the Most Holy. This scene, as presented to the prophet Daniel, must be one of the most awe-inspiring events mankind has ever been privileged to witness. Describing it, Daniel says:

"I beheld until the thrones were cast down (set in place)*, and the Ancient of Days* (God) *did sit,*

whose garment was white as snow, and the hair of His head like pure wool. His throne was like a fiery flame, and His wheels as burning fire. A fiery stream issued and came forth from before Him. Thousand thousand ministered unto Him, and ten thousand times ten thousand stood before Him. The Judgment was set, and the books were opened" (Daniel 7:9, 10).

In vision, Daniel saw thrones being placed into position for some great event which was about to take place. He saw the position of God's throne being changed from the Holy Place to the Most Holy. His attention was attracted by the great wheels which looked like burning fire as they moved beneath the glorious throne of God. Myriads of angels were gathered to witness the grand event.

The apostle John, while imprisoned on the lonely island of Patmos, was given a vision of the throne room of God.

"Behold, a door was opened in heaven . . . and behold, a throne was set in heaven. One sat on the throne. And He that sat was to look upon like a jasper and a sardine stone. And there was a rainbow round about the throne, in appearance like an emerald. And round about the throne were twenty-four thrones, and upon the thrones I saw twenty-four elders sitting, clothed in white raiment, and they had on their heads, crowns of gold.

"And out of the throne proceeded lightnings and thunderings and voices, and there were seven lamps of fire burning before the throne, which are the seven Spirits of God. And before the throne there was a sea of glass like unto crystal: and in the midst of the throne, and round about the throne, were four living beings" (Revelation 4:1-6).

"And I beheld, and I heard the voice of many angels round about the throne" (Revelation 5:11).

> *When the great clock of heaven struck the hour for Christ to begin His work of judgment, God moved His throne from the Holy Place into the Most Holy.*

Christ's Triumphal Entry

Let us now in our imagination watch with Daniel the opening scenes of the judgment as the heavenly court convenes. It appears that something, or someone, is holding up proceedings. Everyone seems to be waiting for the arrival of some great personage before Judgment can begin. Who are they waiting for? On His throne in the Most Holy Place, the Father waits. The covering cherubim on either side of the throne of God wait. The four living beings and the twenty-four elders wait. The vast multitude of angels *"that excel in strength, "* wait. The Judgment is set but cannot proceed. Someone is still missing - the Advocate, Jesus Christ the Righteous, who is to plead His blood on the sinner's behalf.

Now He comes! He comes! *"I saw in the night visions, and behold, One like the Son of Man came with the clouds of heaven, and came to the Ancient of Days, and they brought Him near before the Father"* (Daniel 7:13).

Daniel's attention is drawn to the *'clouds of heaven,'*-myriads of angels who bear the Saviour in triumph to the Father's throne. What an imposing scene! As a mighty conqueror is borne upon the shoulders of his admiring comrades to the place of honour, so clouds of angels escort their victorious General in heavenly state to the Father's throne. There He will begin His final work for the salvation of mankind. No other event of such importance and solemnity has ever taken place in the universe of God. The King of heaven comes to the Ancient of Days to receive *'dominion, and glory, and a kingdom,'* (Daniel 7:14). Our great High Priest enters the Holy of Holies to begin the work of Judgment. [83]

---

83   Selected from The Path to the Throne of God, by Sarah Peck, pp. 207, 208

And so, with songs of adoration and praise, the angels accompany Christ in His flaming chariot and present Him before the Ancient of Days, and there proceeds from the throne *"lightning and thunderings and voices"* (Revelation 4:5). As the Judgment begins, the Father welcomes His beloved Son and bids Him to sit with Him on His throne at *"the right hand of God,"* the place of authority (Revelation 3:21; Colossians 3:1).

Who is to judge the World?

God the Father presides in the Judgment, the holy angels stand as witnesses to the great tribunal, but Christ is Judge. Only He who has taken on humanity, only He who *"was in all points tempted like as we are, yet without sin,"* only He who has been *"touched with the feeling of our infirmities,"* is qualified to be not only our High Priest, but also our Judge (Hebrews 4:15). *"The Father judges no man, but has committed all judgment unto the Son . . . And has given Him authority to execute judgment also, because He is the Son of man"* (John 5:22, 27).

3) THE CHRISTIAN ENTERS THE MOST HOLY PLACE

The sanctuary model teaches us that those sins which have been confessed and forgiven are transferred to the sanctuary in heaven where a record of them is kept. Why does God keep such a record? Is it possible for a *'born again'* man or woman to lose his or her salvation? The answer is 'yes.'

A simple example may help to clarify matters. When you purchase a home, you make an agreement with the bank or mortgage company to make regular payments on that home until the debt is fully paid. As time passes you may tire of the payments and the accountability, and decide you are not going to pay any more. What happens? The bank will repossess the house and begin negotiations with another, hopefully more trustworthy client. And so, it is with God. Salvation is always conditional upon repentance and perseverance in the Christian walk. What if we tire of our walk, and return to our old ways and bad habits?

Every child of God has a home in heaven waiting for him. His name is on the door while he keeps to his side of the agreement, his covenant to obey God's law. Unlike the mortgage company, God even offers to make our payments for us. That is, to empower us by His grace to keep our promise to obey Him. He promises all the resources of heaven to aid us in our Christian walk, but if we persist in our refusal to take hold of God's sanctifying power there will come a day of reckoning - a day of judgment. The question will then be asked, *'Does this person really value his mansion in heaven?'* His file will be pulled, and his record examined.

If all his sins are forgiven and forsaken, they will be blotted from the book of records and remembered no more. He will then be given full and legal ownership to his heavenly investment. If, however, after being forgiven and cleansed, the Christian returns to his old sinful ways - like a dog to its vomit, or a washed sow to her mud hole (2 Peter 2:22) - then his record of sin remains, and his inheritance is given to another. His home is repossessed, as it were, and given to one who values the heavenly treasure. For this reason, Christ bids us, *"Hold that fast which thou hast, that no man take thy crown"* (Revelation 3:11). And again, He warns, *"No man, having put his hand to the plough, and looking back, is fit for the kingdom of God"* (Luke 9:62).

We all have legal right to eternal life as this was fully purchased for us at Calvary (John 3:16). Christ's death ensures salvation for all, but men can change their minds, as an army of backsliders testify. The gift of eternal life is bestowed on condition of accepting Christ as a living part of one's life - an ongoing connection.

In earthly circles it is acknowledged that there is a big difference between the existence of a legal right and its application. In legal terms it is called an <u>interlocutory judgment</u>. A provisional judgment which is not necessarily reflective of the final judgment as the situation may change.

It is a court order that is not final until the judge decides on other matters related to the case, or until enough time has passed to see if the interim decision is working. A person, for example, may be entitled to a divorce, unless this person changes his mind. The outcome hinges entirely upon his or her own actions and decisions. And so, it is with salvation. We have all been issued with interlocutory judgments - our legal right to eternal life. However, the outcome is determined by our response to the Saviour's invitation. In the judgment this is revealed to all, and the decision is final.[84]

There is great danger in receiving the truth but not being sanctified by it. In other words, in accepting the courtyard

experience, that is, forgiveness for sin, but refusing to embrace the Holy Place experience where the life is transformed. Such a person refuses to let go of the doubtful attractions of this world, and usually ends up becoming an even greater sinner than he was before he accepted Christ.

"For if, after they have escaped the pollutions of the world through the knowledge of the Lord and Saviour Jesus Christ, they are again entangled therein, and overcome, the latter end is worse with them than the beginning. For it had been better for them not to have known the way of righteousness, than, after they have known it, to turn from the holy Commandment delivered unto them" (2 Peter 2:20, 21).

Please read Matthew 13:3-9, 18-23; Matthew 12:43-45; and Matthew 7:21-23, carefully.

The Judgment examines our commitment to Jesus from the moment we are *'born again'* into the family of God. The prophet Ezekiel explains it very clearly.

---

84   Attorney Lewis R. Walton, Decision at the Jordan, pp. 59-76. See also John 1:12, 8:31; Luke 21:34; Matt. 13:3-9, 18-23; Rom. 5:10; Rev. 3:11, 12; Col. 3

> *"When the righteous (man) turns away from his righteousness and commits iniquity, and does according to all the abominations that the wicked man does, will he live? All the righteous deeds that he has done will not be mentioned. In his trespass that he has trespassed, and in his sin that he has sinned, in them will he die"* (Ezekiel 18:24).

The opposite is also true. If a wicked man forsakes his evil ways, *"all his transgressions that he has committed, will not be mentioned"* (v.22). They will be cast into the depths of the sea, never again to be remembered (Micah 7:9). <u>The judgment simply respects the choice that every person has made</u>. <u>At that time, the decisions we have made for or against Christ will be sealed for eternity.</u>

How Does God View 'Life' and 'Death?

Another question may be asked at this point. Why are we not simply judged the moment we die? Many people believe that when a person dies his soul is transported straight to heaven or hell. This belief makes a future judgment totally unnecessary and illogical. It also denies the reality of a bodily resurrection when Jesus comes again. However, the Bible is very plain on this subject. There is a resurrection at the end of time, and there is a judgment which precedes it.

A right understanding of the true state of the dead is vitally important, so I challenge every reader to take up his Bible and a concordance and study this subject thoroughly for himself. Because of its importance, we will take a moment to review what the Bible says about life and death.

First, we need to understand what the *'soul'* is. In the Bible the term soul simply means a living human being. *"The Lord God formed man from the dust of the ground, and breathed into his nostrils the breath of life, and man became a living soul"* (Genesis 2:7). By combining the *'dust of the earth'* with *'the breath of life'* from God, man became a living, breathing, active being - a soul.

The animals and birds were also formed *'out of the ground,'* and had the *'breath of life'* in their nostrils (Genesis 2:19; 7:15, 21,22). Hence the Bible also refers to animals as souls (Revelation 16:3). It is written of both man and animals that, *"as the one dies, so dies the other. Yea, they have all one breath . . . all are of the dust, and all turn to dust again"* (Ecclesiastes 3:19, 20). A soul is a composite thing, an earthly body plus life from God. Take away the life, the breath, and the soul ceases to exist.

Creation is the making of man. Death is the unmaking of man. It is the reverse of creation. *"Thou* (God) *takest away their breath, they die, and return to their dust"* (Psalm 104:29).

> *"His* (man's) *breath goeth forth, he returneth to his earth, in that very day his thoughts perish"* (Psalm 146:4).

"The living know that they shall die, but the dead know not anything. . . their love, and their hatred, and their envy is now perished, neither have they any more a portion forever in anything that is done under the sun. Whatsoever thy hand finds to do, do it with thy might, for there is no work, nor device, nor knowledge, nor wisdom, in the grave, whither thou goest" (Ecclesiastes 9:5, 6,10)

"The dead praise not the Lord, neither any that go down into silence" (Psalm 115:17; see also Isaiah 38:18, 19).

The only hope for man is the resurrection, when God will once again unite the dust of the ground with the breath of life, and man will become a living soul once more.

Nowhere in the Bible is the term *'immortal soul'* found. Instead, we are told that *"the soul that sinneth, it shall die"* (Ezekiel 18:4, 20), and that only God has *'unconditional immortality'* (I Timothy 1:17; 6:15, 16). The concept of an immortal soul is a pagan philosophy which was popularized by Plato in the fifth century before Christ. It comes directly from the *'father of lies,'* *"that old serpent called the Devil, and Satan, who deceives the whole world"* (John 8:44; Revelation 12:9). It was he who told the first lie to humanity when he said to Eve in the garden of Eden, *"Ye shall not surely die"* (Genesis 3:4).

> *"The doctrine of natural immorality can be traced through the muddy channels of a corrupted Christianity, a perverted Judaism, a pagan philosopher, and a superstitious idolatry, to the great instigator of mischief in the Garden of Eden. The Protestants borrowed it from the Catholics, the Catholics from the Pharisees, the Pharisees from the pagans, and the pagans from the old serpent, who first preached the doctrine amidst the lovely bowers of Paradise, to an audience all too willing to hear and heed the new and fascinating theology, "Ye shall not surely die."* [85]

How Does God View 'Life' and 'Death?'

We may find the answer as we consider a few texts.

> *"He that hears My word and believes on Him that sent Me, has everlasting life. . . and is passed from death into life"* (John 5:24).

> *"Whosoever lives and believes in Me shall never die"* (John 11:26).

The Bible tells us that only God has immortality. So, what did Jesus mean? Simply this. Our short life span is not counted as a *'life'* by God. Compared to eternity, it is but

---

85   Amos Phelps, Congregationalist minister, 1805-1874.

a drop of water in the vast ocean of time. He refers to our life on earth *as "a vapor that appears for a little time, and then vanishes away"* (James 4:14). To the God of eternity there is only <u>one 'life,'</u> that is eternal life, and there is only <u>one 'death,'</u> that is eternal death. Jesus taught that the death His followers experience on planet earth is only a short *'sleep,'* soon to be interrupted by the return of our Lord. In fact, the Bible refers to death as a *'sleep'* sixty-six times in seventeen books in both the Old and the New Testaments.

After Lazarus died, Jesus said to His disciples, ***"Our friend Lazarus sleeps**, but I go that I may awake him out of sleep."*

As the death of the wicked is eternal, so the life of the righteous is eternal.

The disciples were confused, wondering why Jesus would awaken the sick man, so *"Jesus said unto them plainly, **Lazarus is dead**"* (John 11:11-14). All through the Scriptures are similar references to death being just a *'sleep.'* [86]

As our life on this earth is too brief to be considered true life, so our death is too short to be considered true death. It is just a temporary interruption, a sleep, before resurrection and eternal life.

As <u>the **death** of the wicked is eternal, so the **life** of the righteous is eternal</u>.

The future life of the saved will be like that of Adam and Eve in the Garden of Eden. It will be like our present life, except it will be lived in a beautiful, new, re-created world, without sin, suffering, and death.

While awaiting judgment, or investigation, the dead sleep peacefully in their graves. The passing of the years is but a moment of time to them. It will seem to be only an instant after death that the trumpet call is heard, and the righteous dead rise to meet their Redeemer in the air. **See Colossians 3:4; 1 Thessalonians 4:16-17; 2 Timothy 4:6-8.**

"This mortal life is a pilgrimage, and our body is a

---

86   See 1 Thessalonians 4:13; 1 Corinthians 15:18,20; Daniel 12:2; Ecclesiastes 3:20; 9:5,6,10; Psalm 146:4; 115:17; Acts 2:34

tent, so slight, so transitory, so easily taken down; but what does it matter since there is awaiting us, a mansion prepared by God? Often in this veil of flesh we groan. It cages us, anchors us down to earth, hampers us with its needs, obstructs our vision, and becomes the medium of temptation. How good it would be if our physical body could be suddenly transmuted into the glorified ethereal body which would be like the resurrection body of our Lord! **It would be sweet to escape the wrench of death** *(that is, to be translated).* **But if not, then through death we shall carry with us the germ of the glorified body.**

"The gate of death may look gloomy on this side, but on the other it is of burnished gold, and opens directly into the presence-chamber of Jesus. We long to see Him and to be with Him; and such desires are the work of the Holy Spirit and the first fruits of heaven. But remember that just inside the door there is Christ's judgment seat where He will adjudge our life and apportion our reward. Prepare, my soul, to give an account of thy talents!" [87]

"God . . . hath appointed a 'day' in which He will judge the world in righteousness by that Man (Jesus) whom He hath ordained." Acts 17:30, 31

If God is Omniscient, Why Does He Need the judgment?

God does not need the Judgment. He knows the outcome of every case. He does not ordain the outcome, but He knows in advance who will be saved and who will not. *"The Lord knows them that are His"* (2 Timothy 2:19). However, the angels and the sinless inhabitants of unfallen worlds are not omniscient. They do not know the heart of man, so God deals with sin in a way that will eradicate it forever from the universe by answering the questions in every mind. The universe needs reassurance that sin will not rise a second time and start the deadly process all over again.

---

87   F.B. Meyer commentary on 2 Cor 5:1-8.

What about David? He began well, but in later life committed murder and adultery. How can he be saved? What about Aaron, who in a weak moment made the golden calf and stood by as Israel worshiped it? What about Abraham and Isaac, who both lied about their wives? Are these men safe to save?

Thousands, though converted, have fallen into serious sin. Among the saved will be those who have committed evil, not only before their conversion, but afterwards as well. A universe of sinless beings could well be nervous about having the redeemed from earth living among them. God knows our motives. He knows those who are *'safe to save.'* But the sinless inhabitants of unfallen worlds do not, and therefore we are all judged before the intense scrutiny of the on-looking universe. When the judgment is over, all questions about each one of us, and about God's justice in each case, will have been satisfactorily answered, and the angels and unfallen beings will praise God for His justice and fairness.

> *"Thou art righteous O Lord, which art, and was, and shall be, because Thou hast judged thus." "Even so, Lord God Almighty, true and righteous are Thy judgments"* (Revelation 16:5, 7).

> *"The deepest interest manifested among men in the decisions of earthly tribunals but faintly represents the interest evinced in the heavenly courts when the names entered in the book of life come up in review before the Judge of the earth."* [88]

Preparation for Judgment

God has specified four duties which He requires His people to obey to fortify them against the attacks of the enemy and to prepare them to stand in the Judgment. These are the same duties which were given to ancient Israel on the Day of Atonement.

---

88   White, E., The Great Controversy pp. 483, 484

1) **"The Day of Atonement. . . shall be a holy convocation unto you"** (Leviticus 23:27).

The word 'convocation' means an assembly of people. God is calling on His last day people to press together as never before, to support each other, and not allow the enemy to divide them. When a wolf attacks a flock of sheep, their safety lies in pressing together closely and protectively so that the wolf cannot separate off one of the weaker members to destroy it. We are told to *"bear one another's burdens,"* and not to *"forsake the assembling of ourselves together as the manner of some is. But to exhort one another. And so much more as ye see the day approaching"* (Galatians 6:2; Hebrews 10:25).

Christ's last great prayer for His disciples, and for His children to the very end of time, was a prayer for unity. *"That they may be one, even as We are one"* (John 17:21-23).

There is a special blessing in worshiping with and encouraging others, for God promises to be in their midst even if only two or three are gathered together (Matthew 18:20).

"Press together, press together, press together," is God's clarion call to His people today.

2) **"Ye shall afflict your souls."**

On the Day of Atonement, everyone was required to search his or her heart for any hidden and unforsaken sins. Men and women spent the day in prayer, confession, and fasting, putting away every transgression, so that there would be no unconfessed sins to stand against them. Abstinence from food was considered so important by the Jews in connection with this ordinance, that even today many fast during Yom Kippur.

Today God requires His people to gain control of their appetites. Satan tempts us to over-indulge, even of good food, so that our minds will be dull and unable to discern or appreciate spiritual things. God desires His people to be masters of their appetites, and to keep their bodies in subjection to the higher powers of the mind (I Corinthians

9:27).

It was on the point of appetite that Adam and Eve fell, and it was because of the power of appetite over humanity that Christ suffered in the wilderness for forty days without food. All this, so that He could gain the victory over appetite on our behalf. If we allow Him, Christ will help us develop self-control over our appetites and passions.

The prophet Isaiah, looking down through the centuries, saw our day. He describes it thus:

> *"In that day did the Lord God of hosts call to weeping and to mourning* (heartfelt repentance)*, and to baldness, and to girding with sackcloth* (deep humility)*. And behold, joy and gladness, slaying oxen, and killing sheep, eating flesh, and drinking wine . . . Then it was revealed in my hearing by the Lord of hosts, surely for this iniquity there shall be no atonement"* (Isaiah 22:12-14, NKJV).

No atonement means that our sins remain on the record books in heaven. Unfortunately, Isaiah's picture of unbridled gluttony vividly portrays conditions as they exist today. Our Saviour specifically warns His people against giving loose rein to appetite during this time when the life record of everyone is being examined to determine if his sins are covered by the blood of the Lamb.

> *"Take heed to yourselves, lest at any time your hearts be overcharged with surfeiting and drunkenness, and cares of this life, and so that day* (judgment) *come upon you unawares . . . Watch ye therefore and pray always that ye may be accounted worthy to escape all these things that shall come to pass, and to stand before the Son of man"* (Luke 21:34-36).

The word *'surfeiting'* means to overeat. *'Drunkenness'* refers not only to intoxication due to alcohol, but also to eating foods that injure the system. Overeating, even of the best foods, can injure the health and cloud the mind. Christ desires His people to be careful regarding both the quantity, and the quality, of the food they eat.

To eat in a way that will develop spiritual strength is the Bible rule for all followers of Christ. In the book of Proverbs, the book of wisdom, we find three principles regarding eating honey which apply to all foods that are good to eat.

a) *"My son, eat thou honey <u>because it is good</u>"* (Proverbs 24:13).

b) *"Hast thou found honey? <u>Eat so much as is sufficient for thee</u>"* (Proverbs 25:16).

c) *"It is <u>**not good**</u> to eat much honey"* (Proverbs25:27).

The one who follows the above formula, who eats only the food God created for him to eat, and only as much as he needs, will enjoy abundant health and a clear mind. *"Whether therefore ye eat or drink or whatsoever ye do, do all to the glory of God"* (1 Corinthians 10:31).

The transgression of the laws of our physical being are just as serious in God's sight as is the transgression of His moral law, for these *"fleshly lusts war against the soul"* (I Peter 2:11).

3) *"An offering made by fire."*

The offerings made by fire were entirely consumed upon the altar. For God's people today this means that the Lord desires that our *"whole spirit* (mind), *and soul* (heart - seat of the emotions), *and body* (physical organism), *be preserved blameless unto the coming of our Lord Jesus Christ"* (I Thessalonians 5:23).

He desires that we completely dedicate all that we are and all that we possess to the Lord to be used as He directs. He asks that every idol of our hearts, every secret sin, and every evil thing be placed upon the altar of sacrifice to be completely consumed. In other words, God gave all for us, and He asks us to give all for Him.

> *"Time is rapidly passing into eternity. Let us not keep back from God that which is His own...He asks for a whole heart- give it to Him. It is His, both by creation and by redemption. He asks for your intellect, give it to Him, it is His. He asks for your money - give it to Him for it is His. 'Ye are not your own, for ye are bought with a price,'" (1 Corinthians 6:19, 20). He asks us to be absolutely and completely for Him in this world as He is for us in the presence of God."* [89]

4) *"Ye shall do no work* (no secular work) *in that same day"* (Leviticus 23:25).

In God's Word there is much written regarding diligence in work, so He is not here suggesting that His people be idle. Instead, He asks them to lay aside all enterprises not in harmony with His will, and all work which is performed purely for selfish purposes. He promises to bless His people in material things if they will put His work and service first, and their own needs second.

> *"Take no thought, saying, 'What shall we eat?' or 'What shall we drink? 'or 'Wherewithal shall we be clothed?'. . . For your heavenly Father knows that ye have need of all these things. But seek ye first the kingdom of God and His righteousness, and all these things shall be added unto you"* (Matthew 6:31-33).

God is calling upon His people to develop a special faith relationship with Him. He asks us to put His work and service first, and to trust Him to supply all our daily needs. Paul worked as a tentmaker to sustain himself, but his first work was preaching the gospel. William Carey worked as a cobbler to pay his expenses, but the great object of his life was to take the gospel message to India. Several of Christ's disciples worked as fishermen to sustain the needs of their families, but when the call came for full time ministry, they unhesitatingly left their boats, and entered the Lord's service. With such an Employer as our heavenly Father, we

---

89   White, E., Acts of the Apostles, p. 566

need not have any fear that our needs will not be supplied. King David was well able to testify:

> *"I have been young, and now am old, yet have I not seen the righteous forsaken, nor his seed begging bread" (Psalm 37:25).*

> *"Today the Judgment is set, and the books are opened. Today the cases of the dead who have professed to love and serve God, and whose names have at some time been written in the Book of Life, are coming in review before the great Judge. Small and great stand before Him and are being 'judged out of those things which were written in the books, according to their works'" (Revelation 20:12).*

> *"We are nearing the end of the journey. We are in the time when 'there shall be a great shaking in the land of Israel* (Ezekiel 38:19 - spiritual Israel, God's church). *For many, probation is now closing. 'Cleansed' or 'cut-off'- which shall it be for me? which shall it be for you?"* [90]

If you have truly repented and accepted Jesus as your Saviour, the Judgment is good news. It is the climax of the gospel story, for you do not have to stand before the God of the universe in your own righteousness, but in the righteousness of Christ. The work of our Advocate is not to condemn but to defend His people. He pleads their cause and vanquishes the accusations of Satan by the mighty arguments of the cross. To the accuser of His people, He declares: *"The Lord rebuke thee, O Satan... is this not a brand plucked out of the fire?"* And to those who rely upon Him in faith He gives the comforting assurance: *"Behold, I have caused thine iniquity to pass from thee, and I will clothe thee with change of raiment"* (Zechariah 3:1-5).

---

90   Peck, S., The Path to the Throne of God, p. 216

THE SANCTUARY EXPERIENCE SUMMARIZED

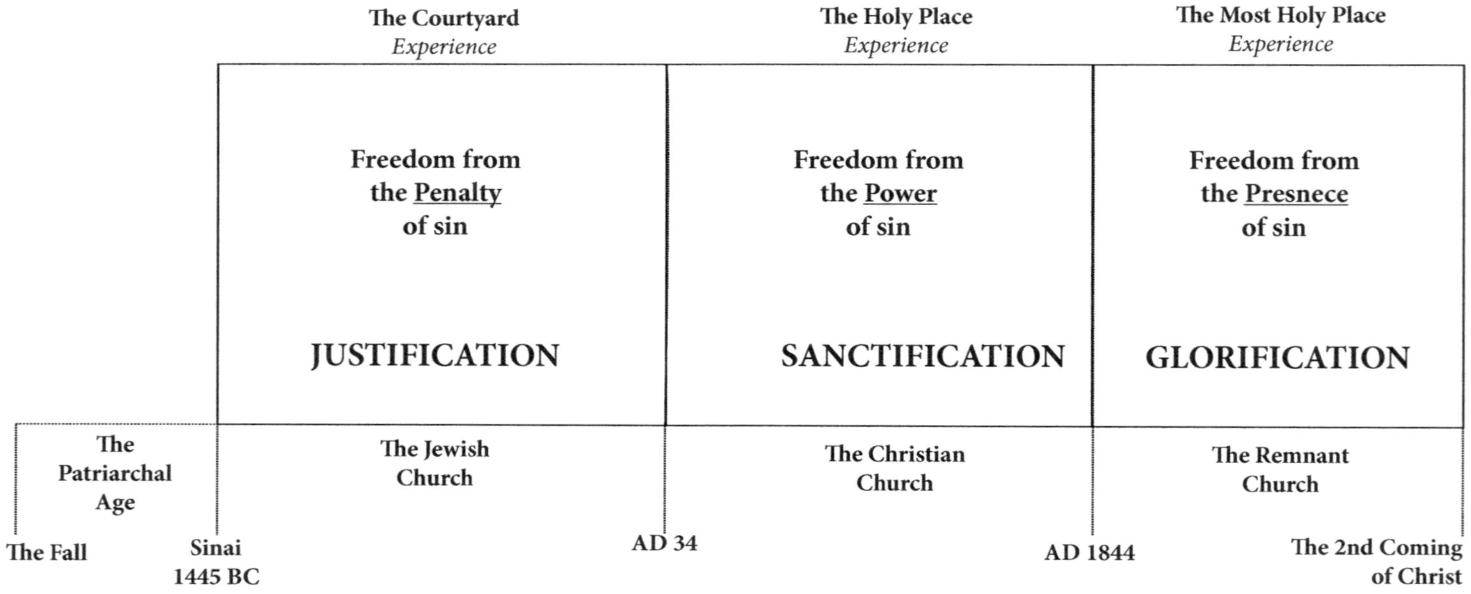

The Courtyard *Experience*	The Holy Place *Experience*	The Most Holy Place *Experience*
Freedom from the <u>Penalty</u> of sin **JUSTIFICATION**	**Freedom from the <u>Power</u> of sin** **SANCTIFICATION**	**Freedom from the <u>Presnece</u> of sin** **GLORIFICATION**

The Patriarchal Age	The Jewish Church	The Christian Church	The Remnant Church

The Fall — Sinai 1445 BC — AD 34 — AD 1844 — The 2nd Coming of Christ

THE HISTORY OF GOD'S PEOPLE
as it relates to the Sanctuary

Chapter 9

Locating the Day of Judgment

"Unto two thousand three hundred days, then will the sanctuary be cleansed" (Daniel 8:14)

For year after year, century after century, the work of ministration in the first apartment of the heavenly sanctuary continued. Sins confessed were forgiven, transferred to Christ, and recorded in the sanctuary above. In the earthly model, on one day of each year, the Day of Atonement, these sins were removed from the sanctuary and placed on the head of the scapegoat, which was then sent away from the camp, never to return. This in effect 'cleansed' the sanctuary and the people from the defilement of sin. Any Israelite who failed to confess all his sins before and on this day was *'cut off'* from the camp of Israel. He never again had a place among the people of God. His fate, like that of the scapegoat, was sealed. Therefore, the Jews looked upon the Day of Atonement as a day of Judgment, as indeed it was.

That which is symbolized by the earthly model occurs in heaven. Accordingly, there must come a day when Christ will finish His work in the Holy Place and move into the Most Holy to perform a similar work to that done by the high priest on the Day of Atonement. The Bible is not silent on this matter of judgment, known also as the *'cleans-*

ing of the sanctuary'. It is spoken of by every Bible writer. In fact, it is mentioned more than a thousand times in the Scriptures. For example:

> *"The Lord hath prepared His throne for judgment. And He shall judge the world in righteousness"* (Psalm 9:7, 8).

> *"God will judge the righteous and the wicked. For there is a time for every purpose and for every work"* (Ecclesiastes 3:17).

> *"The Lord will judge His people"* (Hebrews 10:30).

What is the purpose of the judgment? What does it involve? Simply put, the judgment is a time when Christ examines the life records of everyone who has ever claimed to be a child of God. If he has repented of his sins and remained true to God, then on Judgment Day his sins are *"blotted "* from the heavenly records. If, however, he has turned aside from following Christ, and has returned to his old sinful practices, then his sins will remain on the record books, and his name will be erased from the Lamb's Book of Life. This work of examining the records must occur before Christ returns, because when He does, He brings His reward with Him, *"to give every man according as his work shall be"* (Revelation 22:12).

Jesus confirms that the Judgment must take place before He comes in the parable of the marriage supper (Matthew 22:2-13). In this story Jesus tells of a certain King (God) who has invited many people (His church) to the wedding feast of His Son (Jesus). Most ignore the invitation, being too concerned with worldly affairs. These are judged *"unworthy"*, and the invitation is extended further afield. The Lord's messengers are bidden to go out into the *"highways and byways"* of this world and entreat as many as are willing to come to the marriage supper of the Lamb. Now both *"good and bad"* are gathered in, and the wedding is furnished with guests. Before the wedding takes place, the King comes in to examine the guests. Each one is carefully inspected to see if he has on the wedding garment - the spotless robe of Christ's righteousness. Those who are not properly attired are *"cast into outer darkness".*

The inspection of the guests prior to the marriage represents the judgment prior to Christ's reception of His kingdom. All are carefully examined to determine if they have made the necessary preparation - that is, by faith accepted the robe of Christ's righteousness in place of their filthy rags. Those who are judged worthy make up that large company which is represented as the bride of Christ. These are the subjects of His future kingdom. These are they *"which are called unto the marriage supper of the Lamb, "* and are *"arrayed in fine linen, clean and white"* (Revelation 19:7-9)

a) **When Does Christ Enter the Most Holy Place?**

The Word of God does not leave us in darkness as to the timing of this great event. Daniel's description of *"One like the Son of man coming with the clouds of heaven"* to begin the work of judgment, is a vivid and dramatic portrayal of Christ entering the Most Holy Place. Malachi also foretold this coming to Judgment. To the question, *"Where is the God of judgment?"* the answer is given:

"The Lord, whom ye seek, will suddenly come to His temple, even the Messenger of the covenant whom ye delight in" (Malachi 2:17; 3:1). Here the coming of the Lord to judge His people is said to be sudden and unexpected.

Malachi continues:

> *"Who may abide the day of His coming* (in judgment)*? Who shall stand when He appears? For He is like a refiner's fire, and like fuller's soap. And He shall sit as a refiner and purifier of silver and He shall purify the sons of Levi* (His people)*, and purge* (cleanse) *them as gold and silver that they may offer unto the Lord an offering in righteousness"* (Malachi 3:2, 3).

Here is vividly portrayed the cleansing of God's people in preparation for final judgment. While the judgment is going on in heaven, while sins are being removed from the record books, there is to be a special work of cleansing taking place in the hearts of God's people on earth. They are to *"afflict their souls"* (Leviticus 16:29) by confessing and forsaking all sin through faith in Christ's righteousness. When this work is accomplished, *"then will the offering of Judah and Jerusalem* (spiritual Israel, God's church), *be pleasant unto the Lord"* (Malachi 3:4).

Then the church, which the Lord claims as His bride, will be *"a glorious church, not having spot, or wrinkle, or any such thing,"* but will be *"holy and without blemish"* (Ephesians 5:27). She will *"look forth as the morning, fair as the moon, clear as the sun, and terrible as an army with banners"* (Song of Solomon 6:10). She will be *"arrayed in fine linen, clean and white, for the fine linen is the righteousness of saints"* (Revelation 19:8).

When the 'bride' of Christ fully accepts His sacrifice on her behalf, and finally believes His promise to cleanse her from all unrighteousness, then Christ will come to take His loved one home. The Lord's coming is pictured by John the Revelator as a rescue mission with Christ riding on a *"white horse"* followed by the armies of heaven. He will come to rescue His bride and to wreak vengeance on those who are plotting to destroy her (for a full description, see Revelation 19:11-21).

> *"Behold the Lord cometh with ten thousand of His saints, to execute judgment upon all"* (Jude 14, 15; Malachi 3:5).

b) Daniel's Vision

When does earth's judgment begin? The Bible clearly reveals not only the time when judgment in heaven begins, but also the startling fact that judgment has already begun!

Probably the Bible's greatest and grandest prophecy

is the one found in Daniel chapters eight and nine. This prophecy announced the very year when Jesus would begin His earthly ministry five hundred years before the event. It pinpointed the year of His crucifixion, set the date for the final rejection of the Jewish nation (not individuals) as God's special people, and announced the beginning of judgment with these solemn words, *"Unto 2300 days, then will the sanctuary be cleansed"* (Daniel 8:14).

In the vision of Chapter 8, Daniel is shown a great battle between two powerful nations represented by a ram and a goat. Eventually one nation is overwhelmingly defeated and the other grows to be a world power. In its growth to world dominance, its great warrior prince is *"broken",* and the kingdom divided.

As Daniel watches, he sees another nation growing to prominence in the west. This power he *calls "the little horn,"* which after a time becomes *"exceeding great"* (Daniel 8:9). This new nation far exceeds the others in power, greed, and cruelty. Not only does it *"cast down the truth to the ground"* and prosper but it also dares to *"magnify itself even to the Prince of the host,"* and to cast down *"the place of His sanctuary"* (v.11, 12).

At this point in the vision, Daniel sees two Heavenly Beings conversing. One, the angel Gabriel (v.16), addresses a question to the other, known as Palmoni, or the Wonderful Numberer (8:13 margin). This can be none other than Jesus Christ, who knows and numbers every *"time appointed".* Gabriel asks Christ, *"How long shall be the vision concerning the daily sacrifice, and the transgression of desolation, to give both the sanctuary and the host to be trodden underfoot?".* Christ answers, *"Unto 2300 days then will the sanctuary be cleansed"* (8:13,14).

Daniel is naturally puzzled by what he has seen and heard, and as he seeks to comprehend, Christ commands Gabriel, *"make this man to understand the vision"* (V.16). Gabriel immediately commences to carry out this command, but first he explains that the vision in its entirety reaches to

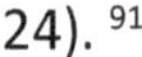

"the time of the end" (v.17). He then back-tracks to the beginning of the vision and explains that the two world powers Daniel saw in conflict, were the nations of Medo-Persia and Greece (v. 20, 21). When the Grecian king Alexander the Great died, or was *'broken,'* his kingdom, explained the angel, would be divided between his four leading generals *"toward the four winds of heaven,"* - that is toward the four points of the compass. From one of these directions, the west, a nation called the *'little horn'* power would eventually emerge. This new nation would be *"mighty,"* and would *"destroy wonderfully, "* and would *"prosper and practice, and* destroy *the mighty and the holy people"* (v. 24). [91]

History testifies, and Christ confirms (Matthew 24:15, 16), that this new nation could be none other than Rome, which followed next in world dominance after the fall of Greece. It began small but grew into a powerful nation, dominating the nations of Europe. The prophecy declares that this power would be a crafty proud nation which would even dare to stand up against the *"Prince of princes"* (v. 25).

Who is this *"Prince of princes?"* Revelation 1:5 tells us that Jesus Christ is *"the Prince of the kings of the earth,"* and Revelation 19:16 declares Him to be *"King of kings, and Lord of lords".* How did Rome stand up against the Prince of princes? Both Herod and Pontius Pilate, as representatives of Rome, stood up against Christ. Herod, in an attempt to kill the baby Jesus, issued a decree that all the children of Bethlehem less than two years of age should be put to death. Pontius Pilate, the governor of Judea, delivered the Saviour to the Jews, and passed the death sentence upon Him.

> *"Why do the heathen rage, and the people imagine vain things? The kings of the earth stand up, and the rulers were gathered together against the Lord,*

---

91   See Daniel 8:19; 10:1; 11:27, 29; 12:9-12.

and against His Christ. For of a truth against Thy holy child Jesus, whom Thou hast anointed, both Herod, and Pontius Pilate, with the Gentiles, and the people of Israel, were gathered together " (Acts 4:25-27).

As Gabriel continued to unfold the sorry history of the *'little horn'* power, and the course it would pursue against the Saviour and God's people, Daniel *"fainted and was sick certain days"* (v.27). Knowledge that *"a king* (or kingdom) *of fierce countenance"* would *"destroy the mighty and the holy people,"* as predicted by Moses many centuries before (see Deuteronomy 28:49, 50), was more than the prophet could bear. He could no longer endure the scene. Gabriel's work of explanation was interrupted. He had clearly explained the first four parts of the vision, but the part pertaining to the 2300 days would have to wait for another time.

c) **490 Years Allotted to the Jews**.

Chapter nine begins with Daniel searching the prophecies of Jeremiah where Israel's exile in the land of Babylon for seventy years is clearly set forth, together with the promise of its restoration after that time.[92] Daniel had entered the court of Babylon as a captive at the beginning of this *'seventy-year'* period. He had served the Babylonian empire loyally as elder statesman and Prime Minister. However recently, as foretold in two previous visions, the Babylonian empire had fallen to the Medes and Persians,[93] and this was considered a signal to the Jews that their captivity was about to end. But Daniel is perplexed. What about the vision of the 2300 days? How did that fit with the seventy years? He was troubled by the vision which seemed to predict further desolation for the temple of God. He understood that in symbolic prophecies, like the one he had been given, a *'day'* represented a literal year. Was the temple in Jerusalem now to lie in ruin for a further 2300

92   Jeremiah 25:8-13; 29:10-14

93   Daniel 2:39; 7:4-5,17

years? Had God changed His mind? In his distress, Daniel sought the Lord for more light by *"prayer and supplication, with fasting, and sackcloth and ashes"* (Daniel 9:3). He was now about ninety years old and was president of the mighty universal empire of Medo-Persia. He was chief of the 120 princes of the realm and one of the three presidents appointed by King Darius. His responsibilities were many and taxing. Yet a great burden lay upon his mind, a desire to understand the part of the vision pertaining to the 2300 days and the cleansing of the sanctuary. He set

aside his robes of state, clothed himself with sackcloth and ashes, and confessed his owns sins and the sins of his people. The burden of his prayer was for the restoration of the Jewish sanctuary and its services.

"O Lord, ... I beseech Thee, let Thine anger and Thy fury be turned away from Thy city Jerusalem, Thy holy mountain . . . Now therefore, O our God, hear the prayer of Thy servant, and his supplications, and cause Thy face to shine upon Thy sanctuary which is desolate, for the Lord's sake.

O my God, incline Thine ear and hear. Open Thine eyes, and behold our desolations, and the city which is called by Thy name. . . O Lord, hear. O Lord, forgive. O Lord, hearken and do. Defer (delay) *not, for Thine own sake, O my God. For Thy city and Thy people are called by Thy name"* (Daniel 9:16-20).

How Heaven must have delighted in the earnestness and sincerity of this aged servant of God! Gabriel is immediately dispatched to convey to Daniel the message that he is *"greatly beloved"* by heaven. And, in answer to Daniel's prayer on behalf of the Jewish nation, he explains that part of the vision which had previously been interrupted by Daniel's state of mind. Without any further preliminaries, Gabriel comes straight to the point, *"I have now come to give thee skill and understanding . . . therefore understand the matter and consider the vision. Seventy weeks are determined upon thy people and upon thy holy city"* (v.21-24).

Daniel would immediately understand from this introductory statement that the Jews, *'thy people,'* would be given an extension to their probationary time. He would understand from the writings of Moses and Ezekiel that a day in symbolic prophecies is equal to one literal year, so seventy weeks of time would equal 490 years (7x70=490).[94] This period of time, he was told, was to be *'determined,'* the Hebrew word for which is *'chathak'* meaning *'cut off'* or *'decreed.'* So, the 490 years, allocated especially to the Jewish nation, were to be cut off- but from what? Obviously from the 2300 days or years. This is the time period which had caused Daniel so much grief, and was the reason for his earnest appeal to heaven for more understanding.

The vision of the 2300 days is now effectively cut into two periods of time, 490 years, and the remaining 1810 years. We will consider the 490 years allocated to the Jews first, as these confirm the validity of the rest of the prophecy. If you have not already done so, it would be helpful to open your Bibles at this point and follow along as the angel reveals future events to Daniel.

During the 490 years appointed to the Jewish nation, the following events would occur:

1) The Jewish nation would *"finish the transgression"*. The Hebrew expression for this phrase is *'lekalle happesha"*[95] which literally means *"to make full the transgression"*. That is, the Jews would fill up the cup of their sins by rejecting and crucifying the Son of God. This would be the crowning act of all transgressions.

2) The coming Messiah would *"make an end of sins"*. The Hebrew expression *'chattath'* is translated *'sins,'* but it also means *'sin offerings.'* Sin offerings would come to an end

---

94   See Numbers 14:34 and Ezekiel 4:6. A day for a year in symbolic prophecies has been well established by Biblical scholars, both Jewish and Christian, for hundreds of years.

95   All Hebrew expressions come from Messiah in His Sanctuary, the work of Jewish scholar F. C. Gilbert.

when our Saviour died on Calvary's cross. See Matt 27:50-51.

3) He would *"make reconciliation for iniquity"*. By His death, Christ would reconcile the world unto God (Colossians 1:20). He would make salvation available to all who would believe on Him.

4) He would *"bring in everlasting righteousness"*. Everlasting righteousness would be made available for all, Jew, and Gentile, because of our Savior's life and death (I Corinthians 1:30).

5) Christ's mission would *"seal up the vision and prophecy"*. The events predicted by this prophecy would be fulfilled so dramatically and on time, that it would make the whole of the vision, including the rest of the 2300 days, sure and solid.

6) *"Anoint the Most Holy"*. The Hebrew words, *'qodesh haq-qodashim'* translated *'the most holy'* are applied to things, not to people. So, this expression refers to the heavenly sanctuary which would be anointed when Christ began His ministry in the Holy Place.

The next question to come to Daniel's mind would naturally be, when are the 490 years going to begin? This is a very important question, and since the 490 years are cut off from the 2300 years, it is obvious that these two time periods must begin together. As if reading Daniel's mind, Gabriel's next statement tells God's people exactly when they can begin counting, *"Know therefore and understand, that from the going forth of the commandment to restore and to build Jerusalem unto the Messiah the Prince, shall be seven weeks, and three score and two weeks . . . and He shall confirm the covenant with many for one week"* (Daniel 9:25, 27). After giving the key for locating the beginning of the 2300 days, the angel then proceeds to divide the seventy weeks into three specific periods of time.

7 weeks + 62 weeks + 1 week = 70 weeks

49 years + 434 years + 7 years = 490 years

Let us look first at the starting point for this prophecy. The Hebrew expression for *"to restore and to build"* is *'lehashib welibnoth,'* meaning *"fully to restore and to build again".* [96] The command must be one that would fully restore Israel as a nation in the Holy Land - that is with full autonomy to govern itself and to worship the God of heaven. This command was given by the Persian emperor Artaxerxes Longimanus to Ezra the scribe in the seventh year of his reign in the autumn of **457 B.C.** (Ezra 7:7,8). This date is established by exhaustive research and is confirmed by many undeniable proofs, such as the canon of Claudius Ptolemy. Ptolemy was a mathematician, astronomer, geographer, and chronologist who lived in Alexandria, Egypt, and who died around A.D. 151. Ptolemy compiled a list of kings of the ancient world together with the years of their reign which he confirmed by astronomical observations such as eclipses of the sun or moon. The God who created the heavenly bodies *"for signs, and for seasons, and for days, and for years"* (Genesis 1:14), uses His works to confirm His divine word.

Three Persian kings acted a part in the issuing of this decree regarding the restoration and building of Jerusalem. Cyrus, in 536 B.C., issued an edict granting permission to rebuild the temple at Jerusalem.

In 519 B.C. this edict was reaffirmed by Darius after construction had been halted due to intense opposition from neighboring countries. And finally, in 457 B.C., Artaxerxes commanded the full restoration of the Jewish state. This decree in full is found in Ezra 7:12-23.

Let us now examine the three periods of time given by the angel.

I) **"Seven weeks" or 49 years.** After quickly mentioning the most important feature of the prophecy the coming of Messiah the Prince, Gabriel refers to the *'seven weeks,'*

---

96   Gilbert, F. C., *Messiah in His Sanctuary*, p. 134

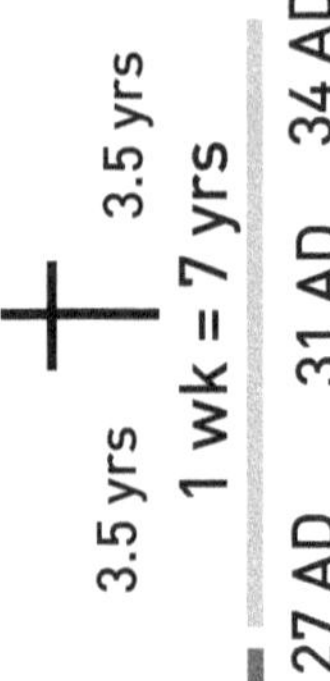

or 49 years, during which the streets and walls of Jerusalem would be built in *"troublous times".* Both Ezra and Nehemiah detail these *'troublous times'* as Jewish workers battled against determined opposition in order to get the project finished. These books read something like a modern-day news report on the continuing conflict between Israel and her neighbors. Finally in 408 B.C., during the fifteenth year of Darius Nothus, the work of rebuilding and restoring Jerusalem and its temple was completed.

2) *"Threescore and two weeks".* After the 7-week period, another 62 weeks were to be added making a total of 69 weeks or 483 years. This period of time, said the angel, would bring us to Messiah the Prince, who would be *"cut off"* a short time after this.

By comparing the Bible calendar with the Gregorian calendar, Bible scholars have been able to ascertain that the decree of Artaxerxes went into effect during our month of October in the year 457 B.C. Adding 483 years to this date, we come to October, A.D.27.

What major event in world history occurred at this time? Gabriel tells us that Messiah the Prince would then begin His public ministry and this is exactly what happened. The word *'Messiah'* in Hebrew and *'Christos'* in the Greek, both mean the *'the anointed one,'* (Psalm 2:1,2; John 1:41; Acts 4:27). At the beginning of His public ministry Jesus was anointed by the Holy Spirit after His baptism in the river Jordan (see Luke 3:21, 22; 4:18; Acts 10:38). After His baptism, *'Jesus came into Galilee preaching the gospel of the kingdom of God, and saying, **'The time is fulfilled".*** (Mark 1:14, 15).

More than 500 years before this, the prophecy of Daniel 9:25 had foretold that in the autumn of **A.D. 27**, *'Messiah the Prince'* would begin His public ministry. And when the clock of time struck the predicted hour of history, Jesus of Nazareth was revealed to His people as the Messiah, or the Anointed One. With His own lips, Jesus announced the termination of the 69 weeks and cited this very prediction as proof of His Messiahship. In reply to the woman at the well who stated, *"I know that Messiah cometh,"* Jesus said, *"I that speak unto thee am He"* (John 4:25, 26).

Gabriel next reveals that a short time after the Messiah began His work, He would be *'cut off'*. What does this mean? In Isaiah 53:8 we read, *"For He* (the Messiah) *was **cut off** out of the land of the living. For the transgression of My people was He stricken"*. Sometime after the 69 weeks, Jesus would be *'cut off'* by crucifixion.

3) **"One Week" or 7 years**. *"And He will confirm the covenant with many for one week"*. Jesus confirmed his covenant with the Jewish people for 7 years from the beginning of His ministry in A.D. 27. Although our Saviour does not favour one person above another, His work was specifically limited to the Jewish nation until its 490 years of probationary time had expired. This was Israel's last chance as a national group to accept her Saviour and to remain as God's especially chosen people. For this reason, Jesus told the Canaanite woman that He was sent to minister *"to the lost sheep of the house of Israel,"* and commanded his disciples to confine their preaching at this time *"to the lost sheep of Israel"* (Matthew 15:24; 10:5, 6). After His rejection and crucifixion, Jesus gave His disciples a worldwide commission. *"Ye shall be witnesses unto Me . . . unto the uttermost part of the earth"* (Acts 1:8).

'And in the midst (middle) *of the week, "* continued Gabriel, *"He shall cause the sacrifice and the oblation to cease".* Three and one-half years into His ministry, Jesus was crucified during the Passover of *A.D.31* - in the month we call April. At His death, the great temple curtain was *"rent in twain from the top to the bottom"* (Matthew 27:50, 51). God destroyed the beautiful hanging so that all might know that sacrifices and offerings had come to an end. The sacrificial system was finished. The Messiah's death caused *"the sacrifice and oblation"* (offerings) to cease forever.

Three and one-half years remained to complete the 70th week. Adding that time to the spring of AD 31, we come to October AD 34 - the termination of the 490 years. During this 3 ½ year period, Christ, through His disciples, continued to preach the gospel message to the Jews. During this time not one sermon preached outside of Jewish territory is recorded. The nation was given one more opportunity to accept the salvation offered by Jesus Christ. How merciful and long-suffering is our God!

Unfortunately, history records that the nation rejected Him once again by persecuting and killing His disciples. In A.D.34, the Jewish Sanhedrin, the governing body of the nation, formalized its rejection of Christ by stoning Stephen, His representative, to death. Stephen, a man described as *"full of faith and power"* who *"did great wonders and miracles among the people"* (Acts 6:8), was a type of Christ. He had a brilliant mind. Not one of his learned opponents, including the scholarly Saul of Tarsus, could match *"the wisdom and the spirit by which he spoke"* (Acts 6:10). So, as in the case of Jesus, the religious leaders stooped to the devil's tactics. They *"stirred up the people"* and *"set up false witnesses,"* and condemned him to die without any charges being laid. Before his accusers his face shone like *"the face of an angel"* (Acts 6:15), and as the stones smashed into his unresisting body; *"he knelt down, and cried with a loud voice, Lord, lay not this sin to their charge. And when he had said this, he fell asleep"* (Acts 7:60). With his dying breath Stephen echoed Jesus' last appeal for the Jewish nation, *"Father forgive them for they know not what they do".*

Thus the 70th week came to a close, and the gospel message was now carried to Samaria, and from there to the *"uttermost part of the earth". "And at that time there was a great persecution against the church which was at Jerusalem. They were all scattered abroad throughout the regions of Judea and Samaria . . . They that were scattered abroad went everywhere preaching the Word"* (Acts 8:1-4).

Philip preached in the cities of Samaria and converted the Ethiopian treasurer. Peter opened the gospel to the God-fearing Cornelius and his household, and the ardent Paul was commissioned to carry the glad tidings *"far hence unto the Gentiles"* (Acts 8:5-40; 10:1-35; 22:21). From the ashes of the Jewish church God raised up the Christian church to take the message of His saving grace around the world.

The formal rejection of the Messiah spelled the doom of the Jewish nation. Gabriel declared, *"and the people of the prince that shall come shall destroy the city and the sanctuary. . . and unto the end of the war desolations are determined . . . and for the overspreading of abominations, he will make it* (the temple) *desolate* (a ruin), *even until the consummation* (the end)" (Daniel 9:26, 27).

 In AD 70, the city of Jerusalem was destroyed by Titus, the commanding general of the Roman armies, and the sanctuary was burned to the ground. *"From that day to this, the Jewish people have never offered sacrifices".* [97]

How earnestly did Jesus admonish, counsel, and plead with the people! With tears running down His cheeks, Jesus wept over the holy city which would not repent, and over the temple which would soon be destroyed. In vain did He warn the people of their approaching doom.

> *"When ye therefore shall see the abomination of desolation, spoken by Daniel the prophet, stand in the holy place (whoever reads, let him understand), then let them which are in Judaea flee into the mountains* (Matt 24:15-16).
>
> *"When ye shall see Jerusalem compassed with armies, then know that the desolation thereof is nigh. Then let them which are in Judea flee to the mountains. And let them which are in the midst of it depart out . . . For these be the days of vengeance, that all things which are written* (in Daniel 9:26, 27)

---

97   Gilbert, E C., Messiah in His Sanctuary, p. 139

may be fulfilled" (Luke 21:20-22).

"O Jerusalem, Jerusalem, thou that kills the prophets, and stones them which are sent unto thee, how often would I have gathered thy children together even as a hen gathers her chickens under her wings, and ye would not! Behold, your house is left unto you desolate . . . And Jesus went out, and departed from the temple" (Matthew 23:37, 38 -24:1).

After Jesus departed from the temple, the glory of God never again entered it. Just forty years later, the city and the temple lay in ruins.

d) **The 2300 Days Explained.**

The legitimacy of the 490-year prophecy is confirmed by the events of history which it pinpointed so accurately. And this prophecy in turn establishes the termination point of the 2300 years with which it is linked. By adding the remaining 1810 years to October, AD 34, we come to October 1844. Then, said the angel, the sanctuary would be *"cleansed"*- the Hebrew word for which is 'tsadaq,'meaning *'purified'* or *'purged.'*

From the foregoing evidence, we must conclude that in October 1844, Jesus entered the Most Holy Place of the heavenly sanctuary to judge His people, and earth's Day of Atonement began.

In Daniel chapter 10, we find the aged prophet again praying and fasting for more light on the 2300 years. Once more Gabriel comes in response to the prophet's plea and provides an outline of events as they affect God's people from his day until the close of human probation. This historical outline is found in Daniel chapters 11 and 12. It 'rounds out' the prophecy of the 2300 days which the angel declared would be *"sealed"* or 'closed up' until the time of the end when *"knowledge shall be increased"* (Daniel 12:4).

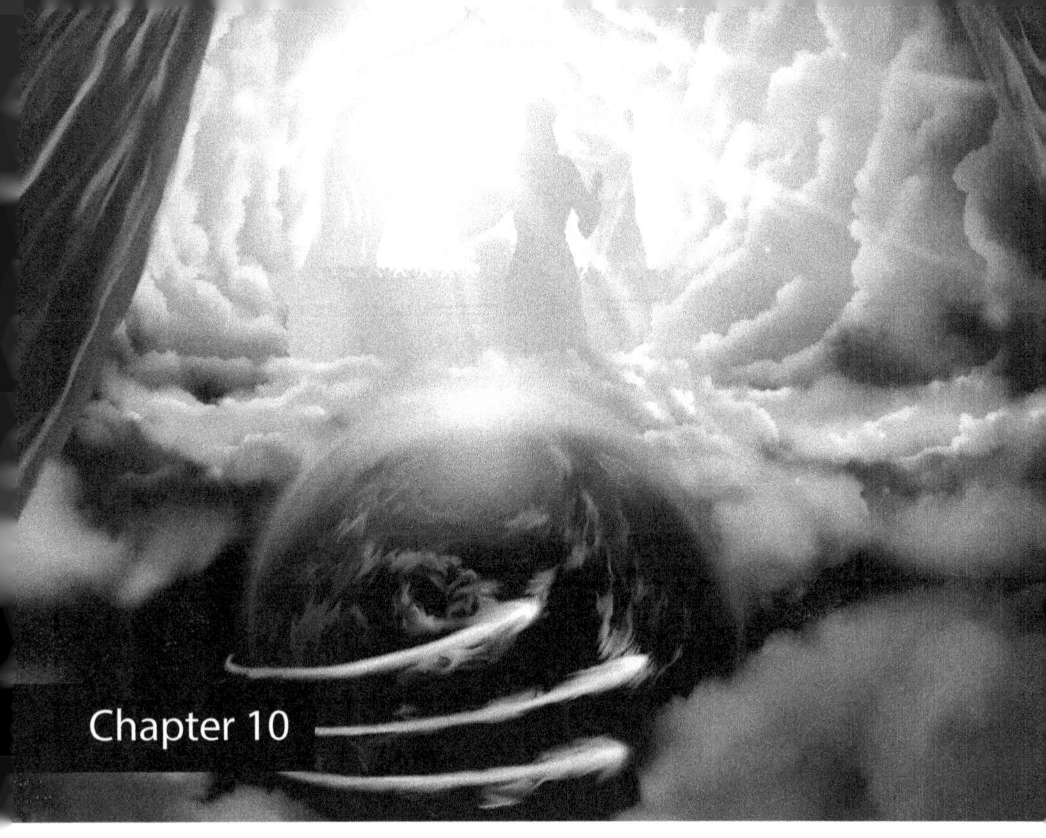

"The Hour of His Judgment is Come"

If indeed earth's Day of Atonement began in the autumn of 1844, would we not expect God to warn the world of this great event? After all, has He not promised, *"Surely the Lord God will do nothing, but He reveals His secrets unto His servants the prophets"* (Amos 3:7)? Did He not reveal *'His secrets'* regarding Christ's first Advent to the world through His prophet Daniel? And has He not given us the sanctuary model so that we may better understand *'His secrets'* regarding our salvation? Did He not warn Israel of the approach of the great Day of Atonement by commanding that silver trumpets be blown throughout the land ten days prior to this event (Leviticus 23:24)? Then surely we can expect God to warn the world of the approach of that even greater day when He would judge not only Israel, but the whole world. We can, and He did!

Not just for ten days did He warn the world of approaching judgment, but for ten years! From 1833-1844 the message, *"the hour of His Judgment is come"* (Revelation 14:7), was proclaimed like a trumpet blast around the world. Men in different countries, under the guidance of the Holy Spirit, diligently studied the Scriptures and discovered, independently of each other, the great prophetic truths of Daniel 8 and 9. Tracing through the 2300 days from the close of the Jewish era, each one came to 1844. Not fully understanding the sanctuary message, many earnest Bible students wrongly concluded that the *'cleansing of the sanctuary'* meant the coming of Christ to this world in Judgment. Although a mistake was made regarding the event to take place at the end of the 2300 days, the message as to the timing of the judgment was correct, so God blessed it.

For ten years the Judgment/2nd Advent message circled the globe. In America it was preached by approximately 300 ministers belonging to various evangelical denominations, and in England some 700 ministers from the Church of England proclaimed a judgment day message. Dr. Joseph Wolff, a converted Jew, preached the soon return of our Lord throughout the Middle East, Turkey, India, and to the regions beyond. He traveled from Tibet to Turkmenistan, from New York to the Netherlands, warning audiences around the world to *"Get Ready."* It is said that he preached *"among Jews, Turks, Muhammadans, Parsecs, Hindus, Chaldeans, Yesedes, Syrians, and Sabeans. From pashas to sheiks and shahs, even to the kings of Organtsh and Bokhara, and the queen of Greece."* [98]

In Scandinavia the message was proclaimed by both the written word and by the living preacher. When the preachers were silenced by government law, God put His Spirit upon little children. As they were under-age the law could not restrain them, so these child-preachers became God's messengers to arouse the people from their careless se-

---

98   Loughborough, J. N., The Great Second Advent Movement, p. 101

curity. Thus the tidings were spread, until virtually every mission station in the world had heard the warning message, *"Fear God and give glory to Him, for the hour of His Judgment has come"* (Revelation 14:7).

God added His very own signature to the work. Jesus told His disciples that one of the signs of His return would be the stars falling from heaven, *"even as a fig tree casts her untimely figs when she is shaken by a mighty wind"* (Matthew 24:29; Revelation 6:13). Such a trumpet blast of warning was given during the early hours of November 13, 1833, in the form of a great meteoric shower, the most extensive and the most wonderful ever recorded.

> *"From the Gulf of Mexico to Halifax, until daylight with some difficulty put an end to the display, the sky was scored in every direction with shining tracks and illuminated with majestic fireballs. At Boston, the frequency of meteors was estimated to be about half that of flakes of snow in an average snowstorm."* [99]

> *"Its sublimity and awful beauty still linger in many minds . . . Never did rain fall much thicker than the meteors fell toward the earth. East, west, north, and south, it was the same. In a word, the whole heavens seemed in motion . . . The display as described in Professor Silliman's Journal, was seen all over North America . . . From two a.m. until broad daylight, the sky being perfectly serene and cloudless, an incessant play of dazzling brilliant luminosities was kept up in the whole heavens."* [100]

> *"I witnessed this gorgeous spectacle and was awestruck. The air seemed filled with bright descending*

___

99   Agnes M. Clerke, A Popular History of Astronomy (1885), p. 369

100   R. M. Devens, The Great Events of the Greatest Century ch. 28, pars.1-5

messengers from the sky . . . I was not without the suggestion at the moment that it might be the har-binger of the coming of the Son of Man. And in my then state of mind I was prepared to hail Him as my friend and deliverer. I had read that 'the stars will fall from heaven,' and they were falling now." [101]

While these students of prophecy were wrong in their expectation that Christ would return in 1844, they were correct in their counting of the days in Daniel's prophecy. They accepted the then popular, but unscriptural view, that the earth was the sanctuary and that its cleansing would be by fire when Christ returned a second time. They also overlooked the fact that the only sanctuary in existence in 1844 was the one in heaven.

Such misunderstanding of prophecy is not without precedence in Scripture. When Jesus rode triumphantly into Jerusalem, His disciples hailed Him as their King and joyfully looked forward to His reign on the throne of David. However, a few days later Jesus was condemned and crucified, and how bitter was their disappointment. They were mistaken in their expectations, but their rejoicing and Christ's triumphal entry into Jerusalem were both in fulfilment of Bible prophecy (Zechariah 9:9).

Likewise, the giving of the message of the soon return of Christ was according to God's purposes. People everywhere were awakened to the fact that some great event was about to take place, and they were roused to forsake their sins and to diligently study the Bible for themselves. This was as God designed. Their disappointment in not seeing the Lord return was foretold in the Scriptures (see Revelation 10:8-11). The *"little book"* here mentioned is the Book of Daniel. Understanding its prophetic periods was indeed *"sweet as honey,"* and the disappointment that followed, intensely *"bitter"*.

---

101   F Douglass, Life and Times of Frederick Douglass (1941), p. 117

Many of these early believers found comfort in the words of Christ spoken through the apostle Paul:

> *"Cast not away therefore your confidence, which hath great recompense of reward. For ye have need of patience, that, after ye have done the will of God, ye might receive the promise. For yet a little while, and He that shall come will come, and will not tarry. Now the just shall live by faith. But if any man draw back, My soul will have no pleasure in him. But we are not of them who draw back unto perdition; but of them that believe to the saving of the soul"* (Hebrews 10:35-39).

A bitter disappointment launched the Christian church, and a bitter disappointment launched the Remnant church. Thus it was that God tested the faith of His true believers and gave them their great commission. To the infant Christian church He said, *"Go ye therefore, and teach all nations, baptizing them in the name of the Father and of the Son, and of the Holy Spirit, teaching them to observe all things whatsoever I have commanded you"* (Matthew 28:19, 20).

To the infant Remnant Church He said, ***"Thou must prophesy again before many peoples, and nations, and tongues, and kings"*** (Revelation 10:11). The end was near, but the world must first be warned.

Our Day in Court

The supreme court of the universe is now in session, and the character and lives of men and women are passing in review before the Judge of all the earth. Who are being judged at this time? The Bible tells us that *"judgment must begin at the house of God"* (I Peter 4:17). Those whose names are recorded in God's family record book, the Book of Life, are the first to be judged. These are those from Adam down to our day who have professed faith in the saving grace of Jesus Christ, and who have their names *"written in heaven"* (Hebrews 12:23). Those who have never professed faith in Christ, and therefore do not have their names written in *"the Lamb's Book of Life"* (Revelation 13:8; 21:27), will have their cases dealt with later.

Daniel's description of the Judgment in Daniel 7:9-10, is particularly meaningful. Let us look once again at the key players in this awesome event.

- **"The Ancient of Days"** - The Ancient of Days is God the Father. *"From everlasting to everlasting, Thou art God"* (Psalms 90:2). He is the source of all life, truth, and wisdom. He is the supreme authority, the fountain of all law. God the Father presides in the Judgment.

- **"Behold One like the Son of man"** - Jesus appears as man's representative at the bar of God. *"If any man sin, we have an Advocate with the Father, Jesus Christ the Righteous"* (I John 2:1). Jesus is our heavenly Attorney and also our Judge, *"For the Father judges no man, but has committed all judgment to the Son"* (John 5:22).

- **"Thousands ministered unto Him."** - These are the angel attendants and witnesses who have faithfully recorded the life history of every man, woman, and child.

With the key players now in position, **"the books were opened."** What are these 'books' that were opened on Judgment Day? Daniel would no doubt have envisaged huge scrolls of handwritten text. Later readers would picture large bound volumes. Today's readers may imagine huge computer data bases where massive amounts of information are stored. Whatever this means, we can be sure that *"God has a system of record keeping beyond any-*

thing mortal man can imagine." [102]

Moses was the first Bible writer to reveal that God keeps a record of every man's life in heaven. After the children of Israel sinned against God by making and worshipping a golden calf, God told Moses that He planned to destroy the whole nation and begin again with Moses' descendants. In one of the most moving entreaties of all human history, Moses pleaded for the life of the people who had so wronged God, even offering to die in their place.

"Yet now, if Thou wilt forgive their sins . . . (here the great leader pauses, and we can imagine him breaking into tears, unable for a moment to continue), *and if not, blot me, I pray Thee out of **Thy Book which Thou hast written**"* (Exodus 32:32).

1. The Book of Life

The 'book' to which Moses referred, can be none other than the Lamb's Book of Life in which are recorded all the names of those who have been adopted into the family of God. Several Bible writers refer to this book.

Luke records these words spoken by Christ to His disciples - *"Rejoice, because your names are written in heaven"* (Luke 10:20). Paul wrote of faithful fellow workers *"whose names are in the Book of Life"* (Philippians 4:3). Daniel, looking down the ages to *"a time of trouble, such as never was,"* declared that at that time God's people would be delivered, *"everyone that is found written in the book"* (Daniel 12:1). And John makes it abundantly clear that only the righteous will have their names retained in the Book of Life and will be privileged to eat once again from the Tree of Life.

> *"He that overcomes, the same shall be clothed in white raiment. And **I will not blot out his name***

---

102   Standish, R. & C., Adventistism Unveiled, p. 141

from the Book of Life but I will confess his name before My Father and before His angels" (Revelation 3:5).

"And there shall in no wise enter into it (the Holy City, the New Jerusalem), *anything that defiles, neither whatsoever worketh abomination, nor makes a lie, but they which are written in the Lamb's Book of Life"* (Revelation 21:27).

"And if any man shall take away from the words of this book of prophecy, God shall take away his part out of the Book of Life" (Revelation 22:19).

From these texts it is clear that some names will be *'blotted out'* from the Book of Life. Such disinheritance is not uncommon in human history. It is possible for a family member to be disowned or disinherited because of conduct which has disgraced the family name. God will likewise disinherit those members of His family who have disgraced and dishonoured His name. His command is, *"Thou shalt not take the name of the Lord Thy God in vain"* (Exodus 20:7). **"Whosoever hath sinned against Me, him will I blot out of My Book"** (Exodus 32:33).

John tells us that there are other books, besides the Book of Life, which will be opened and examined on Judgment Day. *"And the books* (plural), *were opened"* (Revelation 20:12).

2. The Book of Remembrance

"And a Book of Remembrance was written before Him for those that feared the Lord, and that thought upon His name. And they shall be mine, saith the Lord of hosts, in that day (Judgment Day), *when I make up My jewels"* (Malachi 3:16, 17).

This is a book which God especially delights in because it records all the good deeds of His children. Every word of faith and encouragement, every act of kindness, every temptation resisted, every victory gained, every pain and sorrow endured for Christ's sake, all are faithfully chronicled and immortalized in this book. Everyone whose name is in the Book of Life has his good deeds recorded in this book by his guardian angel.

Nehemiah referred to the Book of Remembrance when he exclaimed, *"Remember me, O my God . . . and wipe not out my good deeds that I have done"* (Nehemiah 13:14). The Psalmist also refers to it, *"Thou remember my wanderings. Put Thou my tears into Thy bottle. Are they not in Thy Book?"* (Psalm 56:8)

Christ tells us plainly that God will take into account our small, almost insignificant acts of kindness in the final Judgment.

> *"And whoever gives one of these little ones only a cup of cold water . . . assuredly I say to you, he shall by no means lose his reward"* (Matthew 10:42, NKJV).

> *"Then shall the King say unto them on His right hand, Come, you blessed of My Father, inherit the kingdom prepared for you from the foundation of the world. For I was hungry, and you gave Me **food**. I was thirsty, and you gave Me a **drink**. I was a stranger, and you took Me in, naked and you **clothed** Me. I was sick and you **visited** Me. I was in prison, and you came unto Me. Then will the righteous answer Him saying, Lord, when did we see Thee hungry and feed Thee, or thirsty and give Thee a drink? When did we see Thee a stranger and take You in, or naked and clothe Thee? Or when did we see Thee sick, or in prison, and come unto Thee? And the King will answer, and say unto them, Verily I say unto you, insomuch as you have done it unto one of the least of these My brethren, you have done it unto Me"* (Matthew 25:34-40).

In the Judgment, Christ points to the small, often forgotten acts of human kindness, as deeds done to Himself. So much does He identify with the human family.

3. The Book of Sins

All the sins of both the wicked and the righteous are recorded in heaven. These deeds can be erased only by a divine act of God. The righteous have nothing to fear in the Judgment, for during this time their sins are blotted out. But the sins of the unsaved remain to condemn them.

Both David and Isaiah refer to this record of sin. After David's great sin against Bathsheba and her husband Uriah, he cried in deep remorse, *"Have mercy on me, 0 God, according to Thy loving kindness. According to the multitude of Thy tender mercies, **blot out my transgressions**."* *"Hide Thy face from my sins, and **blot out all my iniquities**"* (Psalm 51:1, 9).

Isaiah records God's response to such a prayer of deep, heartfelt repentance: ***"I, even I, am He that blots out thy transgressions for mine own sake and will not remember your sins."*** *"I have blotted out, as a thick cloud, thy transgressions, and, as a cloud thy sins. Return unto Me for I have redeemed thee"* (Isaiah 43:25; 44:22).

Solomon tells us that God will bring every deed into judgment, both good and bad. *"For God shall bring every work into judgment, with every secret thing, whether it be good, or whether it be evil"* (Ecclesiastes 12:14).

And Jesus tells us that we must account for even our words. *"But I say unto you, that every idle word that men shall speak, they shall give account thereof in the day of judgment. For by thy words thou shalt be justified, and by thy words thou shalt be condemned"* (Matthew 12:36, 37).

Paul admonished the Corinthians not to judge one another, but to leave such things to God *"who will bring to light the hidden things of darkness and will make manifest (openly known) the counsels (thoughts) of the heart"* (1

Corinthians 4:5).

When a person rebels against God and turns away from following Him, his name will be erased from the Book of Life when his case comes before the heavenly court, and all his good deeds will be blotted from the Book of Remembrance. His evil deeds, however, will remain in the Book of Sins to stand against him on that day when the wicked are judged.

> *"When a righteous man turns from his righteousness and commits iniquity . . . he will die in his sins, and his righteousness which he has done will not be remembered"* (Ezekiel 3:20, also 18:24-26).

> *"And whoever was not found written in the Book of Life was cast into the lake of fire"* (Revelation 20:15).

> *"Every man's work passes in review before God and is registered for faithfulness or unfaithfulness. Opposite each name in the books of heaven is entered, with terrible exactness, every wrong word, every selfish act, every unfulfilled duty, every secret sin, and every cunning deception. Heaven-sent warnings or reproofs neglected, wasted moments, unimproved opportunities, the influence exerted for good or for evil, with its far-reaching results, all are chronicled by the recording angel".*[103]

Some people think that our sins are blotted out every time we confess them...To be consistent, God would have to blot out our names every time we sinned!

There are only two possible outcomes from the Judgment. Either our sins will be blotted out, or our names blotted out. It is up to us. Will we, by the grace of God, overcome sin, or will sin overcome us? Are we still in love with our sins, or do we wish to be set free from them? If we want to have our sins blotted out and our name retained in the Book of Life, then Jesus, and only Jesus is the answer. *"But thanks be to God which giveth us the victory through our Lord Jesus Christ"* (I Corinthians 15:57). *"Whosoever is born of God overcomes the world. This is the victory that*

---

103   White, E., The Great Convertrovesy , p. 482

overcomes the world, even our faith" (I John 5:4).

Some people think that our sins are blotted out every time we confess them, but the sanctuary message teaches us that this is not so. To be consistent, God would have to blot out our names every time we sinned! We have on record both David and Rahab's transgressions centuries after the sins were   committed (Matthew 1:6; Hebrews 11:31). Not until they are judged will their sins be forever erased and forgotten, even by God Himself.

"I will forgive their iniquity, and I will remember their sin no more" (Jeremiah 31:34).

"In those days and at that time, saith the Lord, the iniquity of Israel will be sought for, and there will be none, and the sins of Judah, and they will not be found" (Jeremiah 50:20).

"Thou wilt cast all their sins into the depths of the sea" (Micah 7:19).

Peter, in his sermon in the temple following the healing of the lame man, explains the redemptive process in a few short sentences.

> *"**Repent** ye therefore and **be converted**, that **your sins may be blotted out**. So that times of **refreshing** shall come from the presence of the Lord. And **He shall send Jesus Christ**, which before was preached unto you"* (Acts 3:19, 20).

1. *"Repent"* - to be sorry for and to turn away from sins, which are then covered and forgiven, and transferred to the great Sin Bearer in heaven (*Justification*).

2. *"Be converted,"* literally 'to turn about,' - Sins are overcome by the power Jesus freely bestows if we believe

(*Sanctification*).

3. Sins are *"blotted out"* - Sins are erased from the Record Books during the Day of Atonement (*Judgment*).

4. *"Times of refreshing"* - The Holy Spirit is poured out upon the living saints at the end of time (*latter rain power*).

5. *"He will send Jesus"* - The second coming of Christ when He will *"change our vile body, that it may be fashioned like unto His glorious body"* (Philippians 3:21). *'We shall be like Him, for we shall see Him as He is"* (I John 3:2) (*Glorification*).

a) A Graphic Picture

John Shuler, in his classic study *The Great Judgment Day,* gives a vivid word picture of the heavenly court in session as it considers its first case.

"A word of command, and an angel turns the first leaf of the first mighty volume. The gigantic task of examining the lives of God's professed people has begun. *'The hour of His Judgment is come.'*

"The Judgment begins with the first members of the race. As the Book of Life is opened, the name of Abel, the first man who ever died appears. The case of Abel is brought before the bar of God. The records are carefully examined. All his words and deeds are rehearsed from the accurately preserved records in the books. Beside every sin is found recorded *'confessed and forgiven.'*

"Jesus now steps forward and pleads on his behalf. *'This man confessed Me before men',* He says, *'and I confess Him before Thee, Father, and before these angels . . . I plead My sacrifice, My blood for him. Father, receive him."*

"The Father listens joyfully to such a plea as this, and Abel's sins are forever removed from the heavenly record, and his name retained in the Book of Life. His reward in the kingdom of heaven is decided upon.

"Other names are mentioned, however, at which Jesus remains silent. The names of men like Nadab, Abihu, and Saul, who ran well for a time and then fell away, are passed by in silence. No record is found of sincere, lasting repentance before their probation closed, so God sorrowfully decrees that their names be stricken from His book. The words of David are now more than verified, 'The wicked will not stand in the Judgment' (Psalm 1:5).

"Thus, through the years since 1844 this investigative Judgment has been going on. The lives of millions of people whose names were once written in the Book of Life, have come up one by one for review before this great tribunal. All who have ever taken upon themselves the name of the Lord, must pass its searching scrutiny. Every name is called, and every case closely investigated. Names are accepted, names rejected.

"At some point of time the cases of all the dead will have been adjudicated, and the court will turn its attention to the records of men and women who are alive today. One by one these will be dealt with, and finally, when the last case has been settled, the door of mercy will be shut, and the Judge will issue the decree which declares that everyone's future is eternally fixed: 'He that is unjust, let him be unjust still; and he which is filthy, let him be filthy still. And he that is righteous, let him be righteous still; and he that is holy, let him be holy still" (Revelation 22:11).[104]

---

104   Shuler, J. L. The Great Judgment Day, pp. 107. 108

b) Weighed and Found _____?

The Judgment will forever separate the great mass of mankind into two classes. One group will be taken to heaven when Jesus comes again. The other group will be left upon the earth and slain by the brightness of His coming (see Matthew 13:47-49; 25:32-33).

> *"Then shall two be in the field. The one shall be taken. and the other left . . . Two women shall be grinding at the mill. The one shall be taken, and the other left"* (Matthew 24:40, 41).

Two men may work together in the field, or the office, or on a construction site. Two women may work together in business, or in a hospital, or in the school canteen. Both may have their names on the church records, but one will be taken, and the other one left. One has lived up to all the light received from heaven. The other has accepted some truth while rejecting other truth and therefore not fully surrendered to God.

Many choose to ignore God's requirements as expressed in His law and would rather follow the teachings of men which have no foundation in Scripture.

> *"Not everyone that saith unto Me, Lord, Lord, shall enter into the kingdom of heaven, but he that doeth the will of My Father which is in heaven. Many will say to Me in that day, Lord, Lord, have we not prophesied in Thy name? And in Thy name have cast out demons? And in Thy name done many wonderful works? And then will I profess unto them, I never knew you. Depart from Me, ye that work iniquity"* (Matthew 7:21-23).

However, if we do the will of God by the power of God, we will have an *"abundant entrance"* into the heavenly kingdom.

> *"Blessed are they that do His commandments, that they may have right to the Tree of Life and may en-*

ter in through the gates into the city" (Revelation 22:14).

Are we ready to meet our life record in heaven? When Jesus wrote the sins of Mary Magdalene's accusers in the dust of the ground they fled from the sight. They were ashamed to come face to face with their record. It need not be that way with us. We cannot change what is written in the books of heaven, but our record, no matter how wretched it may be, need not condemn us. This is the good news of the gospel. There is *"no condemnation to them which are in Christ Jesus . . . for the law of the Spirit of life in Christ Jesus has made me free from the law of sin and death"* (Romans 8:1-2).

"Jesus answered them, 'Verily, verily, I say unto you, whosoever commits sin is a slave of sin . . . but if the Son shall make him free, he shall be free indeed'" (John 8:34, 36).

c) "Worthy" or "Wanting?"

"In a certain old-fashioned village in Germany is a cathedral which is no longer used as a place of worship. It serves only as a museum. On the wall is a picture which represents the Judgment.

"Seated upon His throne of magnificence is Christ...And just in front of Him is a great crowd of people - just as far as you can see there are heads. Standing in front of the people is an angel, a beautiful form, bearing in his hands a pair of balances. Over this picture of balances, a hand has written, 'Thou art weighed in the balance, and found ___?' The writing hand has paused with the word 'found.' The next word is missing. The hand appears to be waiting for the decision before writing the final word.

"We are living today in the time of Judgment. Your case and mine will soon come before the

great Judge. Your life will be weighed by the standard of His law. The sentence will be pronounced: "Thou art weighed in the balance, and found ___ ?" The blank must be filled by one or the other of two words, 'worthy' or 'wanting.' What will it be for you? What will it be for me?" [105]

"The great day of the Lord is near. It is near, and hastens greatly" (Zephaniah 1:14).

> The Judgment is set, and the books have been opened,
> How shall we stand in that great day.
> When every thought, and word, and action,
> God, the righteous Judge, shall weigh?
>
> How shall we stand in that great day?
> How shall we stand in that great day?
> Shall we be found before Him wanting?
> Or with our sins all washed away?
> - F. E. Belden.

d) The Judgment of the Unsaved

The Bible speaks of not one but two Judgments, not one but two resurrections, and not one but two deaths. The first Judgment, the first death, and the first resurrection are for the righteous. The second Judgment, the second resurrection, and both the first and second deaths are reserved for the unsaved. We have already looked at the first Judgment, that of those who have had their names recorded in the Lamb's Book of Life. This Judgment takes place just prior to Christ's second coming, and Daniel 8:14 tells us that it is already in progress. When Jesus comes again the righteous dead will be resurrected and will join the living righteous to meet our Lord in the air (1 Thessalonians 4:16-18). They will then accompany Christ back to heaven where they will *"live and reign with Him for a thousand years"* (Revelation 20:4).

---

105   Shuler, J. L., The Great Judgment Day, pp.121, 122

The second Judgment, that of the unsaved, will take place during this 1,000-year period called the Millennium. This Judgment will involve an examination of their life record by the saints of God who have been redeemed from the earth.

John the Revelator saw this Judgment scene in vision:

> *"I saw thrones, and they* (the redeemed) *sat upon them, **and judgment was given** unto **them** ... and they lived and reigned with Christ a thousand years"* (Revelation 20:4).

Not only are unsaved men and women judged during this time, and their punishment appointed them, but so are wicked angels. *"Do ye not know that the saints shall judge the world? . . . Know ye not that we shall judge angels?"* (I Corinthians 6:1-3).

The Bible speaks of not one but two Judgments, not one but two resurrections, and not one but two deaths.

Why does God allow the saints to judge the lost? After all, their cases have already been decided. God has a very special reason for allowing the saints to examine the record books. In a sense He is placing His judgments on trial before the universe. His created beings will be allowed to evaluate the fairness and justice of God in condemning the lost. Therefore, David could exclaim:

> *"That Thou may be found just in Thy words, and blameless when You judge"* (Psalm 51 :4).

And Paul echoes this thought, *"That You may be justified in Your words, and may overcome when You are judged"* (Romans 3:4, NKJV). Or as the NEB words it, *"win the verdict when Thou art on trial".*

God puts His judgments on review before the universe that they may examine the reasons for His condemnation of the lost. He does not want to run the risk of having any of the redeemed question His justice in any particular. Maybe someone we have known, and loved, and prayed for, is not among the redeemed. We wonder why. God allows us to check the heavenly records. Here the curtain is drawn aside, and it will be clearly seen that our friend was guilty of secret sins of which we had no knowledge. We will see every effort that God has put forth to save that individual and we will conclude that this person did not want to be saved and would not have been happy in heaven. We will see that God has been just and we will be satisfied that justice has been done.

"God will wipe away every tear from our eyes" (Revelation 7:17). It is not on this earth that God will wipe away every tear, but in heaven. There is no reason for tears in heaven, except for the sorrow we will naturally experience when we see that some loved one is not there.

The angels also have a part in this Judgment. They have passed through some sad experiences because of sin. They have witnessed the fall of Lucifer, the brightest and fairest of all the angels; they have seen millions of their fellow angels lost. They have seen their beloved Commander die on the cross and know something of the agony of God. They have recorded the good and evil deeds of every man and woman who has ever lived and were present when the cases of the righteous were decided. They are intensely interested in who should, and who should not, be admitted into the paradise of God. All questions must be forever settled. Sin must not rise up the second time! (Nahum 1:9).

When all the evidence has been examined by both men and angels, the verdict is given:

> *"Even so, Lord God Almighty, true and righteous are Thy judgments"* (Revelation 16:7).

The redeemed from all ages join the angels in extolling the praises of God, *''Alleluia! Salvation, and glory, and honour, and power, unto the Lord our God. For true and righteous are His judgments"* (Revelation 19:1, 2).

And as God resumes the throne, *"a great multitude ... as the voice of mighty thunderings"* shout, *''Alleluia! For the Lord God omnipotent reigns"* (Revelation 19:6).

e) The Two Resurrections and the Second Death

The Bible speaks of two resurrections. "There shall be a resurrection of the dead, **both** of **the just and the unjust"** (Acts 24:15).

Jesus specifically mentions these two resurrections:

> *"The hour is coming, in which all that are in the graves shall hear His voice and shall come forth.*
>
> *They that have done good, unto **the resurrection** of **life**, and they that have done evil, unto **the** resurrection of damnation"** (John 5:28, 29).*

We know that the righteous dead are resurrected when Jesus returns and that they accompany Him to heaven, but what of the lost? When are they resurrected? Of the righteous dead it is written, *"and they **lived*** (lit. 'came to life') and *reigned with Christ a thousand years . . . This is the first resurrection. Blessed and holy is he that has part in the first resurrection. On such the second death has no power, but they will be priests of God and of Christ, and will reign with Him a thousand years"* (Revelation 20:4-6).

The beginning of the millennium is marked by the resurrection of the righteous. This is very clear. The narrative continues, **"but** *the rest of the dead **did not live again** until the thousand years were finished"* (Revelation 20:5). From this we can see that the *'rest of the dead',* the lost, will come forth in the *"resurrection of damnation"* at the end of the millennium. At this time the lost will be raised to receive their punishment which was determined when their life histories were examined.

What will be their reward? The Bible is very plain on the matter. *"The wages of sin is death"* (Romans 6:23). *"The soul who sins shall die"* (Ezekiel 18:4).

By what means will the wicked die? Again, the Bible is very clear. John the Baptist, speaking of that great day, warned the people, *"He* (Christ) *will . . . gather His wheat into the garner, but He will burn up the chaff with unquenchable fire"* (Matthew 3:12).

The prophet Malachi foresaw that same *'day,'* a time when the earth will *"burn as an oven. And all the proud, yea, and all that do wickedly, shall be stubble. And the day that comes shall burn them up, saith the Lord of hosts, it will leave them neither root* (Satan) *nor branch* (his evil angels and followers)" (Malachi 4:1).

John the Revelator saw the destruction of the wicked in vision. He describes the scene very succinctly - *"And fire came down from God out of heaven and devoured them."* Further on he adds more details. *"But the* cowardly, *and unbelieving, and the abominable, and murderers, and sexually immoral, and sorcerers* (spiritualists), *and idolaters, and all liars, shall have their part in the lake which burns with fire and brimstone, which is **the** second **death"** (*Revelation 20:9; 21:8).

The final, and everlasting destruction of the lost, is called the *'second death.'* From this death there is no return, no resurrection. As the reward of the righteous is eternal life, so the reward of the wicked is eternal death. Some people believe in an eternally burning 'hell', but this is not a Bible doctrine. God says, *"The wages of sin is **death"*** not forever burning in hell. Death is the punishment for sin, not hell. Fire is the means to bring about the destruction.

The fire is said to be *'everlasting'* because it is everlasting in its effects. It is *"unquenchable,"* meaning that only God can extinguish it, and this He will not do until all the results of sin are forever eradicated from the earth. *"Eternal fire"* is said to have reduced the wicked cities of Sodom and Gomorrah to ashes, but Sodom and Gomorrah are not burning today (compare Jude 7 with 2 Peter 2:6).

So, what will be the final end of the lost? Simply this: *"And ye* (the saints) *shall tread down the wicked. For they shall be ashes under the soles of your feet"* (Malachi 4:3). They will be reduced to ashes, eternally dead. The wicked will become part of the elements which form the soil of this earth. Their destruction is an act of love and mercy on the part of God, for to perpetuate their lives would be to perpetuate sin, sorrow, suffering, and misery, and such a thing would be abhorrent to a just, merciful and loving God.

> *"For God so loved the world that He gave His only begotten Son, that whosoever believeth in Him should not perish but have everlasting life.*
>
> *"For God sent not His Son into the world to condemn the world; but that the world through Him might be saved.*
>
> *"He that believeth on Him is not condemned: but he that believeth not is condemned already, because he hath not believed in the name of the only begotten Son of God.*
>
> *"And this is the condemnation, that light is come into the world, and men loved darkness rather than light, because their deeds were evil.*
>
> *"For everyone that doeth evil hates the light, neither cometh to the light, lest his deeds should be reproved"* (John 3:16-20).
>
> *"God exercises justice upon the wicked for the good of the universe. And even for the good of those upon whom His judgments are visited. He would make them happy if He could do so in accordance the laws of His government and the justice of His character. He surrounds them with the tokens of His love, He grants them a knowledge of His law, and follows them with the offers of His mercy; but they despise His love, make void His law, and reject His mercy . . .*
>
> *"A life of rebellion against God has unfitted them for heaven. Its purity, holiness, and peace would be torture to them; the glory of God would be a con-*

suming fire. They would love to flee from that holy place. They would welcome destruction, that they might be hidden from the face of Him who died to redeem them. The destiny of the wicked is fixed by their own choice. Their exclusion from heaven is voluntary with themselves, and just and merciful on the part of God." [106]

In the execution of God's judgments on the wicked, Satan and his rebellious angels are also destroyed. *"For God did not spare the angels that sinned, but cast them down to hell, and delivered them into chains of darkness* (during the Millennium), *to be reserved unto ... the day of judgment to be punished"* (2 Peter 2:4-9).

"And the angels who kept not their first estate (heaven), *but left their own habitation, He has reserved in everlasting chains under darkness, unto the judgment of the great day"* (Jude 6).

"Then shall He say unto them on the left hand, Depart from Me, ye cursed, into everlasting fire, prepared for the devil and his angels" (Matthew 25:41).

The experiment of sin is now over, and God's original plan of peopling the earth with a race of holy, happy beings will be carried out. *'We, according to His promise, look for new heavens and a new earth, wherein dwelleth righteousness"* (2 Peter 3:13).

f) What of the Scapegoat?

As on the Day of Atonement, the scapegoat, laden with the sins of the people, was banished from the camp of Israel never to return, so will Satan be forever banished from the camp of the saints when Jesus comes the second time. The sins of God's people, which he has caused them to commit, will be placed upon the great originator of all sin.

---

106   White, E., The Great Convertrovesy , p. 541-543

"His mischief will return upon his own head, and his violent dealing will come down upon his own crown" (Psalm 7:16).

As the scapegoat was sent away by the hand of a fit man into a land ***"not inhabited"*** (Leviticus 16:21, 22), so when Jesus returns, an angel from heaven will bind Satan and cast him into the *"bottomless pit"* or *"abyss,"* that is, a desolate earth devoid of population. (See Revelation 20:1-3). How does the earth become depopulated?

A series of terrible calamities, plagues like those which destroyed Egypt, will precede the second coming of Christ. *"Grievous sores"* will break out on the incurably rebellious. The sea, rivers, and streams will become as *"the blood of a dead man."* The sun will scorch men *"with great heat,"* and darkness will cover part of the earth. The most devastating earthquake this planet has ever experienced will cause islands to *"flee away,"* and mountains to disappear. *"A great earthquake, such as was not since men were upon the earth, so mighty an earthquake and so great."*

As the battle of Armageddon is fought, God will cause *"great hail out of heaven, every stone about the weight of a talent* (100 lbs or approximately 45 kg)" to fall upon wicked men who are planning to destroy His faithful people (see Daniel 11:44-45 and Revelation 13:15). *"The plague thereof was exceeding great."* These plagues are described in greater detail in Revelation 16 and are called the seven last plagues. The earth will be reduced to a desolate, chaotic, uninhabited wilderness. All the righteous will be taken to heaven, and all the wicked will be dead upon the ground.

Jeremiah was given a view of the earth during the Millennium. He describes it thus:

> *"I beheld the earth, and, lo, it was without form, and void, and the heavens, and they had no light. I beheld the mountains, and, lo, they trembled, and all the hills moved back and forth. I beheld, and, lo, **there was no man,** and all the birds of the heavens had fled. I beheld, and, lo, the fruitful place was a wilderness, and all the cities were broken down at the presence of the Lord and by His fierce anger. For thus has the Lord said, 'The whole land will be desolate, yet I will not make a full end ... Every city will be forsaken, and **not a man dwell therein"*** (Jeremiah 4:23-29).

> *Isaiah describes the same scene. "Behold, **the Lord makes the earth empty**, and makes it waste, and turns it upside down, and scatters abroad the inhabitants . . . and the land will be **utterly emptied**, and **utterly spoiled.** For the Lord has spoken this word"* (Isaiah 24:1-3.)

Because there will be no human beings on the earth during the thousand years, Satan's work will be interrupted by this *'chain'* of circumstances, *"so that he should deceive the nations no more, till the thousand years should be fulfilled"* (Revelation 20:3). There will be no one left alive upon the earth for him to tempt. For one thousand years Satan will be confined to this dreary prison. During this time of forced meditation, he will have time to contemplate his rebellion and its terrible consequences. Around him will be the result of his attempt to wrest control of this planet from its rightful Owner. Around him will be the end result of his rulership. The advantages he promised men if they would only follow him and disobey their Maker, are nowhere evident. An outcast, an exile, abandoned, forsaken by God and by man, Satan for an entire millennium will reap the fruit of his sinful course, and of the "good time" he promised his followers.

At the close of the Millennium, he will be *'loosed a little season"* when the wicked are resurrected to receive their punishment. The final act of God will be to destroy Satan, his angels, and the wicked together in the lake of fire. Sin and sinners will be wiped out of existence, and sin will not *"rise up a second time"* (Nahum 1:9).

"Our God Shall Come"

Psalm 50:3

Let us for a moment draw aside the curtain which veils the not-too-distant future, and picture in our minds the coming of our Lord, and the reception of His people into the Paradise of God.

Judgment is over. The life records of all those who have ever claimed to be the children of God have been closely examined. Names have been accepted, names have been rejected, and now the work is finished. Christ takes His golden censer, fills it with coals from off the golden altar and hurls it to the earth. Immediately there follows *"voices, and thunderings, and lightnings, and an earthquake"* (Revelation 8:3-5). Christ thus signals to the inhabitants of earth that His work as High Priest has ended. Probation has closed, and there is to be no more intercession for sinners.

He exchanges His High Priestly robes for those of a conquering King, and prepares to fulfill the promise made to His disciples many years ago - *"I go to prepare a place for you, and if I go and prepare a place for you, I **will** come* *again, and receive you unto Myself, that where I am, there you may be also"* (John 14:2, 3).

On earth a remnant out of *"all nations, and kindreds, and people, and tongues"* (Revelation 7:9), wait for the *"glorious appearing of the great* God *and our Saviour Jesus Christ"* (Titus 2:13). Many have been forced to flee their homes because of persecution (Revelation 13:15-17). They have found refuge in secluded places in the rocks and mountains where, with prayerful hearts, they wait.

All nature seems turned out of its course. The earth shakes violently, great hail pounds the cities to ruin, and there are fearful sights and sounds in the heavens. Mountains are sinking and islands disappear, the shrieking of the hurricane fills the air with violence, and the sea is lashed to a fury (Luke 21:25). All the earth is convulsed. Its very foundations seem about to give way (Psalm 46:1-3; Revelation 16:17-21).

At last there appears the sign the righteous have been waiting for, *"the sign of the Son of man in heaven"* - a small, black cloud, which grows larger and brighter as it comes nearer and nearer, until it fills the heavens with indescribable glory. *"And the Son of man shall come in His glory, and all the holy angels with Him."* He will come in *"the clouds of heaven with power and great glory." "For as the lightning cometh out of the east and shineth even unto the west, so shall also the coming of the Son of man be." "And every eye will see Him"* (Matthew 25:31; 24:30, 27; Revelation 1:7).

The *"armies of heaven,"* a vast unnumbered throng of angels, attend the King of glory. The very firmament seems filled with radiant forms, as *"ten thousand times ten thousand, and thousands of thousands"* surround heaven's glorious King (Revelation 19:14; Daniel 7:10).

> *"No pen can portray the scene. No mortal mind is adequate to conceive its splendour . . . As the living cloud comes still nearer, every eye beholds the Prince of life. No crown of thorns now mars His sacred head, but a diadem of glory rests on His holy brow. His countenance outshines the dazzling brightness of the noonday sun. 'And He hath on His vesture and on His thigh a name written, KING OF KINGS, AND LORD OF LORDS' (Revelation 19:16) ."* [107]

With reverent and holy awe, the ransomed of the Lord look up toward heaven and exclaim: *"Lo, this is our God. We have waited for Him, and He will save us"* (Isaiah 25 :9).

Now comes the event for which the people of God have waited so long - the resurrection of the righteous dead — that *"glorious hope."*

> *"For the Lord Himself shall descend from heaven with a shout and with the voice of the Archangel* (Christ) [108], **and** *with the trump of God. And the dead in Christ shall rise first.* **Then** *we which are alive and remain shall be caught up together with them in the clouds to meet the Lord* **in the air,** *and so shall we ever be with the Lord"* (1 Thessalonians 4:16, 17).

> *"Awake and sing ye that dwell in dust . . . the earth shall cast out the dead"* (Isaiah 26:19).

> *"Behold, I show you a mystery. We shall not all*

---

107   White, E., The Great Controversy, pp. 640, 641

108   Compare with John 5:25, 28-29 where the voice of Jesus is said to raise the dead. Also note Daniel 12:1-2 and Revelation 12:7-8.

sleep, but we shall all be changed. In a moment, in the twinkling of an eye, at the last trump. For the trumpet shall sound, and the dead shall be raised incorruptible, and we shall be changed. For this corruptible must put on incorruption, and this mortal must put on immortality. So, when this corruptible shall have put on incorruption, and this mortal shall have put on immortality, **then** *shall be brought to pass the saying that is written, Death is*

swallowed up in victory" (I Corinthians 15:51-55).

Now is fulfilled the final act of the sanctuary drama, the glorification of God's people. The old body with all its weaknesses and infirmities is put away forever, and a glorious, new, immortal body is given to the saints of God. *"Then the eyes of the blind shall be opened, and the ears of the deaf shall be unstopped. Then shall the lame man leap as a hart* (deer), *and the tongue of the dumb sing"* (Isaiah 35:5,6).

As we have just read in 1 Thessalonians 4:16, 17, two classes will be redeemed when Jesus returns to bring His saints home to glory. Of one class it is written, *"I will redeem them from the power of the grave. I will redeem them from death"* (Hosea 13:14). Paul refers to this class when he exclaims in triumph, *"O death, where is thy sting? O grave, where is thy victory"* (1 Corinthians 15:55)?

Of the other class, the living saints, it is written, *"These were redeemed from among men, being the first fruits unto God and to the Lamb"* (Revelation 14:4). These living saints are gathered from around the world - "And *He shall send His angels . . . and they shall gather together His elect from the four winds, from one end of heaven to the other"* (Matthew 24:31).

Both the resurrected dead and the righteous living are caught up together to meet Jesus in the air. Our Lord will not touch the earth at this time. In the air they will form one great company *"which no man can number,"* and surrounded by millions of shining angels, they will ascend with shouts of praise and joy to the heavenly home waiting for them. *"Even so, come, Lord Jesus"* (Revelation 22:20).

a) What About the Wicked?

The return of Jesus will not be an event welcomed by all.

"And then shall appear the sign of the Son of man in heaven. And then shall all the tribes of the earth mourn" (Matthew 24:30).

"Behold, He cometh with clouds. And every eye shall see Him, and they also which pierced Him. And all kindreds of the earth will wail because of Him" (Revelation 1 :7).

"The great day of the Lord is near, it is near, and hastens greatly . . . The mighty men will cry there bitterly ... Neither their silver nor their gold shall be able to deliver them in the day of the Lord's wrath. But the whole land shall be devoured by the fire of His jealousy. For He shall make even a speedy riddance of all of them that dwell in the land" (Zephaniah 1:14, 18).

"And they shall go into the holes of the rocks, and into the caves of the earth, for fear of the Lord, and for the glory of His majesty, when He arises to shake terribly the earth. In that day a man shall cast his idols of silver, and his idols of gold, which they made each one for himself to worship, to the moles and to the bats; to go into the clefts of the rocks and into the tops of the ragged rocks, for fear

of the Lord, and for the glory of His majesty, when He arises to shake terribly the earth" (Isaiah 2:19-21).

The wicked will be slain by the brightness of Christ's coming and by the plagues which will be poured out upon them just prior to this time. For a full description, see Revelation 16.

"And I saw an angel standing in the sun. He cried with a loud voice, saying to all the birds that fly in the midst of heaven, Come and gather yourselves together unto the supper of the great God. That ye may eat the flesh of kings, and the flesh of captains, and the flesh of mighty men, and the flesh of horses, and of them that sit on them, and the flesh of all men, both free and bond, both small and great" (Revelation 19:17, 18).

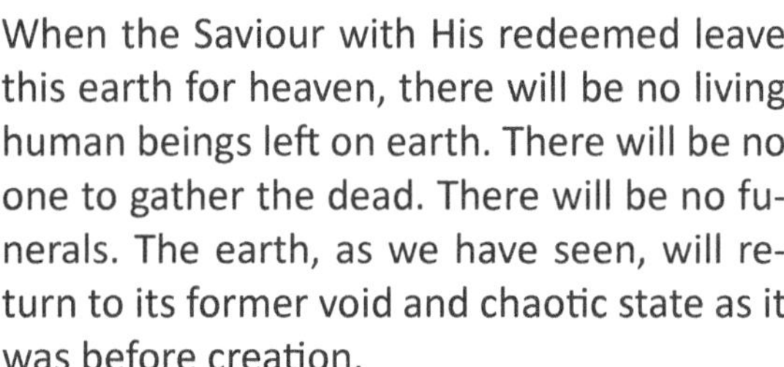

When the Saviour with His redeemed leave this earth for heaven, there will be no living human beings left on earth. There will be no one to gather the dead. There will be no funerals. The earth, as we have seen, will return to its former void and chaotic state as it was before creation.

"And the slain of the Lord shall be at that day from one end of the earth even unto the other end of the earth. They shall not be lamented, neither gathered, nor buried. They will be dung upon the ground" (Jeremiah 25 :33).

b) The Glorious Homecoming of the Redeemed [109]

As we turn our minds from the sad fate of those who refused to accept Jesus as their Saviour, let us re-join that

---

109   Selected from The Path to the Throne of God by Sarah Peck, pp.314-327

happy group traveling through limitless space on their way to the Holy City.

At last, the triumphant procession reaches the city of God, the New Jerusalem. Surrounding the city is a vast area like transparent glass, which appears to the apostle John to be like *"a sea of glass mingled with fire"* (Revelation 15:2). On this glittering expanse which surrounds the city on all four sides, stands the innumerable company of the redeemed. Before them rise the magnificent walls of the New Jerusalem. They are built of jasper, *"a stone most precious"* and, as they are *"clear as crystal,"* the beauties of the city within can be seen by the redeemed (Revelation 21:11, 18). The walls are high and thick. The length of the walls is said to be 12,000 furlongs, or 1500 miles (Revelation 21:16). Some commentators claim that this is the distance around all four sides of the city. Others believe that each side is 1500 miles in length! Which view is correct the redeemed will know soon enough!

The walls have twelve foundations which are garnished with *"all manner of precious stones"* - jasper, sapphire, chalcedony, emerald, sardonyx, sardius, chrysolite, beryl, topaz, chrysoprase, jacinth, and amethyst. The wonderful effect of all these precious stones with their interplay of colours as they reflect upon the sea of glass, defies the imagination. As the redeemed stand before these magnificent walls with their gates of shining pearl, how their hearts must thrill with the prospect of soon passing beyond them into the City of God.

There are twelve massive gates leading into the city, three on each side. Each gate is made from one immense pearl (Revelation 21:12, 13, 21). Why did God choose pearl? A pearl is formed by pain and suffering. If a grain of sand, or some other foreign substance, gets inside the shell of an oyster, it cannot expel it. Trying to do so will tear and lacerate its soft body, so the oyster quietly submits to the irritation. Soon the cruel substance is covered with a secretion from its own body which gradually develops into a beautiful, polished, and costly gem. Likewise,

the redeemed have passed through trials, disappointments, suffering, and sorrow, caused by the grain of sin. But they have *"fought a good fight"* through the mighty power of God (2 Timothy 4:7; Ephesians 6:10-18). Through submission to God, each one has been transformed into *"a pearl of great price,"* and now they stand in triumph before the gates of pearl (Matthew 13 :46).

A command is given for the Israel of God to advance, and that great company, in perfect order, passes over the brilliantly lit sea of glass and through the gates of pearl. Each long line enters through the gate on which is written the name of the tribe to which he or she belongs (Revelation 21:12). As these jubilant processions, twelve in number, enter the pearly portals, they are welcomed by the angel of the gate. Clothed with dazzling white robes, waving *"palms (of victory) in their hands,"* with glittering crowns upon their heads, and holding onto shining harps, the company advances, bathed in the glory streaming from the throne of God (Revelation 7:9). They are a sight wholly beyond human language to describe, or even the most vivid imagination to picture, for *"eye hath not seen, nor ear heard, neither has entered into the heart of man, the things which God hath prepared for them that love Him"* (1 Corinthians 2:9).

Now they pause. Every eye is fixed on the mighty throne of God, *"high and lifted up"* (Isaiah 6:1). As the earthly high priest, at the close of the Day of Atonement, came out of the sanctuary to bless the forgiven and cleansed children of Israel, so Jesus, our heavenly High Priest, now comes forth to bless His children. The *"Alpha and the Omega, the beginning and the end, the first and the last* (Revelation 1:8, 11)" now stands in all His majesty high above every saint and angel. His countenance beams with love as He lifts His hands in blessing over the redeemed multitude, saying *"Blessed are they that do His commandments, that they may have right to the Tree of Life, and may enter in through the gates into the City"* (Revelation 22:13, 14).

That voice, richer than any music that ever fell upon human ear, is heard saying, *"Your conflict is over. Come ye blessed of My Father, inherit the kingdom prepared for you from the foundation of the world"* (Matthew 25:34). Never, until we ourselves actually hear the voice of Jesus giving this blessed welcome home, never until we actually enter the gates of pearl, can we realize the wondrous thrill of this experience.

> *"O brother, be faithful, soon Jesus will come."*
> "In a little while we're going home.
> In a little while, in a little while,
> We shall cross the billow's foam.
> We shall meet at last,
> When the stormy winds are past -
> In a little while we're going home."
> - Eliza E. Hewitt (1851-1920)

c) The Coronation of King Jesus

Occupying the centre of the Holy City is the throne of God where sits the Father in His *grand and calm eternity.* Beside Him is Jesus. So great is the glory radiating from them that the City *"has no need of the sun ... to shine in it: For the glory of God did lighten it, and the Lamb is the light thereof"* (Revelation 21:23; Isaiah 30:26).

''And *there was a rainbow round about the throne, in sight like unto an emerald"* (Revelation 4:3). The brilliance of the light flashing forth from the throne of God, is tempered by the soft green light of an encircling rainbow representing the justice and mercy of God.

"In the midst of the throne and round about the throne" are the four *"living creatures," described* by both John and Ezekiel (Revelation 4:6, 7; Ezekiel 1:18; 10:12). These are the mighty cherubim and seraphim, the highest order of angelic beings. These are those who guard the throne of God and hasten like lightening to do His bidding (Ezekiel 1:14), the sound of their going like the sound of thunder. Gabriel is one of these cherubim and Satan himself once belonged to this powerful class of angels. (See Ezekiel 1:18; 10:12).

Next to the four living creatures are the *"four and twenty elders . . . clothed in white raiment,"* and with *"crowns of gold"* upon their heads. They carry *"harps and golden vessels full of incense"* (Revelation 5:8).   These are the representatives of unfallen worlds who help to form the government of God, the heavenly council of Job 1:6 and 2:1-2.

Before the throne of God, surrounded by mighty angels - the seraphim, and cherubim, and the twenty-four elders - stand the great multitude of the redeemed. There are those who had once been zealous in the cause of Satan, but who have been *"plucked as brands from the burning"* (Zechariah 3:2). These now follow their Saviour with deep and intense devotion. The ardent, self-sacrificing Paul, the great reformers like Martin Luther, and John Wycliffe, and the devoted, loving Mary Magdalene, could well be amongst this number. Next are those who have perfected Christian character in the midst of lies and infidelity - the 144,000, who have honoured the law of God when the apostate Christian world declared it void. They stand *'without fault before the throne of God'"* (Revelation 7:13-17; 14:1-5).

Others are now called to take their stand about the throne, the millions of martyrs from all ages, and the *"great mul-*

titude which no man could number of all nations, and kindreds, and people, and tongues. . . clothed with white robes, and palms in their hands" (Revelation 7:9).

Surrounding the redeemed is the vast number of angels - like a glittering garrison encircling the Israel of God. No earthly pageant can in any way compare, either in numbers, or in dazzling splendour, with this one which is assembled to celebrate the coronation of King Jesus, and the marriage of the Lamb.

The Celebration - A Seven-part Oratorio

Everything is now ready for this magnificent celebration, an oratorio consisting of seven parts. The theme of each anthem is honour and glory to God and to the Lamb. It is one continuous outburst of joyous song and adoring praise. While it cannot be adequately described, we can bring together some of the anthems that are sung by different groups, and perhaps get some faint foretaste of its wonderful inspiration. Our only hope of ever really knowing what it will be like is to be among the redeemed when this celebration takes place.

1. The Anthem of the Seraphim and Cherubim

This group, being so close to the throne, seems to take the lead. With harps in their hands, they strike the keynote of praise and *"give glory and honour, and thanks to Him that sits on the throne"* and *"rest not day and night saying 'Holy, holy, holy, Lord God Almighty, which was, and is, and is to come"* (Revelation 4:6-9). Their continuous melody of thanksgiving and praise seems to harmonize and enhance each anthem to follow.

2. The Song of the Twenty-Four Elders.

These are closely associated with the first group. They also have harps. Casting their crowns before the throne, they reverently sing with grateful praise:

"Thou art worthy, O Lord, to receive glory and hon-

our and power. For Thou hast created all things, and for Thy pleasure they are and were created."

"Thou art worthy . . . for Thou was slain, and hast redeemed them to God by Thy blood out of every kindred, and tongue, and people, and nation. And hast made them unto our God kings and priests. And they will reign on the earth" (Revelation4:10, 11; 5:8-10).

3.   The Song of the 144.000.

This group, *"having the harps of God,"* next take up the refrain. Having *"gotten the victory over the beast, and over his image, and over his mark, and over the number of his name*:

"They sang as it were a new song before the throne, and before the living creatures, and the elders. And no man could learn that song but the 144,000 which were redeemed from the earth" (Revelation 15:2; 14:1-3).

It is the song of their deliverance from the beast and from his image. It is the song of their experience.

"Great and marvellous are Thy works, Lord God Almighty. Just and true are Thy ways, Thou King of saints. Who shall not fear Thee, O Lord, and glorify Thy name? For Thou only art holy. For all nations will come and worship before Thee; for Thy judgments are made manifest" (Revelation 15:2-4).

This anthem, called *"the Song of Moses ... and the Song of the Lamb,"* honours a far more glorious triumph and deliverance than that which Moses sang about after Israel's deliverance from Pharaoh's mighty army.

4. The Song of the Great Multitude.

*"After this I beheld, and, lo, a great multitude, which no man could number, of all nations, and kindreds, and people, and tongues, stood before the throne, and before the Lamb . . . and cried with a loud voice saying, **Salvation** to our **God** who sits upon the throne, and unto the Lamb"* (Revelation 7:9, 10).

And as they, *"with a loud voice,"* repeat again and again the words of their anthem, they make all heaven ring with melody and praise.

5. The Hallelujah Chorus.

As a fitting finale to this greatest of all oratorios comes the hallelujah chorus. *"And after these things"* said John, *"I heard a great voice of many people in heaven, saying*:

> *"Alleluia! Salvation, and glory, and honour and power, unto the Lord our God. For true and righteous are His judgments. For He hath judged the great harlot, which did corrupt the earth with her fornication, and hath avenged the blood of His servants at her hand. And again they said, Alleluia!"*

In response, the twenty-four elders and the four living creatures fall down before the throne of God crying, *"Amen! Alleluia!"*

Now the voice of the great multitude - in a cascade of sound like that of many waters, like the rumble of mighty thunder - raises its voice in a triumphant shout of praise and adoration:

> *"Alleluia! For the Lord God omnipotent reigns. Let us be glad and rejoice and give honour to Him. For the marriage of the Lamb is come, and His wife has made herself ready"* (Revelation 19:1-7).

6. The Amen Sung by the Angels.

> *"And I heard the voice of many angels round about the throne and the beasts and elders saying with a loud voice: "Worthy is the Lamb that was slain to receive power, and riches, and wisdom, and strength, and honour, and glory, and blessing"* (Revelation 5:11, 12).

> *"And all the angels . . . fell before the throne on their faces, and worshiped God, saying: "Amen! Blessing, and glory, and wisdom, and thanksgiving, and honour and power; and might, be unto our God for ever and ever. Amen"* (Revelation 7:11, 12).

How fitting that the *"Amen"* is left for the angels to sing! They have never fallen, so they do not know the experience of redemption, but with all their melodious might they can sing *"Amen"* to all that the other groups have sung. *"Amen"* - a strong, positive assertion, fixing as it were the stamp of truth upon the words of praise. And so, the angels sing the grand *"Amen and Amen."*

7. The Father's Solo

Now comes the climax to this unspeakably marvellous oratorio. It is a solo. *"A voice came out of the throne."* Every other voice is hushed. Now a harp string is touched. Listen! Powerful, melodious, clear, expressive of infinite love, a voice that reaches to the very ends of the universe. He can no longer keep silent. Like the other parts of this oratorio, the Father's solo first expresses praise to His own Son:

> *"Praise our God, all ye His servants. And ye that fear Him, both small and great"* (Revelation 19:5).

> *"Sing, O daughter of Zion! Shout, O Israel!*
> *Be glad and rejoice with all the heart, O daughter*
> *of Jerusalem.*
> *The Lord has taken away thy judgments,*
> *He has cast out thine enemy.*

> *The King of Israel, even the Lord,*
> *Is in the midst of thee.*
> *And thou shalt not see evil anymore . . .*
>
> *For the Lord thy God in the midst of thee is*
> *mighty, He will save,*
> *He will rejoice over thee with joy!*
> *He will rest in His love,*
> *He will joy over thee with singing"*
> (Zephaniah 3:14-17).

8. The Response of the Universe.

Answering the challenge of the Father to *"praise God ... both small and great,"* the whole universe now combines its collective voice in a majestic and powerful surge of praise which resounds throughout the whole of creation:

> *"Blessing and honour; and glory, and power; be unto Him that sits upon the throne, and unto the Lamb* **FOREVER AND EVER"** *(Revelation 5:13).*

Jesus, Wonderful Jesus.

What is Jesus doing during this celebration? The only mention made of Him is that He sits on the throne with the Father. Surrounded by those whom He has redeemed, His lovely countenance beaming with joy and radiating with happiness, His last prayer for His loved ones is now answered, *"Father; I will that they also, whom Thou hast given Me, be with Me where I am; that they may behold My glory"* (John 17:24).

He sees the travail of His soul and is satisfied (Isaiah 53:11). He rests in His love, love and joy too deep for utterance in word or song. Precious Saviour! Wonderful, wonderful Redeemer!

When the crown, the seal of the marriage, is placed upon the Bridegroom, the combined groups of all the redeemed, the innumerable company of angels, and the representatives of unfallen worlds, burst forth in a mighty and prolonged HALLELUJAH! Can you picture the scene? Can you hear the music? O, what will it mean to be there? Surely, we cannot afford to miss it!

d) The New Earth.

Heaven is not the final abode of the redeemed. At the end of one thousand years, the Holy City with the saints of God, will descend to this earth. The earth will then become the centre of God's universal government. But first it must be cleansed by fire, even its polluted atmosphere will be burned up together with every evil thing (2 Peter 3:10-13). When the cleansing fires are finally out, then our Lord will make a new heaven (atmosphere) and a new earth.

*"And I saw a new heaven and a new earth. For the first heaven and the first earth were passed away, and there was no more sea. And I John saw the Holy City, the New Jerusalem, coming down from God out of heaven, prepared as a bride adorned for her husband. And I heard a great voice out of heaven saying, 'Behold, the tabernacle of God is with men, and He will dwell with them, and they shall be His people, and God Himself shall be with them, and be their God.' And God shall wipe away all tears from their eyes. There shall be no more death, neither sorrow, nor crying, neither shall there be any more pain. For the former things are passed away. And He that sat upon the throne said, **'Behold, I make all things new.'***

"And He carried me away in the spirit to a great and high mountain, and showed me that great city, the holy Jerusalem, descending out of heaven from God, having the glory of God. And her light was like unto a stone most precious, even like a jasper stone, clear as crystal" (Revelation 21 :1-5, 10, 11).

"For, behold, I create new heavens and a new earth.

And the former shall not be remembered, nor come into mind . . . And they shall build houses, and inhabit them, and they shall plant vineyards, and eat the fruit of them . . . The wolf and the lamb will feed together, and the lion will eat straw like the bullock, and dust will be the serpent's meat (food). They will not hurt nor destroy in all My holy mountain, saith the Lord" (Isaiah 65:17, 21, 25).

"The Spirit and the bride say Come. And let him that hears say, Come. And let him that thirsts come. And whosoever will, let him take the water of life freely" (Revelation 22:17).

"EVEN SO, COME, LORD JESUS."

We Are Nearing Home

Just over the mountains in the Promised Land,
Lies the holy city built by God's own hand.
As our weary footsteps gain the mountain's crest,
We can view our homeland of eternal rest.

REFRAIN
We are nearing home! We are nearing home!
See the splendour gleaming from the domes afar!
See the glory streaming through the gates ajar!
There we soon will enter, never more to roam,
Hear the angels singing!
We are nearing home! We are nearing home!

In the rolls of the prophets, we have long been told,
Of that wondrous city with its streets of gold.
Now with raptured vision we can see it there,
With its walls of jasper and its mansions fair.

Those who enter that city are the faithful few,
Who keep God's commandments - faith of Jesus, too.
There we'll lift our voices through the endless days,
In sweet songs of gladness and in psalms of praise.

My brother, my sister, will you meet us there,
In that land of sunshine where there'll be no care?
Accept of God's message, and to Him be true.
Then when Jesus cometh He will call for you.

- John R. Sweeny

Bibliography

Andreasen, M. L., *The Sanctuary Service,* Review & Herald Publishing Assoc., Washington DC, (1937).

Australasian Div. Exe. Committee, *Righteousness by Faith,* Signs Publishing, Warburton, Vic.

Behe, M. J., *Darwin's Black Box: The Biochemical Challenge to Evolution,* Simon & Schuster, New York, NY, (1996).

Bible Readings for the Home, Vol. I. Review & Herald Publishing Assoc., Washington DC, & Pacific Press Publishing Assoc., Boise, ID, (1962).

Frazee, W D., *Ransom and Reunion,* Pioneers Memorial Press, Wildwood, GA, (1994).

Gilbert, F. C., *Messiah in His Sanctuary,* Review & Herald Publishing Assoc., (1937).

Goldstein, C., *False Balances,* Pacific Press Publishing Assoc., Boise, ID, (1992).

Hardinge, L., *Shadows of His Sacrifice,* Teach Services, Ruston, NY, (1996).

Hardinge, L., *With Jesus in His Sanctuary,* American Cassette Ministries, Harrisburg, PA, (1991).

Haskell, S. N., *The Cross* & *Its Shadow,* Review & Herald Publishing Assoc., Washington DC, (1984).

Maxwell, C. M., *God and His Sanctuary,* Pacific Press Publishing Assoc., Boise, ID, (1980).

Peck, S. E., *The Path to the Throne of God,* Publisher and date unknown.

Schuler, J. L., *The Great Judgment Day,* Review & Herald, Washington DC, (1923).

Standish, R. & C., *The Big Bang Exploded,* Hartland Publications, Rapidan, VA, (1998).

Standish, R. & C., *Adventism Vindicated,* Historic Truth Publishers, Paradise, CA, (1980).

Walton, L. R., *Decision at the Jordan,* Review & Herald, Washington DC, (1982).

White, E. G., *The Acts of the Apostles,* Pacific Press Publishing Assoc., Boise, ID, (1911).

White, E. G., *Christ's Object Lessons,* Review & Herald Publishing Assoc., Washington DC, (1941).

White, E. G., *The Desire of Ages,* Pacific Press Publishing Assoc., Boise, ID, (1940).

White, E. G., *Education*, Pacific Press Publishing Assoc., Boise, ID, (1952).

White, E. G., *The Great Controversy*, Pacific Press Publishing Assoc., Boise, ID, (1950).

White, E. G., *Ministry of Healing*, Pacific Press Publishing Assoc., Boise, ID, (1942).

White, E. G., *Patriarchs and Prophets*, Review & Herald Publishing Assoc., Washington DC, (1958).

White, E. G., *Steps to Christ,* Pacific Press Publishing Assoc., Boise, ID, (1956).

White, E. G., *That I May Know Him*, Review & Herald Publishing Assoc., Washington DC, (1964).

White, E. G., *The Story of Redemption*, Review & Herald Publishing Assoc., Washington DC, (1980).

White, E. G., *Thoughts From the Mount of Blessing*, Pacific Press Publishing Assoc., Boise, ID, (1955).

White, J. G., *The Christian's Experience*, Northwest Publishing Assoc., Sacramento, CA, (1942).

Woychuk, N. A., *You Need to Memorize Scripture*, Scripture Memory Fellowship, St. Louis, MO, (1993).

Wright E T., *God's Way in the Sanctuary*, Destiny Press, QLD, (1984).